*Stalin
and
His
Times*

Joseph Stalin at the Yalta Conference, February 1945

Stalin
and
His
Times

ARTHUR E. ADAMS

The Ohio State University

DRYDEN PRESS
HINSDALE, ILLINOIS

Cover: From a drawing of Joseph Stalin in 1920 by N. Avvakumov.
(The Mansell Collection; Mercury Illustration Research)

Library of Congress Catalog Card Number: 70–183627
ISBN: 0–03–085094–0
Printed in the United States of America
9   008   9876543

Preface

THIS book describes briefly the history of the Soviet Union while Stalin struggled for and won power and while he ruled. It also attempts to explain why the history evolved as it did, why Stalin succeeded in achieving many of his objectives, and in what ways he failed. Finally, it seeks to assess the significance of Stalin's era (1923–1953) for the Soviet Union and for the outside world.

Although most of the broad outlines of Stalin's influence in the Soviet Union are fairly clear, the effects of his long domination are so far-reaching that they still cannot be finally assessed. As for its impact upon the rest of the world, the Stalin era was one of the most significant periods of modern history. It has changed politics and lives in many lands. The new People's Republics of Eastern Europe, for example, as well as the social and political systems of mainland China, North Korea, North Vietnam, Tanzania, and Cuba are copies or adaptations of the Stalinist prototype. Elsewhere, in backward or developing nations around the world, leaders and rebels alike assiduously study Stalin's accomplishments, striving to learn how best to advance the development of their own nations, whether their aim be revolution or rapid industrialization. For the Western democracies, the appearance of the Stalinist state very early provoked doubts about democracy itself, compelling the searching reexamination of social values and governing methods that still brings conspiratorial groups, students, or citizen masses into the streets to reform or destroy governments.

Stalin's era also brought about a massive reshaping of international relationships. It gave rise to an arms race more costly than the world has ever seen before, it contributed heavily to a Cold War that still wracks the world's nerves, and it directly or indirectly provoked shooting wars in such places as Greece, Korea, and Southeast Asia.

Why has this era had such immense influence upon the rest of the world? While this question is considered at length in this book, it may be useful for the reader to have in mind some of the most obvious answers as he begins reading Chapter One. First and foremost, under Stalin's ruthless hands, a huge, almost helpless Russian nation was swiftly transformed into an industrial and military giant. In less than two decades (1928–1945) the Stalinist experiment produced a world power second only to the United States of America. The almost incredibly rapid creation of this modern nation could not but stir men's minds throughout the world.

A second factor, always puzzling as to its precise effect, has nevertheless registered an equally profound impact upon outside observers. The transformation of Russian society was at least in part the result of the commitment of Stalin and his colleagues to the political ideology most properly identified by the awkward title "Marxism-Leninism-Stalinism." From somewhere in the depths of that ideology, which was at once a philosophy of history and a promise of utopia, men found an intense faith in their ability to change the course of history. Armed with this faith and organized into a disciplined Communist party, they virtually moved mountains. If Marxism-Leninism-Stalinism could thus transform a backward and sleeping giant into a powerful nation, it is no wonder that the young, the oppressed, and the leaders of many nations would spend countless hours seeking to absorb this new wisdom.

A third aspect of Stalin's accomplishment that has fascinated men and women of our time might be termed his *technique of industrialization*. By sheer force of will he drove Russia through the stages of industrialization far more rapidly than any comparable society had previously been able to advance, forcing his people to work, to acquire needed skills and professions, and to create new factories and whole industries. Instead of borrowing from abroad, he found his capital in the energy of the peasants and workers, coercing the society into lifting itself out of poverty by its own labors and sacrifices.

Before Stalin, industrializing a nation was a slow process requiring from fifty to a hundred years or more. With Stalin, a decade sufficed to transform a relatively underdeveloped nation into a great industrial power. Moreover, in the past, development of any sort had usually come to poor nations in the form of imperialist exploitation by Western capitalist powers. Such development often did little more for the exploited nations than to confirm their backwardness and strip them of their economic resources. But Stalin's system of self-help appeared literally to create wealth out of nothing. In addition, while he industrialized, he also modernized the whole social system, changing its values, its institutions, its culture, and attempting to change the very thought processes of its people. His success appeared to promise other poor nations that they too could win independence, power, and prosperity, using only their own courage and the proper techniques, and this is a fundamental reason why Stalin's model for modernization still proves fascinating to these nations.

Finally, Stalin the man contributed much to the great impact of his era. He represents a new type of hero or Great Man. To some he symbolizes the sickness of the twentieth century, to others its salvation. If his special quality can be characterized in a word or two, it may be said that he was a superior administrator, or, more emphatically, he was *The Great Administrator*. He was totally dedicated to the idea that *anything* could be organized and directed, that the administrator with intelligence, courage, and determination could achieve almost any desired goal by means of proper administrative techniques shrewdly applied. One senses that ultimately for Stalin, the individual, the society, the party, and even the nation were all subordinate to his determination to build and direct the perfect administrative machine able to achieve any ends he assigned to it, regardless of financial or human costs.

In the end, one is inclined to see the administrator that Stalin became as an inhuman monster, dedicated to the machinery and its proper functioning rather than to the Soviet citizens whose servant he claimed to be. Nevertheless, the point is often made, and with considerable justification, that the transformation of Russia would not have occurred but for Stalin's fanatic determination, brutal forcefulness, and shrewd administrative skills. In the world in which we live, where for many nations the goals of modernization seem unattainable by other means, the way mapped by the Great Administrator, the man who would be stopped by nothing, still appears to promise salvation.

October 1971   ARTHUR E. ADAMS

Contents

Stalin
and
His
Times

CHAPTER ONE

The First Years

Lenin and His Rule

VLADIMIR LENIN, founder of the Bolshevik party
that seized power in Petrograd on October 25, 1917,
had dreamed of bringing peace, social justice, and
prosperity to Russia. But in the years immediately
following the revolution the task of achieving
utopia proved to be far more difficult than Lenin
had anticipated. Moreover, although he was
totally dedicated to the good of the poor people — in
particular, the urban proletariat of Russia and
the rest of the world — his efforts were hampered
by serious defects inherent in the very means and
ends he championed.

There were flaws in the revolutionary organization that he led. His Communist party, the vanguard of the workers, the select group designated by
him to serve as a dictatorship of the proletariat until

that dictatorship withered away into utopia, created its own problems. The exclusiveness and authoritarian character of the party, while helping to form it into a revolutionary battering ram, also isolated it from the society it sought to improve, exacerbating at every turn its already painful relationships with that society.

There were also flaws deep in the fundamental assumptions of Marxist-Leninist ideology, the political philosophy and practical rules supposed to guide the party's conduct. Lenin, with the kind of arrogance marking the fanatic "true believer" as often as the ferocious conqueror, was convinced that he knew better than the people themselves what they needed for the improvement of their lives. He was Plato's "philosopher king" in the flesh, but Russia's diverse multitudes—spoiled nobles, bourgeoisie, lazy peasants, and hungry workers, Kalmyks, Tartars, and Ukrainian nationalists, to name only a few—cared little for his role or his vision and resented his authoritarian efforts to hammer them into new classes and impose on them the kind of institutions he said they needed.

Possibly the fundamental flaw running through both the party organization and its governing ideology must be attributed to Lenin's own character. Personally he was authoritarian, monstrously impatient with the world as he found it, and totally dedicated to reshaping it to fit his own ideals. He firmly believed himself to be Marx's only legitimate prophet, the one man who knew absolutely how history must unfold, who could interpret its laws accurately, and who had fashioned the instrument uniquely capable of achieving Marxist goals—the Russian Social Democratic Labor Party (Bolshevik). The Bolshevik party, composed of men who accepted Lenin's intellectual authority and elitist precepts even while they bickered with him about details, was his sharp sword of revolution. But Lenin, the philosopher king, never seemed aware that he and his colleagues, though dedicating themselves to the "good" of the Russian people, had chosen autocratic methods. One can force men to be saved against their will only by breaking their spirits and depriving them of the right to think independently.

The flaws of party and dogma and the influence of the

personality of the leader only partly explain why Lenin's years as Russia's ruler were so hectic. Certainly, the historical condition of Russia when Lenin assumed power must also be taken into account. Problems that drove Ivan the Terrible to madness, Peter the Great to orgies of violence, and Catherine the Great's successors to early or violent deaths still haunted Russia's rulers. The nation remained a vast and poor agricultural country, where the peasants had never managed to cultivate the soil efficiently and where the upper classes, long virtually independent of the tsar's political authority, had mismanaged and squandered the nation's resources on a grand scale. With a multinational population of 163 million people in 1917, and a territorial sweep of nearly 6,000 miles from its western borders to the Pacific Ocean, it had been, until Lenin's arrival, virtually ungovernable except by the force of arms and autocracy.

Pre-1917 Russian government was an extensive tangle of offices whose confusions rendered effective rule impossible, and the capricious exercise of authority by the tsars, struggling to preserve the autocracy, had steadily worsened the government's effectiveness. The rapid processes of change introduced by the beginnings of quasi-representative government under the last tsar, Nicholas II, also increased the existing administrative chaos. Industrialization, too, had begun to make its influence felt in the late nineteenth century, and the changes it brought to the economic and social systems in the twentieth had serious disruptive effects.

Although Russia was moving industrially before Lenin seized power, the effort to do so was disjointed and painful. Nevertheless, some industrial enterprises under government patronage and subsidy progressed swiftly; railroads were built and foreign trade expanded; technical and professional schools burgeoned, producing thousands of new technical and scientific specialists, as well as lawyers, economists, businessmen, and professors; and great factories in the major cities brought together the first sizable groups of urban industrial workers, the proletariat. At the same time prices rose, and in the countryside rural taxes stretched the limits of the peasant's ability to pay his debts and stay alive.

Meanwhile whole nations and peoples within the empire—such as the Poles, Finns, Ukrainians, and Georgians—increasingly longed to break away from imperial domination. Still other ethnic groups, some barely literate or following religious and social traditions utterly divorced from Russian culture and tradition, posed political problems of growing complexity, for each group was now faced with the need somehow to make its own adjustment to the rapidly changing environment.

Against this troubled backdrop, Lenin came to power at a particularly unfortunate moment in Russia's history. The society in which he began his struggle to build a socialist utopia had bled profusely during three tragic years of war with Germany, reaching a climax of economic and social chaos in 1917, when peasants seized the property of landowners, soldiers deserted by hundreds of thousands, nationality groups violently struggled for political separation or national independence, and the imperial order simply disintegrated. Immediately after the October Revolution, in the first months of the Bolshevik regime, the power of Germany's armies forced Lenin to sign a damaging treaty of peace at Brest-Litovsk, which permitted Germany to occupy western Russian provinces and the Ukraine and thus deprived Russia of vital food supplies as well as the products of Ukrainian mines and industries.

Almost at the same moment, other enemies of the Bolsheviks within Russia began a civil war, establishing fronts that threatened Lenin's new government from every direction of the compass. These warring forces were strengthened late in 1918 by the intervention of military units dispatched by Russia's former Western allies and Japan. Faced with the need to fight rather than reform, Lenin and his party colleagues conscripted armies of their own, instituted extreme centralization of government, expanded the operations of the Cheka, the Bolshevik agency of Red Terror, and created the economic system known as War Communism, a system best defined as state control for state interests.

The desperate threat posed by civil war and intervention to the very life of the new regime justified and encouraged the militarization of the party. In order to save the revolution, Lenin himself became the new "tsar"; Leon Trotsky, his capable right hand, headed the Commissariat for Military Affairs and soon emerged as a "Red Napoleon," demanding and obtaining for the sake of proletarian military victory the return of military rank and the reestablishment of strict obedience and discipline. Another assistant, Joseph Stalin, came forward in these crisis conditions as a tough troubleshooter, a party tribune ready for dispatch to any front to exert vicious pressures and to force men on pain of death to obey orders.

The impact of civil war upon the party as a whole was to strengthen and exaggerate the authoritarian character that Lenin had already instilled in it. The experience of the war persuaded men who had expected to achieve utopia merely by declaring an end to rank, privilege, and faulty class structures that a nation can maintain itself only by developing a high degree of military organization and discipline, and only by submitting to powerful leaders capable of daring and ruthless action.

For Lenin, the lessons were painful and no doubt disillusioning, although he never permitted disillusionment to show. But if learning how to rule was frequently painful, the need to find new solutions for pressing problems was a constant challenge. As the civil war came to an end, workers and peasants who thought utopia should mean self-government, private profit, and easy living refused to sow or harvest their fields and mounted strikes against the Bolshevik regime. To these common people, the new regime was no more acceptable than the old. Indeed they were profoundly sensitive to the similarities between the two. The new regime had conscripted them into the Red Army and had kept them fighting by means of the Cheka. It had confiscated the peasants' produce by force of arms, and it had regimented workers in their factories, forcing them to work long hours for little pay, deprived of the right to bargain, to negotiate freely, or to campaign for their own political views.

In March 1921, a major rebellion broke out at the island naval base of Kronstadt among sailors who had long been considered bolshevism's most ardent supporters. At Kronstadt good Bolshevik-party men who nevertheless felt that they could no longer tolerate the bureaucratic centralism of the party denounced Lenin as the "new tsar" and called upon the rank and file to rise in the name of the toiling masses and overthrow his "commissarocracy." They spoke for striking Petrograd workers and for millions of rebellious peasants across the nation, as well as for their fellow sailors at Kronstadt, and because their pleas for the immediate establishment of democratic self-government were coupled with a will to fight for their demands, they had to be suppressed. Lenin dispatched Trotsky with his most trusted military units to do the job, and these forces, marching across the ice of the Gulf of Finland, drowned the Kronstadt revolt in blood.

Domestic troubles were not alone in demanding Lenin's attention during the last months of 1920 and the early months of 1921. As he studied political events abroad he was forced to abandon his earlier hope that world revolution would soon follow the spark in Russia. Peace had broken out in the world, and with peace the European nations he had hoped would follow the Bolshevik example now settled down to the work of rebuilding themselves along well-worn capitalistic lines. As hopes diminished for an immediate world revolution that might protect the tenuous Bolshevik experiment in Russia, Lenin had to take his own interim measures to maintain his regime in power. Until enough order could be restored within Russia itself, any advance toward international utopia would have to be postponed. The Kronstadt revolt had demonstrated the dangerous hostility of sailors and urban workers. Even more threatening was the vast and anonymous anger of the peasants. Sick of having their produce taken away from them, they were refusing to sow the land, hiding and hoarding their grain, and fighting local authorities. They possessed the power to destroy Lenin's great experiment by starving it to death, and to save himself Lenin proposed a daring economic retreat.

Responding to these conditions at the Tenth Congress of his party, held in the month of the Kronstadt rebellion, Lenin announced that bolshevism had gone too far during its first years in power by nationalizing industry, taking over responsibility for all trade activities, and forcing the peasant to give up his agricultural products to the state. Criticizing the agricultural policy of the period of War Communism, he said: "Any Communist who thought the economic basis, the economic roots, of small farming could be reshaped in three years was, of course, a dreamer. We need not conceal the fact that there were a good many such dreamers among us. Nor is there anything particularly bad in this. How could one start a socialist revolution in a country like ours without dreamers?"[1]

Having admitted these mistakes, Lenin proposed to correct them at once. To the peasants whose grain had been confiscated during the period of War Communism so that cities and soldiers could be fed, he now returned the rights to buy and sell land, to hire labor, and to sell grain for profit. Most factories nationalized since 1917 were handed back to private owners or to cooperative management, although Lenin shrewdly insisted that the state must retain the all-important heavy industries. In order to bring about a recuperation of the economy, free exchange of goods was encouraged, and for the peasant a tax in kind was established, so that each farmer could count on selling for profit a fixed amount of the produce he raised.

Abroad, this New Economic Policy (NEP) was hailed as the harbinger of communism's failure, and the further reestablishment of private property, capitalism, and good bourgeois sense in Russia was happily anticipated. But for Lenin and his party chiefs, NEP was merely a breathing space bought by compromise and concession in order to heal the wounds of World War I, civil war, and the Bolsheviks' first overambitious efforts to achieve communism all at once. Yet, even though Lenin managed to retain power by making these concessions, for many of his fellow communists the retreat from utopian communism came hard. Some believed their cause had been lost and wondered if there would ever be a return to the ex-

[1] V. I. Lenin, *Collected Works* (Lawrence and Wishart, London, 4th ed., 1965), XXXII, 216–217.

hilarating drive toward a new world that had marked the early days of 1918.

In May 1922, Lenin suffered his first stroke, which prevented him from returning to work until late in the fall. A second stroke in December of the same year kept him confined, an invalid, until his death in January 1924. During the last months of his life, separated from the party and government he had established, and worried by the private reports of party friends and petitioners, he concerned himself deeply with what was to come after his death. The party was his creation. What would it be without him? Who would lead the party and the Russian people to fulfill their promised destiny? As Lenin examined the question, not one of his most trusted lieutenants seemed precisely to fit his requirements.

During this time a triumvirate of communists ruled the party and the country—Grigory Zinoviev, Leo Kamenev, and Joseph Stalin. Trotsky, the most popular man in the country after Lenin, stood in the wings. Lenin studied all these men, reflected upon their strengths and weaknesses and even wrote out some tentative suggestions to the party about their qualifications as leaders. But even while he querulously struggled through his last days, these others were moving beyond him, already caught up in the struggle to rule Russia and to advance themselves.

Lenin's Heirs

Of the men who seemed likely to succeed Lenin, Leon Trotsky was most favored. Born in1879, son of a Jewish farmer near Odessa, he had long been active as a leader of Marxist revolutionary activity, supporting, however, factions opposed to Lenin's Bolshevik party. Joining the Bolsheviks in July 1917, Trotsky instantly became, in the popular mind at least, second only to Lenin as a leader of the revolution. He was a handsome, dramatic man, with a flair for the theatrical and a love of words. Eloquent and overwhelming at the speaker's podium and in debate, he was also brave under fire and a daring and imaginative organizer. In late 1917, it was Trotsky who led the Military

Police photograph of Stalin, 1910

Revolutionary Committee that actually carried out the Bolshevik seizure of power in Petrograd. Later, he brilliantly led the peace negotiations at Brest-Litovsk, staging the proceedings and deliberately calling upon a world audience to witness and condemn the ruthlessness of the German conquerors. Thereafter, he became Commissar of War, and through the civil war, photographed constantly in his dashing leather coat and a helmetlike military cap with a red star, he pounded demoralized conscripts and dragooned peasants, deserters, and former tsarist officers into a military force that helped to save the revolution.

To his misfortune, however, Trotsky had serious disadvantages in the struggle for power that had existed even before Lenin's first stroke. Having joined the party only at the end of July 1917, he was a "New Bolshevik," and his sudden success was bitterly resented by many men who had stood by Lenin over the years. In addition, Trotsky possessed a self-righteous sense of his own superiority that made him imperious toward the failings of lesser men. Through the years before 1917, his biting commentaries about his erstwhile opponents, Lenin and the Bolsheviks, had created undying enmities among the latter. Most of all, after the civil war was over, his popularity and the widespread assumption that he would automatically succeed Lenin made him a natural target of other Bolsheviks who coveted this honor for themselves. Such men considered Trotsky the chief obstacle to their own success.

And there *were* other ambitious men in the party. Three of these contenders joined together some time in 1923 to form the triumvirate within the Politburo of the party that now began to rule both party and government. Each of the three joined with the others because he feared Trotsky's strength. Zinoviev and Stalin each viewed himself as Lenin's true successor. It was a case of the weak banding together to fight off the strong; however, the men who formed the triumvirate were not equally matched. Zinoviev, an Old Bolshevik who had joined Lenin in 1902 and who was famous for his oratorical ability, was not only a member of the Politburo; he was also Chairman of the powerful Soviet at Petrograd and President of the Comintern, the communist international organization established in May 1919 as the General Staff for world revolution. While Zinoviev saw himself as Lenin's closest lieutenant and legitimate heir, he lacked the incisive mind and courage required of the leader. The second member of the triumvirate, Leo Kamenev, was another Old Bolshevik who had been with Lenin since 1902 and now ranked as his deputy. In addition to serving on the Politburo, he was Chairman of the Moscow Soviet. Considered a fine theorist, Kamenev was courageously stubborn in defending his views and competent in the management of his offices, but he was slow, unimaginative, and lacking in daring when compared to Lenin and Trotsky, or to Stalin, the third man of the triumvirate.

Since Stalin is the primary concern of our study, we must examine his antecedents more carefully than those of his competitors. And since it is probable that the ultimate power of this man was rooted to a considerable degree in his personality and character, any clue gleaned from his past may help to unravel the mystery of his ultimate success. Born in 1879 in the Georgian town of Gori in the southern Caucasus, as Iosif Vissarionovich Dzhugashvili, he lived his first years in poverty. His Georgian father was a heavy-handed shoemaker, his mother, an illiterate but deeply religious washerwoman.

Swarthy and blackhaired, the young Dzhugashvili suffered from an attack of smallpox at the age of six or seven and carried the pockmarks on his face through the rest of his life. Only in 1912 did Dzhugashvili adopt the pseudonym "Stalin" (man of steel), but because he is remembered by this name it will be used throughout this book. At nine he entered the ecclesiastical school at Gori, where his work was good, for he had an excellent memory, an aggressive, competitive spirit, and a taste for Georgian literature. In 1894 at the age of fourteen he went to the Theological Seminary at Tiflis with a scholarship to train for the priesthood. At the seminary, however, he apparently absorbed more than clerical knowledge. He quickly learned that he hated external discipline and religion, and his efforts to win justice for himself and others at school soon aroused in him a growing awareness of the broader social injustices and differences between nationalities, Russian and Georgian, to be found outside the walls of the seminary. Although the seminary training left ineffaceable clerical marks upon his mind and manners, his interests widened, he soon began reading books banned by the school authorities, refused to be quelled or to narrow his activities, and in 1899 was expelled from the school.

He became a professional revolutionary, a Marxist. Lecturing to impoverished urban workers, helping to organize strikes at Tiflis and subsequently at Batum, and persistently editing or writing for a variety of clandestine newspapers, he was to live through the years before 1917 as an underground worker, a practical fighter for revolution, and an inmate of several of the tsar's prisons and exile settlements. If there was a significant difference between Stalin and his colleagues, Trotsky, Zinoviev, and Kamenev, with regard to their fundamental characters, the difference may well have stemmed from Stalin's extended underground activity. His revolutionary experience came from inside Russia, predominantly in the Caucasus area, where he lived the quasi-criminal life of the political rebel working to bring down the government, involved at times in the criminal acts of organizing and leading strikes, fighting the police, propagandizing for the revolution, and even planning robberies to replenish the party treasury.

This was the life, as Stalin was to idealize it later, of the "practical," that is, of the down-to-earth, worker. The minds of these underground revolutionaries were taken up with such details as where next to move a clandestine press, or how to find new sleeping places from night to night in order to escape the police. Their days and nights were consumed with efforts to goad the proletariat to social action by endless discussions in crowded rooms, by writing and distributing underground newspapers and leaflets, by fomenting strikes and demonstrations. Ceaselessly on the alert against police informers—of which there were many—the "practical" underground worker learned to give infinite attention to petty details of organization and planning, so that plans were effectively carried out, while those who were known to the police remained free. This life, full of police spies and petty rivalries between oversuspicious men, placed great emphasis on the values of cunning and caution, and it taught a man sooner or later to trust almost no one.

In contrast, Trotsky, Zinoviev, Kamenev, Lenin himself, and indeed most of the other leaders of the party were cosmopolitan revolutionaries, members of the Russian intelligentsia. All these men had lived in the West, moving in the Western milieu as if it were their own. They were sophisticated, Western-oriented theorists, heirs to the romantic and elitist Russian tradition of the intelligentsia—proud of their literary styles, their interest in culture and the arts, and their ability to theorize about Marxism and other political philosophies. With their bourgeois backgrounds and émigré lives taken up with political squabbling over party affairs, they were a far cry from the underground practical worker. And they were prone to look down on the underground men as coarse pawns of the revolution who needed to be led by wiser, more subtle intellects.

Stalin had little interest in the West. Although prior to 1917 he made several short visits abroad, usually to attend a congress of the party or to meet with Lenin, he had spent little time in foreign environments. There was, the others thought, a peculiar, provincial narrowness in his interests. Nor was he much concerned with theories of world revolution, for while he was an internationalist, in the sense that he subscribed to Marxist dogma, the revolution in Russia, a nationalist revolution, was what really appeared to interest him.

By the time he began to be well known in the higher echelons of the party, Stalin's character was well formed. He was secretive and brusque, little given to long and tedious excursions into the realm of theory, remarkable for his devotion to Lenin, his ability to attend to detail, and his mastery of organizational matters in the Caucasus. In January 1912, Lenin persuaded the Central Committee of the party to coopt this Georgian disciple into the Central Committee, even though at that moment Stalin was in the hands of the Russian police. Later the same year, having escaped from exile, Stalin ventured to Cracow to meet with the Central Committee and Lenin. There and at Vienna, during his longest stay abroad, Stalin met and talked repeatedly with Lenin, and fulfilled what was to be one of his most important early assignments. His task concerned the nationality problem in the Russian Empire—"that prison of nations," as Trotsky later called it, and the problem was to develop an acceptable nationality policy for the party. Because Stalin presumably was well acquainted with the nationalities of the Caucasus, Lenin asked him to prepare a statement that could be adopted by the party.

Working at Cracow and Vienna through January 1913, Stalin enjoyed the advice and the editing of Lenin himself, and under the latter's tutelage he produced his first important theoretical effort, the article entitled "Marxism and the National Question." There has been much controversy about the authorship of this article, primarily owing to Trotsky's later charges that the ideas and even the words belonged to Lenin rather than Stalin. Yet the nationality problem had in fact long been one of Stalin's main concerns; he had written on the subject before; and the article contains unmistakable signs of his own awkward phraseology as well as Lenin's formulations.

Briefly, the thesis that Stalin argued was that each ethnic minority within the Russian state should have the right to self-determination, including the right to secede and become an independent state, but such a right, he took pains to make clear, should be enjoyed by the toiling masses of the ethnic group, rather than its bourgeoisie. In a similar vein, he argued that each nationality should enjoy cultural autonomy, with the right to instruct its young in its own language and to govern itself within a larger democratic republic. The endorsement of these views by the party in August 1913 established Stalin as the party's nationality expert, the chief party theorist for nationality problems, whose opinions had to be listened to whenever questions arose concerning the aspirations of nationalities within the Russian Empire. Whether the ideas were originally his own or Lenin's, this single article transformed the rough underground worker into one of the party's foremost theorists in an area where others were hesitant to speak. For Stalin, it was a significant step forward.

Back in Russia, Stalin was arrested again and sent off to exile in Siberia, returning to the capital only in early 1917, when he became one of the editors of *Pravda*, the party newspaper at Petrograd. His writing in the Russian language was stiff and awkward, retaining the repetitive sounds of the Orthodox litany that he had learned so well in the seminary. These qualities, in fact, were to characterize Stalin's writing and speaking throughout his life. He also appeared to think in much the same fashion, slowly and painfully, working out each step as he went, applying principles of logic and evidence almost as if they were foreign to him, but eventually producing his argument in a jerky formulation that was built to trap his audience inescapably with its conclusions. There can be no doubt that he was deeply committed to Marxist-Leninist ideology, yet in his interpretation of the doctrine there was always to be a certain primitive quality — as though a not very well educated priest were abstracting the Holy Writ into words that his most simpleminded parishioner could grasp.

In 1917 and through the years until 1922, Stalin the practical worker, the organizer and hard-bitten administrator, performed many difficult tasks for Lenin and the party. He spoke publicly often enough to have been more widely known in the party than he was, but the Westerners, the Bolshevik intelligentsia, found him crude and boring, almost embarrassing in his harsh, clumsy efforts to play their game. Lenin, of course, saw the other qualities. He made excellent use of the fearless administrator who could organize any bureau and make it work, who could force recalcitrant armies to move forward, who loved to exert his authority and get things done and would stop at nothing in carrying out his missions. Such men were all too rare.

Because of Stalin's talent for organization and administration, and probably also because he carried in his heart immense ambition and a persistent resentment of his colleagues, vast powers came into his hands. One important office after another became his. In 1917 he was appointed Commissar of Nationalities, the responsible overseer of the national minorities — making up some 40 percent of Russia's total population — about whom he was the presumed expert. Through the civil war, he carried out a series of demanding assignments as Lenin's troubleshooter, executing each task with brusque efficiency. These efforts brought him many new friends among the Old Bolsheviks, because in these assignments he often confronted Trotsky, the Military Commissar, and on such occasions frequently became the champion of lesser men who also hated Trotsky. In 1919, he joined the newly established Politburo and the Orgburo, the office that managed the personnel records of the Bolshevik party. Also, in early 1919 he was named to head the Commissariat of State Control (subsequently, the Commissariat of Workers' and Peasants' Inspection), which was given the responsibility of inspecting all government offices and improving the quality of their efforts. Finally, in 1922 he became the General Secretary of the party, and thus came to control the offices that prepared the agenda and the materials for the meetings of the Politburo. At this point, he was the only party leader holding membership in the four highest party offices: Central Committee, Politburo, Orgburo, and Secretariat.

Because Zinoviev and Kamenev recognized Stalin's exceptional abilities to organize and administer, both wanted him in the triumvirate. Neither apparently thought it even remotely possible that Stalin could aspire to the post of leader. To them, as well as to Trotsky, this slightly tongue-tied man who lacked their sophistication was second-rate, a trifle stupid perhaps. As a dull but efficient bureaucrat, he was simply a necessary assistant, a clerk whose files could tell them whom to call if they needed help in some non-Russian province or whom to assign to a difficult party post. The truth was, however, that by 1922, in the party offices Stalin controlled, he already possessed immense power, more strength in fact than anyone then realized. In part this reflected Stalin's own caution. The time had not yet come for him to flex his muscles openly, for Lenin was still alive.

Until 1922, Stalin remained, at least outwardly, completely loyal and dedicated to Lenin, although he had long since begun his struggle to undercut Trotsky and the others. But when the leader suffered his first stroke, the scheming "practical" quietly but definitely abandoned his former allegiance. The struggle for great power had begun in earnest, and the patient, shrewd manipulator of administrative machinery moved stolidly and methodically to consolidate his strength.

Stalin's Struggle for Power

During the tribulations of the civil war and the forceful economic system of War Communism, the party had become militarized and bureaucratized. From a group of radical, visionary leaders of revolution committed to an idealistic goal of creating a people's democratic society, its principal leaders were transformed into ironhanded centralists. They became persuaded that only the fiercest sort of hierarchical command system could govern the Soviet state successfully and that effective direction of such a state demanded a tautly centralized and unified party. But while certain Bolsheviks moved easily to these conclusions, many others within the party, as well as many outside it who had supported bolshevism at the beginning—for example, the Kronstadt sailors and Petrograd workers —were quick to resent what they called "the new autocracy." They longed to turn the party bureaucracy around and hand the reins of government back to the people.

The struggle between these two views about how the party should be run and how the nation should be governed was to be a grave, strife-ridden issue throughout the 1920s, for the tangled threads of conflict were multiple. The conflict over *how* the party should be run was simultaneously a struggle over *who* should run it, whether the bureaucrats in power or their ostensibly more democratic opponents and critics. Just as crucial was the conflict directly related to the *kinds* of state policies—political, economic, social, and foreign—that the opposing sides believed should be developed.

Stalin favored bureaucracy, centralization, and absolute party unity, meaning by the latter term the unquestioning obedience of all party members to the orders of the leaders. He was indeed the perfect successor to Lenin in the sense that he seemed innately disposed to rule a one-party machine. The party Secretariat, which he headed from 1922 onward, moved ahead carefully and systematically to strengthen the party's organization, to make its controls effective, to weed out dissenters and weaklings, and also to place Stalin's supporters in important posts. Thus, while the party apparatus gained in strength, Stalin's own strength within that apparatus gained disproportionately. And thanks to the loyalty of Stalin's supporters, the combined power of the Central Control Commission and the Workers' and Peasants' Inspectorate after 1923 became, next to the Secretariat, his most reliable control instrument.

Careful management of his various offices brought Stalin, at the meeting of the Twelfth Party Congress (April 1923), virtual although disputed control of the party machinery. The Central Committee of the party had been packed with his nominees. He had achieved the power to influence the selection of "elected" delegates who would support him without question in any matter discussed at national party conferences or congresses. The party, in sum, was already ruled by a new dictator, although that dictator was constrained—by his jealous and obstreperous colleagues and by the fact that Lenin still lived—to be circumspect about the way he exercised his strength.

There was still another powerful weapon that could be used against the democratic critics in the party. This was the resolution condemning factionalism within the party passed at the Tenth Congress, in 1920, when a vigorous Lenin had forcefully attacked his own critics. All members of the party were formally required by this strongly worded resolution to accept the will of the leadership. Indeed, the Central Committee was given the authority to expel factionalists from its midst, to reduce their rank, or even to expel them from the party. Party unity thus became a shibboleth enforced by stern measures, which were justified by the argument that the existing problems of survival were too serious to permit endless debate. For Stalin, this was proper; he wanted a political phalanx that would carry out the leaders' orders. But other men wanted to be certain that the orders issued represented the will of the party. They believed that by means of free and open discussion the highest circles of the party should air all issues, and that reason rather than authority should be the criterion for decision making.

Because Trotsky was viewed by many Bolsheviks as the

hated outsider, as well as the man most likely to succeed Lenin, he seemed almost fated to become the symbol of opposition to the new party bureaucracy. During the 1920s, although he was by no means the most effective or dogged critic of bureaucracy, his fame served to make him the natural focus of the conflict. His actions as an oppositionist, therefore, are integral to this struggle. On December 5, 1923, in his letter "On the New Course," he attacked the triumvirate and made clear the main lines of battle, calling for an end to the terror and repression of the party by a few men and for the revival of the right of members to criticize. The challenge was accepted at once by Zinoviev, who, seriously considering himself next in line for the succession, already feared and resented Trotsky. Zinoviev commented publicly that Trotsky should be arrested for his overt factionalism. Then Kamenev joined the fight, and Stalin, lagging only a little, marshalled his party controls for the elections to the Thirteenth Party Conference (January 16–18, 1924), with the purpose of crushing Trotsky's support in the elections. This was achieved. Of the one hundred and twenty-eight delegates sent to that conference "only three belonged to the Opposition."[2] During the conference, the triumvirate, calling themselves "true Leninists," viciously attacked the Opposition movement, labeling their opponents "false Leninists and fraudulent Bolsheviks," men who wanted the party to become a democratic, and therefore feckless, talking shop. The triumvirate further denounced as dangerous the economic ideas of the Opposition and they reviewed Trotsky's career disparagingly. Subsequently Trotsky and his supporters found that *Pravda,* the principal organ of the party press, would not publish their views, for Stalin's Party Control Commission had fired those *Pravda* staff members who believed the controversy should be reported objectively.

Lenin's death, on January 21, 1924, brought home to all party members the genuine need for unity in the face of the new situation. Thus, Lenin's death strengthened Stalin's posi-

[2] Robert V. Daniels, *The Conscience of the Revolution* (Harvard University Press, Cambridge, 1960), p. 233.

tion. And Stalin was not slow to consolidate his gains with ostentatious deference to the fallen leader, appearance at the bier, and his famous rhetorical Te Deum read at the Congress of Soviets on January 26:

> Departing from us, Comrade Lenin enjoined us to guard the unity of our party as the apple of our eye. We vow to you, Comrade Lenin, that this behest we shall fulfil with honour . . .!
> Departing from us, Comrade Lenin enjoined us to guard and strengthen the dictatorship of the Proletariat. We vow to you, Comrade Lenin, that we shall spare no effort to fulfil this behest, too, with honour!
> Departing from us, Comrade Lenin enjoined us to strengthen with all our might the alliance of workers and peasants. We vow to you, Comrade Lenin, that this behest, too, we shall fulfil . . . .[3]

Several more repetitive paragraphs followed, each one ending in that significant phrase, "We vow to you, Comrade Lenin . . ."

With these words Stalin shrugged his shoulders into Lenin's mantle, attempting to cast himself as the true heir of the great leader. In a milieu where other factions were grasping uncertainly at power, he moved with the utmost assurance and daring. By contrast Trotsky, nursing a vague malaise that had taken him off to the Black Sea, did not attend Lenin's funeral. Later he was to charge that Stalin had deliberately kept him away, and in his biography of Stalin he reproduced the following telegram to prove his point: "The funeral will take place on Saturday. You will not be able to return on time. The Politburo thinks that because of the state of your health you must proceed to Sukhumi. Stalin."[4] In fact—as Trotsky learned only later— the funeral was postponed a day, so that he could have returned in time. For Trotsky's career, his absence was a catastrophe.

Precisely whom Lenin had wanted to succeed him is not at all clear. There is some reason to believe that as his illness

[3] J. V. Stalin, *Works* (Foreign Languages Publishing House, Moscow, 1953–1955), VI, 48–50.
[4] Leon Trotsky, *Stalin, An Appraisal of the Man and His Influence,* edited and translated by Charles Malamuth (Hollis and Carter, Ltd., London, 1947), p. 382.

forced him into a relatively contemplative life, he began to look more critically at the party-state structure he had helped to create. As with Trotsky later, the separation from power permitted him to revert to the role he had played so long and so well before 1917—that of critic of the status quo and champion of the revolutionary conscience. The man who was no longer directly responsible for the hard decisions of government found it easy to criticize the man at the controls. Indeed, Lenin's last articles were vitriolic denunciations of the bureaucratic corruption he saw everywhere, even in Rabkrin, the Workers' and Peasants' Inspectorate, which he had devised for the express purpose of wiping out such corruption. And his last political maneuvers were desperate schemes designed to curb or quell rough and autocratic exercises of party authority by Stalin and Stalin's friends.

Deeply concerned with the problem of succession, Lenin pondered long on the question of who might head the party after his death. And during his last years, he managed to dictate a number of brief notes about the party's best men. Unfortunately, his attempts to give judicious advice to the party actually added to its confusion and left evidence of his belief that none of his followers was good enough to succeed him. Thus, in what has long been known as "Lenin's Testament," a note addressed to the party that he dictated in late December 1922, he provided deep insights into the characters of his probable successors, but failed to give any of them his blessing. Expressing his worry that the party might split and noting that the first need was to guarantee its solidarity, he went on to say:

> I think that the fundamental factor in the matter of stability—from this point of view—is such members of the Central Committee as Stalin and Trotsky. The relation between them constitutes, in my opinion, a big half of the danger of that split, which might be avoided, and the avoidance of which might be promoted, in my opinion, by raising the number of members of the Central Committee, to fifty or a hundred.
>
> Comrade Stalin, having become General Secretary, has concentrated an enormous power in his hands; and I am not

> sure that he always knows how to use that power with sufficient caution. On the other hand, Comrade Trotsky, as was proved by his struggle against the Central Committee in connection with the question of the People's Commissariat of Ways and Communications, is distinguished not only by his exceptional abilities—personally he is, to be sure, the most able man in the present Central Committee—but also by his too far-reaching self-confidence and a disposition to be too much attracted by the purely administrative side of affairs.
>
> These two qualities of the two most able leaders of the present Central Committee might, quite innocently, lead to a split; if our party does not take measures to prevent it, a split might arise unexpectedly.[5]

To understand the further development of Lenin's evolving analysis of Stalin, it is necessary to recall that the once-vigorous Lenin was, during his last years, under Stalin's official surveillance. The Politburo had assigned to the master of petty detail the responsibility for seeing that the sick man's needs were cared for. Lenin thus found himself removed from the Kremlin, surrounded by nurses and secretaries and doctors. His principal entry into the Politburo as well as to the various offices of government was through his wife, the Old Bolshevik, Krupskaya, one of whose duties was to importune Stalin for the variety of documents and information that Lenin demanded in order to keep abreast of events.

Inevitably, Stalin's brusque impatience and unwillingness to have Lenin constantly investigating his actions brought him into conflict with Krupskaya. When Stalin bluntly criticized her for encouraging the continued political activity of her husband, Krupskaya, distressed, let her feelings get back to Lenin. Armed with this new evidence of Stalin's character, Lenin on January 4, 1923, dictated a postscript for his "Testament." The postscript said:

> Stalin is excessively rude, and this defect, which can be freely tolerated in our midst and in contacts among us Communists, becomes a defect which cannot be tolerated in one holding

[5] Nikita Khrushchev, *The Crimes of the Stalin Era* (The New Leader, New York, 1962), pp. S66–S67.

the position of the Secretary General. Because of this, I propose that the comrades consider the method by which Stalin would be removed from this position and by which another man would be selected for it, a man who, above all, would differ from Stalin in only one quality, namely greater tolerance, greater loyalty, greater kindness and a more considerate attitude toward the comrades, a less capricious temper, etc.[6]

While Lenin's decision that Stalin should be removed from the office of General Secretary was strongly influenced by Stalin's rudeness to Krupskaya, his judgment was also founded on years of experience and on evidence of more recent, disagreeable efforts by the Georgian to have his way in a number of party matters. Learning of these actions, Lenin pressed forward his own private efforts to halt what he considered their evil and bureaucratic consequences. He personally investigated extensive charges that Stalin and his friends had acted with criminal brutality and autocratic violence in suppressing their enemies within the Georgian party. Similarly he prepared vituperative articles criticizing the functioning of Rabkrin, laying the blame for its shortcomings upon Stalin. The upshot of this continued nagging from Lenin's villa was a new quarrel. Krupskaya, continuing as Lenin's principal liaison agent and defender, again suffered a tongue-lashing from an irate Stalin. And again Lenin learned of the event. This time he replied with a furious personal letter (dictated on March 5, 1923), with copies to Stalin, Zinoviev, and Kamenev:

> Dear Comrade Stalin: You permitted yourself a rude summons of my wife to the telephone and a rude reprimand of her. Despite the fact that she told you that she agreed to forget what was said, nevertheless Zinoviev and Kamenev heard about it from her. I have no intention to forget so easily that which is being done against me, and I need not stress here that I consider as directed against me that which is being done against my wife. I ask, therefore, that you weigh carefully whether you are agreeable to retracting your words and apologizing or whether you prefer the severance of relations between us.[7]

[6] Quoted in Khrushchev, p. S9.
[7] Khrushchev, pp. S11–S12.

Stalin apologized, although the text of his apology is not known, but it was too late for Lenin to forgive, for his next stroke, which came on March 9, paralyzed his right side and brought an end to his political activity.

The tragic mixture of political and personal relationships we have just examined says much about Stalin's grim determination to hold power. Certainly he was not Lenin's choice for the succession. And it is apparent, when one examines the voluminous evidence Lenin had of Stalin's various misdemeanors, that Lenin was just in his criticisms, even though in the last notes he spoke more like an offended husband and an angry sick man than a calm and responsible leader of the party. Whatever over-all political import these criticisms may have had, they reveal in retrospect that by 1923 the ailing leader had lost all power to influence his party effectively.

As we have seen, the man self-selected to be Lenin's successor calmly claimed that honor with the words: "We vow to you, Comrade Lenin . . ." And with dogged patience he rigged the elections for the next major policy meeting, the Thirteenth Party Congress. When that Congress met in May 1924, the degree of the triumvirate's control was overwhelming. Not one member of the Opposition had been elected as a voting delegate, although Trotsky, Eugene Preobrazhensky, and six others were present without the right to vote. Trotsky himself, faced with Stalin's charge that he and the Opposition were declaring war on the party and threatening its destruction, was compelled to protest his loyalty. And since loyalty was construed as silent obedience to the overwhelming majority, Trotsky was ultimately constrained to say: "My party—right or wrong . . . I know one cannot be right against the party . . . for history has not created other ways for the realization of what is right."[8] He had been soundly defeated.

It should be noted that the atmosphere of the Thirteenth Congress was in sharp contrast to that of Lenin's congresses. By May 1924, arguments were stereotyped and monotonously re-

[8] Quoted in Leonard Schapiro, *The Communist Party of the Soviet Union* (Random House, New York, 1960), p. 284.

peated; claques of Stalin's supporters applauded regularly, on cue, harassed the efforts of dissenting members to speak, and mindlessly voted complete approval of the leadership's decisions. The era of debate and democracy was gone. Already Stalin's regime had begun in earnest, and his power was consolidated still further at that congress by the enlarging of the Central Committee and the party's Central Control Committee, both of which were packed with Stalinist delegates. Of special significance was the charge given the latter agency: to "guard the unity of the party and the established line of Bolshevism from any deviations whatsoever."[9]

Trotsky was stripped of real power in the party, both by the machinations of the triumvirate and by his own erratic habit of withdrawing from the fight at moments when he should have stood fast. It remains one of the mysteries of Soviet history why Trotsky, who in 1922–1923 had seemed almost certain to succeed Lenin, was so easily pushed aside by Stalin and his colleagues. In the records of the struggles of these times, one is repeatedly struck by Trotsky's distaste for petty intrigue and factional conflict, and by his refusal to lower himself to Stalin's street-fighting tactics; certainly Trotsky's unwillingness to fight fire with fire for what he believed in contributed to his ultimate defeat.

There is also reason to believe that Trotsky lacked his opponent's ruthless courage. Although in his earlier years and later under Lenin's leadership he had seemed to dare anything, in the struggle with Stalin, repeatedly, when the issues were clear and Trotsky's next step was virtually dictated to him, he found some way to avoid taking that next step and to evade the battle. Fundamentally Trotsky seems to have preferred the role of *enfant terrible,* critic and fiery revolutionary, to that of governing authority; it was as though he secretly feared to assume personal responsibility for the regime and the bureaucracy required to rule Russia. Also there was always a touch of the litterateur, of the dilettante, and of the dashing cavalryman, about him; he could cut and stab in a sharp debate or exchange of letters, but he seemed almost instinctively to withdraw from

[9] Quoted from the Resolution of the XIIIth Congress in Daniels, p. 240.

the tough hand-to-hand combat that might have won him the party leadership. Granted Stalin's advantage in having very early gained control over the administrative machinery, the question still remains: Why did the ambitious Trotsky permit Stalin to secure this advantage without a struggle?

In later years Trotsky pled a vague nervous illness to explain his hesitancy in the contest. But this illness has never been adequately identified. It seems to have been some weakness of spirit or character which acted erratically to deny him the role he thought was his. He was after all a writer who loved fierce words and a fine turn of phrase, but he was irrevocably wedded to theorizing in the endless fashion of the Russian intelligentsia and he had no heart for the tedious and brutally hard job of ruling the Communist party and refashioning the Russian Empire. He was, in sum, a gifted revolutionary, a brilliant theorist, and could be under proper leadership a distinguished administrator; yet he was unable to turn himself into what the Soviet state needed most of all—a ruler who would permit nothing to stand in his way. Further, unlike Stalin, he did not lust for political power with the total concentration of all his being.

He seemed almost anxious to have done with the quarrel. After another brief literary attack, signaled by the publication of his *Lessons of October,* in which he denigrated both Zinoviev and Kamenev, he was forced in January 1925 to give up his chief political base, his office as Commissar of War. He was given instead minor posts dealing with the administration of electrification and of foreign concessions, and he was warned by the Central Committee that further defiance of party norms would result in serious disciplinary action. Examining the lengthy documents of these conflicts one cannot help but wonder if Trotsky accepted these decisions with relief, glad to be separated from the crude world of power, happy in the belief that he could yet win the true revolution with the weapons he loved best to employ—brilliant polemics and conspiratorial agitation.

Even while the struggle with Trotsky was at its height, a second crisis in the party's leadership was building. In the fall of 1924, Stalin turned against his triumvirs, Zinoviev and Kamenev, joining with the right-wing members of the Politburo,

Nikolai Bukharin, Aleksei Rykov, and M. P. Tomsky, to form a new majority. This regrouping placed Zinoviev and Kamenev in the minority and forced them into opposition. Thus the two men who had acted as the defenders of unity and party authority during the fight with Trotsky now found themselves demanding (as Trotsky had before them) the right to defend themselves in party circles and to argue openly with the new party leader and dictator, Stalin. It was too late. They had unwittingly supported the growth of Stalin's bureaucratic power, thinking that it would serve their own interests, and when they realized that he had grown too strong he was already concentrating his efforts upon undermining them in their own strongholds. In this struggle, the defense mounted by the new opposition bore little resemblance to Trotsky's principled stand. The new fight was a simple series of maneuvers for political power by the former members of a tight triumvirate.

Leo Kamenev's power base rested on his position as Chairman of the Moscow Soviet. In late 1924, Stalin replaced the Secretary of the Moscow Party Committee, I. A. Zelensky, a supporter of the Zinoviev-Kamenev bloc, with a new man, N. A. Uglanov, who also received Zelensky's place in the Orgburo and the Secretariat. As a result of Zelensky's displacement, in 1925, when Kamenev sought support on his home ground, he found that Stalin was already in control there.

Zinoviev was made of sterner stuff, and his combined offices gave him strength that Kamenev did not have. Besides belonging to the Politburo and Central Committee of the party, he was Chairman of the Comintern and Chairman of the Leningrad (changed from Petrograd on January 26, 1924) Soviet, the second most important regional division of the party. Stalin's efforts to move into the Leningrad party organization were met and skillfully resisted. Zinoviev, imitating Stalin's own tactics, not only removed the latter's supporters from the Leningrad organization, but subsequently screened the Stalinists from the panel of Leningrad delegates elected for the Fourteenth Congress of the party.

Thus balked in Leningrad, Stalin moved to undermine Zinoviev's position in the Comintern, provoking him into a doctrinal debate that proved embarrassing for the Leningrad leader. At this point, having laid the groundwork for the customary stage-managing of the Fourteenth Party Congress (December 1925), Stalin was ready for an open confrontation. Although he was unable to keep the Leningrad supporters of Zinoviev away from this congress, the latter were overwhelmingly outnumbered and viciously attacked, and opposition speakers who commented were subjected to noisy heckling. Once again, the opposition was charged with factionalism, that is, with illegal organization against the unified will of the party. They were shouted down, and their arguments were discredited. As a result of this struggle, Stalin's strength in the Politburo grew; he was now the acknowledged leader; his erstwhile colleagues, Zinoviev and Kamenev, pushed into opposition, were soon to join Trotsky in the Left Opposition of 1926-1927, or in what was to be known as the United Opposition movement.

Immediately after the Fourteenth Congress, Stalin pushed his attack on the Leningrad party organization more forcefully by assigning a new secretary, Sergei Kirov, to the city *apparat*. When a friend of Zinoviev's, the Deputy Commissar of War, M. Lashevich, was discovered to be directing an opposition group in the Red Army, Lashevich's disgrace was used to smear Zinoviev and secure the latter's expulsion from the Politburo. Stalin was now forcing the issue. Opposition members who attempted to organize mass meetings were met with furious demands from Stalin that they desist, and they did so, caught on the horns of the dilemma that was to destroy them. Loyal to a monolithic one-party system, they had accepted rules about factionalism that made any dissent against the official party line (now dominated by Stalin) tantamount to treason. By definition, under the principles they had accepted, any effort to organize opposition was an effort to establish a new ruling party. Neither the most ardent advocate of democracy nor the most inveterate of Stalin's opponents cared to be labeled a traitor to Lenin's sacred party. In consequence, the embattled oppositionists repeatedly pledged silence, and each time they took this vow, accepting the precept of unity, they weakened the possibility of challenging Stalin in the future.

In October 1926, Trotsky lost his position in the Politburo, Kamenev was dropped as an alternate, and Zinoviev was deprived of his leadership in the Comintern. Apparently victorious, Stalin did not however slacken his efforts to have done with his enemies. He forcefully suppressed the new public demonstrations which the opposition now turned to in desperation. Insisting that all opposition must stop, Stalin threatened dire consequences, but Trotsky and the others had gone too far to withdraw from the struggle. Their punishment accordingly came swiftly. Late in October 1927, Trotsky and Zinoviev were expelled from the Central Committee. Three weeks later, Trotsky was ousted from the party, and by January 1928, he was on his way to exile in the city of Alma Ata in Kazakhstan.

At this time Stalin had already succeeded in making himself the virtual master of the party. Yet in subsequent years (1928-1929) he would go further, turning against the leaders of the Right (Bukharin, Rykov, and Tomsky) and driving them out, very much as he had driven out the others. The party was to have no leader but Stalin.

Questions of Theory and Practice

For the sake of clarity, the preceding paragraphs have emphasized Stalin's struggle to gain control of the party as well as his personal rivalry with the so-called Left Opposition and with various members of the Politburo. In reality much more than the personal ambitions and political postures of the different leaders was involved in these conflicts. At every important party meeting, crucial issues—practical and theoretical, economic and social—were hotly debated, and policies were decided upon, so that while the contenders for power might often defend one or another side in these discussions simply to embarrass an opponent, they also took positions according to their honestly held convictions and on the basis of their conflicting interpretations of doctrine and reality.

One theoretical problem was of major concern. In the mid-1920s, with the civil war in the past, and with the New Economic Policy functioning reasonably well, an urgent question before all communists was whether the party should take steps to advance world revolution abroad or to begin new and fundamental reforms within the Soviet Union. Trotsky's theory of permanent revolution, to which Lenin had subscribed in 1917 and after, argued that the success of the socialist revolution depended upon its becoming international. Thus, according to Trotsky, although the first revolutionary steps had been taken in Russia, this backward nation could not alone withstand the inevitable hostility of the surrounding capitalist world. The spark of revolution ignited in Russia had to be followed by proletarian revolutions in other nations, until a socialist world had been achieved. This theory presented Bolsheviks with a moral imperative: to guarantee their own success in Russia they must necessarily pursue revolutions in other countries. Stated negatively, failure of the proletariat to win their revolutions abroad would doom the Russian experiment to failure. Thus, the charge presented by the theory of permanent revolution was at once internationalist and nationalist: good Bolsheviks were obligated to dedicate much of their energy to working for international revolution in order to guarantee the continued existence of the Russian experiment.

Stalin, hardheaded and nationalist, was concerned primarily with Russia. He was contemptuous of men who, like Trotsky, urged the launching of dangerous adventures abroad in order to save the revolution at home. Better, he thought, to stay home and consolidate Bolshevik power. In 1924 and during the following two years, he formulated a new theory to justify his resistance to the internationalists. It became known as the theory of *Socialism in One Country,* and its tenuous connection to a sentence Lenin had written in 1915 permitted Stalin to insist that it was "good" Leninist theory. Certainly it was good Leninist practice, for it adhered closely to the practical line Lenin had followed after 1917. Stalin argued that world revolution was not the first necessity, but that, on the contrary, it was possible without world revolution to build socialism in one country. It was even a little silly, he said, to assert that since other revolutions had not occurred by 1924–1926, there was no hope for Russian socialism. Quite the opposite was true—there was every hope if only men would set to work and build. The new nationalist leader of Russia literally told his followers: "Stop sitting helplessly waiting for other nations to go communist! If we work and build our utopia here as I know we can, the revolutions out there will follow in good time."

Tactically, the thesis of socialism in one country provided Stalin with an excellent theoretical club for beating down Trotsky and Zinoviev. Trotsky, of course, could not accept the new theory and subsequently paraphrased its substance in these words, "We are not interested in international revolution but in our own safety, in order to develop our economy." In the same paragraph he characterized Stalin's theory as "a conservative nationalistic deviation from Bolshevism."[10] Actually, however, Stalin was careful not to repudiate international revolution outright; instead he simply insisted that the best way to advance toward international revolution was by building socialism in Russia. And Stalin had the best of the argument.

Although Trotsky, Zinoviev, and other oppositionists could protest that Stalin did not believe in the revolution, pointing to his refusal to give adequate and timely support to the German or the Chinese communists, or to Comintern plans elsewhere, Stalin in turn could charge his opponents with defeatism and with repudiating the idea of the continued success of the revolution in Russia. According to Stalin, since communist revolutionary efforts abroad were not succeeding, the only hope left was socialism in one country. And by putting this conclusion into words, Stalin proved himself a profoundly practical theorist. The people of the nation and the ranks of the party were anxious to better their own lives by improving Russia's economic conditions. He showed them how this could be theoretically justified.

Stalin's theory, presented to the Fourteenth Party Congress in late 1925 and accepted as official doctrine by the party at his bidding, was thereafter a fundamental guide to policy. It was also the whipping boy, which oppositionists who believed in permanent revolution continued to flog long after they had

[10] Trotsky, p. 396.

been removed from power. Thus it influenced or determined subsequent positions taken by opposing sides on many important issues.

In the specific area of foreign policy, Stalin's interest in building socialism in one country soon provided justification for oppositionist attacks. Soviet foreign relations were rendered exceedingly difficult by the avowed aim of communism and the Soviet-controlled Comintern to bring destruction to the capitalist countries through worldwide revolution. While Stalin undoubtedly believed in this ultimate goal, he had an empire to rebuild at home, for which he needed peace, allies, and trade. He therefore followed a dualistic policy. He worked for peace and trade, vital for the Soviet state's security and well-being, and he coupled this with the manifestly incompatible policy of seeking to advance communist revolution around the world, often to the disadvantage of the very nations whose friendship he sought. Such fence-straddling made him vulnerable to his critics and immeasurably complicated his foreign policy.

Presumably Stalin followed the dualistic policy because he thought he had to. Certainly it would have been impossible for him to repudiate world revolution openly and still retain leadership in the Bolshevik party. Nor could he forget the sorry state of the Soviet Republic and go adventuring about the world looking for revolutions that might in some distant and unreliable way strengthen the Soviet experiment. Locked into a difficult position, he closed no doors tightly and burned none of his bridges down to the waterline, allowing his foreign policy to reflect, by turns, "socialism in one country" and his own version of "permanent revolution." The consequences, both for Soviet foreign policy and communist revolution, were to be very nearly disastrous in several instances during the 1920s.

In 1923, when the hopes of many ran high that a communist revolution would win in Germany, Stalin read the signs differently and refused to act forcefully in support of the German communists. After the ignominious collapse of that revolutionary effort, he was fiercely castigated by the internationalists. In England, he supported a United Front policy of Anglo-Soviet trade unions, and when the British general strike broke out in 1926, expectations grew that it might end in revolution. But the British workers ultimately proved unready for revolution, Stalin's efforts failed, and Trotsky heaped harsh criticism and blame upon the man who believed in socialism in one country.

Stalin's dualistic policy also failed in China. Following up Lenin's earlier association with Dr. Sun Yat-sen, the nationalist revolutionary leader of China, Stalin continued the policy of the United Front, supporting Dr. Sun's successor, General Chiang Kai-shek. Believing that the tide was running for a bourgeois nationalist revolution in China, Stalin's emissaries and Comintern representatives joined with Chiang in his efforts to seize power and establish a national democratic state. But Chiang, during his march northward in 1926, showed signs of restiveness with his communist alliance, and in early 1927, he turned against his partners, slaughtered many of the Chinese communists and forced the Russians to withdraw. Throughout the Chinese adventure, Trotsky, Zinoviev, and other members of the opposition remained strangely silent or actively supported Stalin's policy. Only in early 1927, with Soviet advisers driven from China and Stalin's policy an obvious catastrophe, did Trotsky characteristically denounce the defeat in China as "not only a defeat for the opportunist line but also a defeat for the bureaucratic methods of leadership."[11]

In the Comintern after the removal of Zinoviev as its leader in 1926, Stalin moved cautiously to assign his own men. To a remarkable degree he was thereby enabled to take over the management of the Comintern and transform its objective from world revolution to the protection of Soviet interests. His fundamentally nationalist attitude toward world communism was made perfectly clear in late 1927 when he said: "An *internationalist* is one who is ready to defend the USSR without reservation, without wavering, unconditionally; for the USSR is the base of the world revolutionary movement, and this revolutionary movement cannot be defended and promoted unless the USSR is defended. For whoever thinks of defending

[11] Daniels, p. 283.

the world revolutionary movement apart from, or against, the USSR, goes against the revolution, and must inevitably slide into the camp of the enemies of the revolution."[12]

Thus in practice and in theory Stalin subordinated immediate world communism to Soviet national interests. By early 1928 he had established formal diplomatic relations and trading agreements with many nations, but had not successfully supported revolution in any other country. Trotsky, of course, roundly condemned Stalin for having betrayed the world revolution.

Meanwhile, on the domestic scene, as the Soviet state moved away from the destruction of civil war and through the first years of the New Economic Plan, economic issues became more sharply drawn. Freed to make a profit from his work on the farm, the peasant produced excellent harvests; but ruined industries recovered less rapidly. While agricultural production by 1923–1924 had reached three-fourths of 1913 levels, industrial production lagged at only one-third of the 1913 figure. This contributed to new difficulties, for as the peasants began to make money they sought to buy the manufactured goods they had gone without for many years; but since the latter were in short supply, prices for manufactured commodities soared, peasant profits were thus seriously diminished, and the peasant continued to feel abused by the new regime.

By 1926–1927 industrial production reached the 1913 level; however, getting back up to prewar levels after almost a decade of postwar effort solved few problems. Industrial plants and machinery were old and worn out, available capital having gone until 1926 primarily to repair old equipment rather than to expand or construct new industries. Moreover, between 1913 and 1926 fourteen million more people had been added to the nation's census, so that the relative per capita product was less in 1926 than it had been before the war. In one important sense, however, NEP had been very successful, for the state continued to control all heavy industries; thus even while state management was inefficient and costly, there

---

[12] Stalin, X, 53–54.

could be no doubt that the Bolsheviks were still in charge and would remain so. Smaller industries (79 percent of the total number in 1926–1927) were still operated under private management, which found itself increasingly the target of strict discriminatory policies—heavy taxation, limited access to raw materials, and restricted use of transportation facilities.

Ideologically, the concessions made by NEP to private property and profit were galling to communist convictions. Sooner or later, everyone in the party believed, Lenin's retreat would have to be halted and the march forward to the socialist state resumed. The fundamental questions were: *When* should the new advance begin? And *how* should it be accomplished? Some form of planned program for industrialization was anticipated by all communists, but as they explored the issues and tried to find answers to the fundamental questions of *when* and *how* to begin the new advance, they fell into controversy over important subsidiary questions: What could be done about the stubborn petty bourgeois majority in the country, the peasantry? Where would capital for investment in industrial growth be found? These questions were crucial, for without satisfactory answers there would be no socialist state; consequently, much study and debate went into their discussion.

In mid-1923, communists of the Left were already advocating a systematic and bold plan for the development of the economy. Trotsky and his brilliant economic adviser, E. Preobrazhensky, insisted that without a well-designed economic plan no serious progress could be made, and Preobrazhensky argued for the development of some form of primitive socialist accumulation. More precisely, he insisted that the peasant population should be heavily taxed in kind; that is, peasants should be compelled to give up their food products at very low prices. The profits from the state's resale of these products could then be used to build new industries. The Left communists, acknowledging that this would create a major social conflict which could escalate to open warfare against the kulak, or rich peasant, nonetheless were prepared to accept these risks in the interest of developing socialist industry.

Stalin's position in the early period (1924–1925) was cautious and hesitant. The peasants had, in 1921, forced Lenin to bow to their will, and Stalin hesitated to provoke them three years later; thus in 1924 he favored slow industrialization and concessions to the peasants, especially to the kulaks, who provided most of the grain surpluses that came into the market. But as industry continued to recover, some drastic action was clearly required to accelerate its further advance. The Soviet Union could not be allowed to stagnate at 1913 levels. At the Fourteenth Congress of the party in December 1925, therefore, Stalin announced that industrialization would be expanded rapidly, particularly heavy industry, so that the Soviet Union could supply its own machine tools and thus lay the base for further growth.

Even this could not satisfy his critics. When Stalin and his right-wing supporters finally accepted the principle of economic planning at a Central Committee meeting in early 1927, the United Opposition seized this occasion to criticize further Stalin's inadequate planning, the backwardness of industry, and the favoritism shown to rich peasants. Later in the year Stalin conceded that higher taxes should be assessed against the rich peasants. By this time, of course, he had won most of his political battles and had consolidated his position. Now he began to borrow the economic theories of his opponents, because they were good theories and the opponents were out of power. He could do as he wished.

The New Party and Its Leader

By the end of 1927 the Communist party had been transformed into an administrative machine that submissively executed Stalin's wishes in most matters. In the Politburo, the main policy-making body which had given him so much trouble in the early 1920s, he had pushed out Trotsky, Kamenev, and Zinoviev, brought in Vyacheslav Molotov, Mikhail Kalinin, and Kliment Voroshilov, and assured himself of the personal loyalty of all candidate members. Thus the Politburo was finally his. The Secretariat, the Orgburo, and the Central Committee worked under his leadership virtually without a hitch, controlling assignments to the important positions in the party and making it possible to rig all elections and stage-manage all meetings.

With the exception of his failure to root Zinoviev's supporters out of the Leningrad party organization in 1925, Stalin controlled party meetings as well as the party press, and therefore he controlled the public understanding of what was going on inside the party. Opposition speeches were shouted down and often cut out of the official reports. Oppositionists could not publish their writings freely and their efforts to hold demonstrations and mass meetings met with rough suppression by the police or by gangs of toughs and rowdies. Meanwhile, at all formal meetings, conferences, and congresses of the party, the carefully selected delegates unanimously approved Stalin's resolutions. Democracy was denounced; unity—that is, disciplined obedience to the decisions of the leadership—was accepted and glorified. A new autocracy had superseded Lenin's tough revolutionary-and-debating society.

The character of the party itself had changed considerably between early 1924 and the beginning of 1928. In numbers, including candidate members, it had grown through these years from 472,000 to 1,304,471. The famous "Lenin's levies," which Stalin had instituted in early 1924 to bring some 200,000 new people into the party even before Lenin's death, had significantly altered its composition. By 1927, it was a party of young and inexperienced people—25 percent of them under the age of twenty-five, more than half under thirty, and over 85 percent under forty. These were predominantly new party members, who had joined after the revolution; indeed, over half of the primary party secretaries (the backbone of the party) in 1927 had entered the party after 1921. These newcomers owed their positions and their loyalties to Stalin and his colleagues; in fact, many had known no other leader but Stalin.

The shifting of opposition supporters away from positions of responsibility, either by Stalin's machinations or by a process of selection that forced out of the party men and women not resilient enough to adapt to its bureaucratization, had profoundly changed the party's inner composition. In the lower ranks,

Stalin, Lenin, and Kalinin at the Eighth Party Congress, March 1919

since almost all these members had joined after the revolution, few had experience like Stalin's in the prerevolutionary underground as "practical" workers. At the higher levels, Stalin's technique of selecting assistants had forced out many of the Old Bolshevik members with Western-Marxist leanings and roots in the intelligentsia. In their places he had put former underground workers, the rough-and-ready types who best understood his motives and methods, and old friends who shared his contempt for the intelligentsia.

In general this new party was poorly educated. Less than 1 percent of its members had graduated from universities, and under 8 percent had completed work at the secondary level. Thus the ranks of the party were composed of young and eager followers who owed their advancement to Stalin and who were persuaded that he was the proper leader, and at the top were Old Bolsheviks handpicked by Stalin because they saw things his way and were prepared to do whatever he demanded. It was a tough and able party, a hardfisted bureaucracy, short on technical and professional competence, bored and uneasy before the theoretical hairsplitting that so fascinated the fast-disappearing party intelligentsia, but capable of hard-driving effort when the leadership sent down its orders.

Despite his unpopularity among opposition circles, Stalin himself by late 1927 had won considerable popularity in the country and in the ranks of the party. While to a Trotsky his speeches and writings were marred by a clumsy, primitive solidity, and his style still seemed to reflect his experience as a Russian Orthodox seminarian, Stalin projected to his underground colleagues, to the ranks, and to millions of ordinary people quite another image. He was the shrewd and patient administrator, a reasonable, moderate man, utterly devoted to Lenin, to Lenin's ideals, and to Russia. Calm, thoughtful, and successful, he might not be a spellbinder in the pulpit, but his ideas were simple and clear and sound; they made sense for Russia.

Within the party, he encouraged a primitive and formalistic interpretation of Lenin's theories and practices. More and more apparent became his tendency to categorize roughly, casting into the camp of the enemy all who did not agree with him absolutely. Related to this tendency was an equally strong penchant for viewing life in highly mechanistic terms that over-simplified complex realities and left no room for exceptions, deviations, or "tedious" qualifications. The core of his thought seemed to be a habit of seeing reality his way, insisting that it be his way, and regarding any resistance to his perception as an imperfection that could be corrected by tightening up administrative laxity and rooting out dissenters.

While the men who opposed Stalin denied his right to rule because he was not a "true Leninist," he probably was, on the contrary, Lenin's most faithful disciple. For Stalin in the late 1920s, as for Lenin earlier, the party was the decisive agency of change; to be effective it had to be as disciplined and instantly responsive to commands as the most precisely tooled military machine. To accomplish its mission of guiding (or driving) the proletariat to the promised utopia in the Russia in which it found itself, the party required total efficiency coupled with forceful leadership at the top. And although Trotsky accused Stalin of ushering in the Thermidorian (reactionary) era of the revolution with his new bureaucracy, it can be argued far more convincingly that Stalin carried the party forward the only way possible at the time, even though in the process he inadvertently may have destroyed the possibility that Russia could ever become *socialist* in the egalitarian and humane sense of the word.

Stalin defeated the oppositionists primarily by inflexibly claiming that the leadership which he personified was Leninist. The oppositionists failed largely because loyalty to the party silenced their efforts to criticize, criticism being considered proof of disloyalty. To be loyal, Stalin tirelessly argued, one must obey without question. The opposition also lost because its leaders could not fight Stalin's kind of fight—the ceaseless, underground maneuvering of the ward boss, the Machiavellian, the intriguer. Trotsky and his friends, contemptuous of Stalin because he lacked the Western-European graces of the émigré revolutionary and the elitist self-righteousness of the traditional intelligentsia, failed to realize that Stalin fought to win at any cost. While they continued their wars of words, Stalin worked for power, not only for himself, but for Russia.

The machine politician mastered the machine and drove out the theorists, whom he could not help but scorn as rash and wordy adventurers. With an instinct having little or nothing to do with Marxism, he developed the party into an effective ruling organization. And with unswerving concentration, he guided his national policies toward making Russia powerful, self-sufficient, and independent. Russia wanted what Stalin promised and followed him because he permitted no alternative.

At the beginning of 1928, although the administrative machine capable of ruling Russia had been created, socialism was still only a word representing something to be achieved in the future. The economy, incapable of advancing further under its existing power, could not be moved except by daring innovations and great courage. Utopia had still to be reached, and Stalin, soberly peering ahead, determined to take the risk in order to achieve the impossible.

CHAPTER TWO

The Second
Bolshevik
Revolution

The Decision to Industrialize

As Stalin maneuvered for power in the years after Lenin's death, the main issues of conflict were not based solely upon personal rivalries, but were more often concerned with complex political and economic problems. Central to all issues was the need for economic growth. Until 1925, the nation's economic target remained simply to bring industrial and agricultural production back to the high levels of the prewar years. By 1926, however, when the period of restoration was judged to be over, the question that concerned all men and women in the Soviet state was: Where do we go from here?

As we have noted in the previous chapter, the New Economic Policy introduced by Lenin in early 1921 was disparaged by many communists as a disgraceful retreat. To preserve communist power, Lenin had restored to the peasant the right to buy and sell his products for profit, to lease land and hire laborers; Lenin had in fact returned the rural economy to the petty bourgeois peasantry, and some thought he had thereby sold out the revolution. Moreover, to encourage the recovery of industry, he had, while preserving state control over the important big industries and the lion's share of the labor force, nevertheless permitted private industry to take over approximately 85 percent of all industrial plants.

Dedicated and literal-minded communists chafed under this mixed economic system, which permitted the "Nepmen"—private entrepreneurs, speculators, and middlemen—to grow rich. Many party members longed to rid themselves of these evil profiteers and get back on the high road of the revolution. In 1921 a compromise had been necessary. But what about 1926 and 1927—when the economy had recovered and when it was obvious to everyone that if further advances were to be made, vigorous and decisive steps must be taken? The general feeling in the ranks of the party in these latter years was that it was time to stop treading water, time to take hold of the economy and move it forward.

The socialist dream of economic equality and social justice for all men was based on an assumption of plenty, on the belief that a better life could be achieved only if the land itself escaped from poverty and hunger. Thus, fundamental to the kind of society Soviet communists wanted was a modern system of industrial production, which could provide consumer goods, raise standards of living, and thereby bring socialism a step nearer. After nearly ten years the Soviet economy had reached a plateau where it became possible to consider moving ahead toward the goals of revolution. In the years immediately after 1925, therefore, it was the consensus of Soviet communists that the time had come to begin the march toward greater industrial production.

As important as the dream of plenty in driving the party to take action to achieve new economic growth was a widespread concern about the position of the nation in the system of nation states. Lacking the capacity to arm and defend the Soviet Union, panicked frequently by rumors that the Western imperialists were preparing new military interventions, party members fervently argued that Russia must industrialize rapidly, at almost any cost. Since world revolution quite obviously was not going to save them, and since the doctrine of socialism in one country implied that they must save themselves, their course was clear: they must attempt to build a heavy industrial productive capacity that could provide the necessary armaments.

A third problem, primarily economic but also in part ideological and of deep concern to party leaders, was the overwhelming agrarian character of the Russian nation. In the late 1920s Russia remained a peasant nation. The party—vanguard of the proletariat—and the Soviet government were fully aware that they existed only at the sufferance of the peasantry—the hated, profit-seeking, capitalist-emulating, rural petty bourgeoisie. And in the years 1926–1927, the affluent upper portion of that peasantry, intent upon higher prices for its produce, was refusing to send its grain to market, displaying once more its power to starve the cities and threaten the very life of the regime. The peasants' refusal to sell their grain unless they received a good profit clearly presented Soviet leaders with a dilemma. Either the Soviet state could go along with the peasants as it had in the past, producing low-priced consumer goods to keep them satisfied, and as a consequence industrializing very slowly, or the peasants would somehow have to be forced to pay the costs of a more rapid industrialization by selling a large proportion of their produce to the state at low prices. And if economic progress depended upon the state's ability to compel the peasants to yield up their grain so that the state could use the profits from selling this grain for industrial investment or ship it abroad in exchange for new machine tools, the question Soviet leaders now had to ask themselves was: How fast can we advance? And this was only another way of asking: How much pressure dare we put on the peasant?

In December 1927, at the Fifteenth Party Congress, Stalin put an end to the years of discussion and debate that had kept party members endlessly occupied with the writing of tentative plans. He abruptly initiated a program of industrialization that emphasized heavy industry and was intended to be supported in part by the introduction of a new kind of agricultural system. "The way out," he said, "is to turn the small and scattered peasant farms into large united farms based on cultivation of the land in common, to go over to collective cultivation of the land on the basis of a new and higher technique. The way out is to unite the small and dwarf peasant farms gradually but surely, not by pressure, but by example and persuasion, into large farms based on common, cooperative, collective cultivation of the land with the use of agricultural machines and tractors and scientific methods of intensive agriculture. There is no other way out."[1] Underlying this statement were the unspoken assumptions that the new system would turn out greater quantities of agricultural produce than the dwarf farms and that the government would find ways to procure the surpluses at its own prices.

Having long rejected the radical suggestions made by Trotsky and the Left for dealing with the peasants, Stalin finally adopted them. Why he had not done so earlier can probably be explained in terms of his sense of timing, the status of his own power before 1927, and his interpretation of domestic and international conditions. When at last he had no doubt about the strength of his personal control over the party, and when it was evident to everyone that the economy had to be driven forward, he decreed that the great advance should begin.

The magnitude of the advance he was proposing became clear only eight months later, when in August 1928 the First Five-Year Plan for the Industrialization of the Soviet Union was presented in its optimum version. A document of nearly a thousand pages, it had been written and rewritten for many months, and its chapters contained detailed programs for an immense economic effort. Within five years, overall industrial production was to increase by 250 percent above that of

[1] J. V. Stalin, *Works* (Foreign Languages Publishing House, Moscow, 1953–1955), X, 312–313.

1927–1928, and heavy industry was to increase by 330 percent. These were targets that implied social change of almost unimaginable scope. One may begin to comprehend the ambitiousness of the plan, at least in terms of its probable consequences, by trying to visualize what would happen to any moderately industrialized society today if it were to double or triple its industrial production within a period of five years: the accompanying social changes would be cataclysmic. So they were to be for the Soviet Union.

Detailed sections of the plan prescribed how the processes of industrialization would be financed and how production costs and the labor force would increase; they specified an immense expansion in capital construction, established production targets for old industries and for new enterprises yet to be constructed, and directed the training of new technicians and specialists. In sum the effort was to plan and control massive changes in all aspects of the economy and the society, an aim at once audacious, admirable, and even somewhat frightening in its connotations. Emphasis was placed above all upon the almost overnight achievement of what must be called "superindustrialization."

Undoubtedly, many members of the carefully rigged party meetings honestly agreed with Stalin that industrialization had to be driven forward rapidly, and even former members of the opposition returned to support what they considered was essentially their own policy. Probably, however, few party members thoroughly realized the vast significance of the decision they had taken or the ramifications that the First Five-Year Plan (formally begun in October 1928) was destined to have for Soviet society and for the rest of the world.

Nor could Stalin himself have had any clear concept of the magnitude of his decision or of the consequences it would have for himself and for every aspect of Soviet life. But while the men of the Left and Right, the Trotskys and Bukharins who had every reason to dread the ruthless willfulness of Stalin, could not have foreseen its many results, some of these men soon began to question the costs of its excessive pace. Stalin, however, once the decision had been confirmed, refused ever to question it; and indeed, because his subsequent commitment to the prolonged and fanatical crusade to transform the Soviet nation with breathtaking speed remained so steadfast, his initial decision must be accounted one of the most momentous political decisions of the twentieth century. For Russia, it marked the beginning of the Second Bolshevik Revolution.

Many of the intended and unintended consequences of this new revolution followed naturally from the simple postulates of socialist theory. From their many discussions, and with Stalin's approval, the Bolshevik party had concluded that socialism meant an abundance of goods for all members of the society. Such abundance could only be achieved through the development of a dynamic industrial productive capacity. The essence of the struggle for socialism, therefore, became the struggle to industrialize. But this struggle, in turn, implied the accomplishment of a transformation of the whole society far greater than anyone could anticipate at the start. In order to lift a backward peasant society out of the mire of its villages and slothful ways and transform it into an ever-changing modern society in step with the twentieth century, much more than a few new industries were required.

Thus Stalin's Five-Year Plan for industrialization and for certain limited changes in agriculture was, simultaneously, a decision that the *whole* society must be modernized. Young men and women had to be educated to the habits and techniques of industrial production. Technical schools and universities had to be created or reconstructed to train the great numbers of engineers, managers, technicians, scientists, and scholars needed to create, run, and improve new and ever more complex industries. Further, given the nature and needs of modern industrial production, it was to be anticipated that many cities would grow by leaps and bounds, that moral and political values would change, that old social institutions would be destroyed and new ones created. In addition the new society would need modern and highly effective governmental control systems, new kinds of intellectual and cultural leaders, and its people would have to learn the new ethics of production to which Western industrial workers had been accustomed for many decades.

In short, starting with the relatively simple aim of industrializing Russia in a hurry, Stalin and the party had committed themselves to modernizing the functions and structure as well as the economic and social thrusts of a great and complex society. That decision has shaken the world with its consequences, and it has also provided a model for other modernizing nations racing to leap into the twentieth century and not overly sanguine about the capacity of democratic procedures to help them proceed at the speed they demand.

Industrialization Plans and Collectivization

The targets established by the First Five-Year Plan for production were based upon very optimistic analyses of the conditions that would exist while the plan was being implemented. The immense rates of growth ordered by the plan required huge increases in the productivity of industries currently in existence, great capital construction programs for new industries, and costly projects for electrification and for the expansion of transport facilities, urban housing, municipal services, and education. In its treatment of the vitally important question of investment, the plan was almost incredibly optimistic. For example, it stipulated that some 90 percent of the massive funds required would be provided by industrial accumulation. These surpluses would result, it was hoped, over the five years after 1928 from a simultaneous growth of industrial production and the successful paring down of production costs. Savings in the cost of production would bring higher profits when manufactured goods were sold, and from these profits, it was planned, would come the money for investment. In order to achieve these goals the plan required that labor productivity increase over five years by 110 percent, that the use of fuels become more efficient, and that construction costs be cut in half.

This optimistic anticipation that industries could fund

their own growth was doomed from the start by a host of difficulties inherent in any such effort to lift a backward economy by its bootstraps. Rural workers who came into industrial work, including many women, were patently incapable of forming a highly productive labor force overnight; in fact they were so ineffective that, ultimately, twice as many workers were needed during the plan as had been stipulated. Similarly wages got out of control and required nearly double the predicted amount. So, too, costs of construction soared beyond all official estimates because of the lack of skilled managers and builders, the rising costs of materials, the chaos in transportation systems, and poor planning that led to frequent delays.

Other nations embarking upon the struggle to build new industries have funded their development with money borrowed from foreign lenders. The initial Soviet plan had in fact anticipated that some 700 million rubles might be sought abroad, but as the plan evolved, and particularly as the world depression spread its pall into Russia, Stalin argued that Russia must lift itself upwards by its own efforts. Foreign loans, in the Leninist lexicon, signified colonialism and loss of the nation's independence to its creditors. For Stalin, one of the principal purposes of the industrialization campaign was to guarantee the Soviet Union's independence, once and for all; by this logic, foreign loans were unacceptable.

In the agricultural area, the First Five-Year Plan proposed a very cautious scheme of collectivization.[2] Approximately 15 percent of the total cultivated land was to be collectivized by 1933, and the plan frankly stated that "in this field we are still

[2] The term *collectivization* refers to the Soviet process of transforming small private farms into large "collective" farms by persuading or compelling peasants to consolidate their holdings and to work the land cooperatively. In utopian and communist theory such collective farms were expected to produce at higher rates than did the small private farms, and peasants who joined the collectives were believed to be entering a more progressive social system than their petty-bourgeois colleagues could ever know. In reality, under Stalin, collective farms were forcefully managed by party-appointed chairmen, and the collective farm system was designed primarily to control the peasants and to procure larger portions of agricultural products for the market than was possible under private farming.

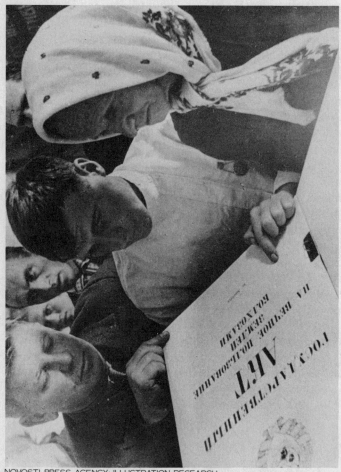

Peasants examining the State Act granting land for use by collective farms

feeling our way, for the fundamental technical principles have not as yet been clearly formulated."[3] In addition to this slow and partial collectivization, the plan called for the establishment of large state farms, which could be operated with hired labor and which, it was anticipated, would turn over 60 percent of their product to the state. Meanwhile, the remainder of the peasantry was to continue on private farms.

During the first year of the plan (October 1928–1929), industrial growth actually exceeded expectations, achieving a 23.7 percent increase rather than the planned 21.4 percent. While problems of quality, cost, and labor multiplied, a good beginning had been made. It now seemed evident that in order to take advantage of this running start, targets should be increased for the following years and the production campaign should be pushed forward as rapidly as possible. This, of course, meant finding more money to import machinery and pay for raw materials, construction, and labor. Once again the fundamental problem was where the money could be found.

Resolutely moving the nation toward superindustrialization, and apparently beginning to forget the plan as planned and to view industrialization as a race to see how fast he could make the process move, Stalin reviewed the situation in 1928 and through 1929 and concluded that the peasantry had to be dealt with. It seemed to him that unless he could finally solve the peasant problem, he and the Soviet Union were doomed to be forever hampered and held back by the peasantry. The issue, as he chose to present it to the party, revolved around the rich peasants, the kulaks. During the autumn and spring sowings of 1927 these kulaks had persisted in cutting down their production and had refused to sell their harvests at the prices offered. In Stalin's view, as he explained to the party, this meant that the stocks of agricultural produce needed to support the development of the Five-Year Plan would not be forthcoming.

To Stalin, therefore, the basic issue was clear. While the

[3] Quoted in Maurice Dobb, *Soviet Economic Development Since 1917* (International Publishers, New York, 1948), p. 225.

industrial side of the Five-Year Plan appeared to be workable, the sullen and uncooperative peasants were once again posing a grave threat to the Bolshevik dream. If they would not produce foods and fibers and sell them at prices the government could afford to pay, the investment funds earmarked for industry would be needed instead to buy food for the rapidly expanding urban population. By hoarding their harvests and demanding higher prices, the peasants were in effect making themselves the dictators of Soviet policy. They possessed the power to bring the First Five-Year Plan to a halt for the sake of their own profit, and they displayed no serious interest in the nation's industrial progress.

One method of overriding peasant resistance was already at hand. Acting in the very months when the plan was being prepared for implementation, Stalin had taken what he called "emergency measures." That is, he reverted to War Communism policies of forceful requisitioning. As he explained to the Leningrad party organization on July 13, 1928, he had turned to "arbitrary administrative measures, the infringement of revolutionary laws, house-to-house visitations, unlawful searches, and so on. . . ."[4] Speculators who were found holding back grain for higher prices, no matter what their economic status, were classified as kulaks, all surplus stocks they held above an established norm were confiscated, and they were subjected to heavy fines.

Sometime during this preliminary skirmish, probably during the summer of 1928, Stalin appears to have reached a private decision that the only solution to the problems arising from the independence of the peasants was the introduction of full collectivization. For him, the enemy was clearly visible, and in such a situation his instinct was to strike unerringly for the jugular. Needing money to invest in his industries, he concluded, as the Left communists had so strenuously argued earlier, that it could only come from capital extracted from the peasants. What better way than finally and squarely to face the issue that had always held Russia back, to confront the peasant

<hr />

[4] Stalin, XI, 215.

with force and to break him once-and-for-all to the centralized commands of the government?

However, since in 1928 Stalin was as yet unable to exert absolute power in the Politburo, he was careful to conceal this decision. Not until the second half of 1929 did he finally force the rightist and propeasant opposition of Bukharin, Rykov, and Tomsky into submission. Then, having undermined their strength in the Politburo and deprived them of other offices, he gained virtually total control over the party machinery and was at last able to do more or less as he wished. At this point, in the summer of 1929, the party began its all-out effort to destroy the rich peasants, who appeared to Stalin and many other communists to be the backbone of peasant resistance—the "vicious rural bourgeois class" that refused under any circumstance to give up its independence and its right to sell its produce for the highest profit.

By late 1929, the party had sent out 25,000 workers "with adequate political organizational experience" to strengthen the efforts of local village communists in implementing the new policy. Speaking to a Conference of Marxist Students of the Agrarian Question on December 27, 1929, Stalin described what the new policy meant in action. He denounced all halfway measures of dealing with agricultural problems and declared, "we have passed from the policy of *restricting* the exploiting tendencies of the kulaks to the policy of *eliminating* the kulaks as a class. This means that we have made, and are still making, one of the most decisive turns in our whole policy."[5]

It was indeed a decisive turn. For the first time in Russia's long history, a political ruler during peacetime was bold enough to attempt to dictate all the vital economic decisions in agriculture, and not only to tell the peasant what he would produce, but also to compel him to hand over his produce to the state. Thus, determined to bend the peasant millions to his will and to force them to give up their grain at his demand, Stalin deliberately and consciously introduced a new period of civil war into the USSR. His effort to have his way provoked a sharp and

[5] Stalin, XII, 173.

bloody conflict, with profound and lasting consequences for the nation.

Following Stalin's announcement of the government's policy of liquidating the kulak (already underway), the Central Committee of the party on January 30, 1930, formally set aside the previous policy of piecemeal collectivization and instituted a drive to achieve complete collectivization as soon as possible. Gone was the cautious and slow development envisioned in the earlier versions of the Five-Year Plan. The drastic character of the new liquidation campaign was spelled out succinctly by the Central Committee of the Ukraine on January 6, 1930, when it ordered its members "to carry out a merciless campaign against the kulaks along the entire front," specifying that "the elimination of the kulaks from the districts of total collectivization and their deportation from the village must be a component part of the struggle waged by collective farms and poor and middle peasants . . ."[6] With the target date for *full* collectivization set for the fall of 1930, or at the latest the spring of 1931, the Soviet countryside during the first months of 1930 became the scene of appalling violence and chaos.

Party organizations were directed to achieve immediate collectivization in the villages. The secret police moved out into the rural areas to compel the kulaks to give up their farms and established facilities for isolating their victims in distant concentration camps. Poor peasants were conscripted for the work of identifying kulaks and organizing new collective farms, and they in turn contributed to transforming the collectivization campaign into a terrifying saga of unprincipled robbery and violence. Poor peasants attacked the households of rich and middle peasants, stole their livestock, furniture, jewelry and other purely personal items, burned houses and other property, and indulged in innumerable acts of wanton savagery. The beleaguered kulaks themselves, rather than give up what they had worked so long to accumulate, slaughtered their own livestock and attempted to defend themselves and their families,

[6] Quoted in Alexander Baykov, *The Development of the Soviet Economic System* (The Macmillan Company, New York, 1948), p. 200.

thus provoking even more ferocious onslaughts by the collectivizers.

The events of the campaign to liquidate the kulak and to achieve full collectivization form an appalling story of the suffering and death of men and women who hardly knew why they were being attacked. It is a story of endless lines of peasants driven away from their homes and carried off like cattle in open freight cars to distant concentration camps. In the unfolding tragedy, men denounced their village neighbors out of spite or because they coveted the neighbors' livestock, and the very word *kulak* quickly lost its original meaning. Although its "rich peasant" connotation was carefully preserved by the communists, the word was soon applied to *anyone who opposed collectivization*. Thus middle and poor peasants quickly found that they too could be branded with the fearful word, that at any moment they too might be set upon by their neighbors or some communist-organized wedge of collectivizers, who might schedule them for the next shipment or list of victims to be deprived of home, citizenship, and freedom, or, too often, their very lives.

During this conflict, millions of peasants were forcefully herded into new collective farms, despite the fact that very few people, including the party members and officials who directed the struggle, knew exactly what a collective farm was supposed to be or how it was supposed to operate. The type of communal organization officially designated for establishment was the *artel*, which would socialize "all draught animals, agricultural machinery, livestock yielding marketable production, seed stocks, fodder to the amount required for the upkeep of the socialized livestock, all buildings necessary for carrying out collective farming and all enterprises processing agricultural produce."[7] But what of the private households of the former rich and middle peasants? Who was to hold these? And how was the work in the new organization to be administered? Which of the "members" were to plant the seed, plow, or care for the cattle? Who would make the principal managerial decisions? And how were the profits to be shared? Answers to all these questions

[7] Baykov, pp. 194–195.

had to be worked out on individual farms during the height of the collectivization struggle while central authorities were trying to develop general instructions.

Stalin and other communist leaders hoped that the new large collective farms would exploit improved agricultural techniques and reap the advantages of modern agricultural science. But in the last quarter of 1929 and the first two months of 1930, the scientists and rural specialists needed for such vast operations were not available; the tractors that were to modernize agriculture had not yet been built; indeed the factories that were to produce these tractors were still in the blueprint stage. Techniques for management and transportation, for the collection and distribution of produce and industrial goods, had yet to be devised; questions of financing and marketing were variously understood; and the masses of peasants who had been forced to move into the collectives had no way to influence their new masters. It was small wonder, then, that many of the newly collectivized peasants, as well as those who were driven into exile, could only wonder what insane mind had engineered this nightmare and could only denounce and resist what they considered to be utter madness.

Suddenly, at what appeared to be the height of the struggle, Stalin, the man who had begun the conflict, the prime mover behind the coercion and violence, brought this civil war to an end. On March 2, 1930, his *Pravda* article, "Dizzy with Success," rudely halted the holocaust. Attacking the lower ranks of the party for overzealously attempting to "socialize everything," he spoke strongly in support of a new *Model Charter for the Artel* that was being published that very day. "We know," he said, "that in a number of districts of the USSR, where the struggle for the existence of the collective farms is far from being over, and where the artels are not yet consolidated, attempts are being made to skip the artel form and to leap straight away into the agricultural commune. The artel is still not consolidated, but they are already 'socializing' dwelling houses, small livestock and poultry; moreover this 'socialization' is degenerating into bureaucratic decreeing on paper, because the conditions which would make such socialization necessary do not yet exist." He ridiculed the overzealous "socializer" who had ordered the registration of every head of poultry in every house-hold, and he took a moment to sneer at "those 'revolutionaries,' —save the mark!—who *begin* the work of organizing an artel by removing the bells from the churches. Just imagine, removing the church bells—how r-r-revolutionary!"[8] Calling such events "blockhead exercises," he ordered a return to voluntarism; in sum, he called a halt to the collectivization campaign, saying that errors had been made and insisting that henceforth the peasants should not be driven into the collectives by force but should be persuaded to join of their own volition.

There were probably several reasons why Stalin halted the campaign when he did. Most obvious is the fact that he had won his first objective; he had already beaten the kulak. By the beginning of March, several millions of the stronger peasants who had the will and ability to resist had lost their lives or their liberty, had been deported to the north or to Siberia, or had slipped away into the cities. Stalin had won this major point.

But for other reasons as well it was unwise to continue the shocking and bloody struggle. Undoubtedly, Stalin was well a-ware of the anarchy that the collectivization campaign had brought to the countryside, anarchy that had already provoked the slaughter of valuable livestock and that, if continued, would have made the spring sowing impossible. He knew, too, that many of the new farms had been thrown together too hastily. Many, because they were economically unfeasible, should never have been created; in others, after the wealthy capable farmers had departed, there was simply no one left with sufficient or-ganizational ability and agricultural competence to take charge and manage the operation successfully. Seed, fertilizer, and farm implements were lacking. Peasants were sullen and seething with anger. It was time for Stalin to pause and consolidate his polit-ical victory.

The Consequences of Collectivization

Regardless of the momentary respite now called in this massive effort to liquidate the kulak and gain maximum col-

[8] Stalin, XII, 203–204.

lectivization, certain effects of the effort were to prove irreversible. Therefore, a more precise estimate needs to be made at this point of the multiple impact of the collectivization drive upon Soviet society and the rural economy. Of first importance, perhaps, were the population shifts that took place in the countryside. The great movement of people that occurred during this struggle may best be indicated by means of the following table:[9]

	October 1929	20 Jan. 1930	10 Feb. 1930	1 Mar. 1930	1 May 1930
Collective farms organized (thousands)	—	59.4	103.7	110.2	82.3
Numbers of homesteads collectivized (millions)	—	4.39	10.93	14.26	5.78
Collectivized peasant households as percentages of total number of peasant households	4.1	17.8	42.4	58.0	24.0

As the above figures show, in the forty-odd days from January 20 to March 1, the number of collective farms almost doubled, increasing from 59,400 to 110,200. During this same period the number of households collectivized rose from 4.39 million to 14.26 million, these figures representing respectively 17.8 and 58 percent of the total number of rural households. In terms of human individuals involved, beginning with an estimated 17 million already in collective farms on January 20, the numbers rose to approximately 56 million on March 1. During these six hectic weeks, some 39 million people had been forced to give up their old ways and to join the new farm organizations.

The figures above also allow us to follow these vast social movements a step further, through the reversals that followed.

[9] Adapted from Baykov, pp. 196, 199; Leonard Schapiro, *The Communist Party of the Soviet Union* (Random House, New York, 1960), p. 384.

With the publication of Stalin's "Dizzy with Success" article, and the permission it granted peasants to leave the farms voluntarily, millions of peasants expressed their choice in the ensuing "action plebiscite" by voting negatively with their feet. Two months after Stalin stopped the "blockheads" he had put to work, about 23 million peasants had returned to private farms.

Meanwhile, however, the peasants who fled back to private farms found their situation greatly changed from what it had been earlier. The plots they returned to were often simply pieces of land separated from the local collective rather than the farms they had been forced to abandon. And most who left the collectives returned to private farming empty-handed, lacking poultry and livestock that in the meantime had been slaughtered, stolen, or allowed to expire on the mismanaged collective farms. The situation of the private farmers, therefore, was now much worse than before. It was to prove fairly easy for Stalin to compel many of them to rejoin the collective farms "voluntarily" in 1931, when the percentage of peasant households collectivized again rose—to 61 percent.

In terms of economic and human costs, the collectivization campaign had been disastrous. The kulaks, that is, the most competent and self-reliant farmers, were either in labor camps, in hiding, or dead. Also, during the cataclysm, livestock had been wantonly slaughtered, either from pique, or the naive faith of many peasants that henceforth the government would furnish everything necessary to collective farm members. In some cases poultry and livestock were slaughtered simply because, in the midst of terror and confusion, many peasants chose to gorge themselves on their own livestock rather than give it up to collective ownership. Again a table (see page 60) best demonstrates the seriousness of the slaughter. Subsequent totals of livestock in 1934 are also shown, for the disastrous effects of what happened in the first years of collectivization were to continue for many years.

By January 1, 1931, the number of cattle had decreased 30 percent, sheep and goats 37 percent, and hogs 50 percent, and these drops were to produce still greater losses in succeeding years. The food shortage resulting from these losses seriously aggravated the nation's food problem. And because of the large

LIVESTOCK *(millions of head)*
(1 January)

	1928	1931	1934
Cattle	60.1	42.5	33.5
Hogs	22.0	11.7	11.5
Sheep and Goats	107.0	68.1	36.5
Horses	33.1	—	15.4

number of horses slaughtered, the input of tractors could not improve the agricultural situation in the early 1930s; instead, tractors simply replaced the draft power that had been lost.

Far more significant, politically and morally, was the cost of the collectivization campaign in terms of human lives ruined or lost. These costs have been variously established by scholars around the world. It is believed that at least five million families were deported or destroyed during the months of the kulak liquidation campaign and in the subsequent years of the First Five-Year Plan. Stalin himself, discussing the matter with Sir Winston Churchill at Teheran in early 1945, said that the collectivization effort had cost at least ten million lives and was comparable to the suffering caused by his country's struggle with Hitler. The famine that struck the land in 1932 and 1933 was a product of the chaos and disturbance of the collectivization efforts, as well as of drought. It has been estimated that some five million more peasants died of malnutrition during these latter years.

Whatever the precise number of human lives involved, Stalin's collectivization campaign intensified the peasants' bitter hatred for the regime and established a state of seige between communism and countryside. After 1930, as before, the peasants looked upon the communists in the way helpless natives in other lands view the foreign conqueror who occupies their country and robs it of its goods. Given, first, the need Stalin felt to use coercion and violence to achieve his ends, and second, the rage and hatred created by his tactics, the collectivization campaign introduced new factors that further exacerbated the bad relations already existing. Using force to achieve his ends, Stalin soon found it necessary to use more force; thus, his collectivization policies led directly to the expanded use of police, to the greater suppression of freedom, and the *continually* increasing need to exercise more stringent controls over every activity in the countryside. In sum, while Stalin achieved collectivization, in the process of doing so he lost the opportunity to direct the USSR's development by peaceful means. He had taken not the first, but perhaps the greatest, step of his career toward building the Soviet totalitarian system of government.

But from his own perspective, Stalin had won his chief objectives. The back of kulak resistance was broken, and the further point had been made—there would be collective farms. In the years that followed, this point was hammered home, for over the months and years after the campaign to liquidate the kulak, while peasants withdrew from the collectives and attempted to begin where they had left off, the government continued sober but forceful efforts to win volunteer members. Credits were made available to collective farms, livestock on the collectives was exempted from taxes, members of the collectives were given privileged claims to available consumer goods, and efforts were made to increase supplies of tractors and specialists to the Machine Tractor Stations. Private farmers on the contrary paid discriminatory taxes for the horses they owned and the grain they marketed and were unable to procure the supplies and services they needed. Slowly, under these kinds of pressures, private peasants who found they had no other viable alternative "volunteered" to return to the collectives.

Thus, in the final analysis, Stalin succeeded in his overall effort to control the peasantry. And although his effort had been detrimental to the all-important goal of greater agricultural production, in one sense at least control was all that he had wanted. With the establishment of state and collective farms, despite the fall of agricultural production, the regime was able to siphon off a high percentage of produce for the market at exceedingly low prices. Thousands of urban party workers remained in the countryside; Soviet management organizations were strengthened; a network of Machine Tractor Stations became a system for regulating and supervising almost every activity on the collective farms, from plowing, sowing, and other production tasks, to the development of technical education and surveillance of the peasants' political activities. The Great Administrator had evolved a system for modernizing and managing the peasants and drawing off their agricultural produce with very little payment, and while his struggle had been brutal and terrible, ultimately it secured him the grain he needed for the support of industrialization.

Industrial Achievements of the First Five-Year Plan

Quantitatively, substantial gains were made in industrial production during the period of the First Five-Year Plan. While Soviet statistics, by employing a system of measuring growth based on the fixed prices of goods in 1926–1927, obscure actual achievements, they at least give us a Soviet evaluation of what was accomplished. The value of all large-scale industry in 1932 was 218 percent greater than it had been in 1928, heavy industry had increased 257 percent, and large-scale consumer industries by 187 percent. Within these general areas there had been considerable variation. The output of machinery had increased four times; electrical power had doubled; some 25 percent of the coal produced in 1932 came from new mines; and most of the refining and cracking plants of the oil industry were also new. While figures were never provided for the smaller industries, it is generally assumed that their production decreased.

In general the figures given above represent an almost unbelievable rate of growth for backward Russia. Within a time span of less than five years—for Stalin had impatiently shortened the plan period to four and one-quarter years—heavy industrial production had been more than doubled. This was an accomplishment of such magnitude that its announcement was to evoke a varied response from observers. Many men and women around the world at once acclaimed Stalin as one of the great leaders of history, while others, more skeptical, simply refused to believe that such achievements were possible.

Throughout the first plan, Stalin repeatedly urged acceleration of the tempo. As he directed the process, planned growth fell into the background, and under his impetuous insistence the effort to achieve greater production became a wild race in which each industry or group of industries endeavored to advance as rapidly as possible. Those enterprises achieving assigned production targets ahead of schedule were assigned new, higher targets and hustled along their way. Lagging industries or those which could not get properly started were melded with larger groups or discarded.

In an environment in which force and compulsion came to rule more and more in both industry and agriculture, Stalin's driving determination whipped forward the whole society. And he found much to justify his urgency. Above all there was, he argued, the threat of war, and in 1931 when Japan invaded the Chinese mainland, the plan was altered to put greater emphasis upon arms production. There was also need, he insisted, for more tractors, more electricity, more managerial efficiency, more trade, and more skilled laborers, and all these needs required greater dedication and effort. Typical of his exhortations and of his conviction that the nation must push forward the industrialization campaign no matter what the cost, was the following passage from his speech at the First All-Union Conference of Managers of Socialist Industry on February 4, 1931. Arguing that the rising tempo of industrialization must not be slackened for one moment, he described what seemed to him to have been Russia's tragic destiny in the past:

> One feature of the history of old Russia was the continual beatings she suffered for falling behind, for her backwardness. She was beaten by the Mongol Khans. She was beaten by the Turkish beys. She was beaten by the Swedish feudal lords. She was beaten by the Polish and Lithuanian gentry. She was beaten by the British and French capitalists. She was beaten by the Japanese barons. All beat her—because of her backwardness; because of her military backwardness, cultural backwardness, political backwardness, industrial backwardness, agricultural backwardness. They beat her because to do so was profitable and could be done with impunity.[10]

Stalin went on in this speech to quote Lenin's admonition: "Either perish, or overtake and outstrip the advanced capitalist

[10] Stalin, XIII, 40–41.

countries." And his conclusion, underlined for the new Soviet industrial managers he spoke to, was succinct and terrifying: "We are fifty or a hundred years behind the advanced countries. We must make good this distance in ten years. Either we do it, or we shall go under."[11]

Driven by such fears, Stalin seemed unable to pause to contemplate the terrible costs and side effects of the process he had set in motion. And there were indeed many problems and pitfalls, many difficulties and shortcomings, in the way the plan was implemented. Pushed too rapidly, the scheduled increase of production was achieved quantitatively, but in almost no other way. At the same time the plan's obsessive emphasis upon growth created managerial conduct that was counterproductive. In order to fulfill and overfulfill production goals, managers simplified their products. A shirt factory could produce more shirts if it left off pockets and cuffs, or even buttons, and its director would receive a bonus if he thus overfulfilled the plan. Similarly, a locomotive could be assembled and set down on the charts as one more locomotive for the plan, even though its wheels would not turn. Just as long as a factory produced the volume of goods specified by the plan, success was sure and rewards would follow for its manager. Unfortunately, the manufacture of goods that could not be used only added to the overall costs of production.

Labor problems also plagued the working out of the plan. Instead of doubling the labor capacity per capita as had been projected, in the heavy industries only a 51 percent increase was achieved, and in the construction industry, only 66 percent. This meant an increase in the hiring of laborers, with the result that the number of workers employed in the heavy industries alone rose from 2.7 million in 1928 to a little over 5 million in 1932. In this larger number there were many young and inexperienced workers and nearly a million and a half women new to industrial work. These additions to the labor force had many serious consequences. More workers meant greater demands for urban housing, food, and manufactured consumer goods. Their appetites forced up prices in the urban markets, and led to cries for higher wages, which, in turn, drove up the

[11] Stalin, XIII, 41.

cost of wages. In general, the plan had anticipated an increased wages bill of 50 percent. In fact, the cost of wages doubled, and this, added to the concurrent expense of providing more food and shelter for more urban workers than had been planned, substantially inflated the costs of industrialization.

The behavior of the swelling labor force was also a source of serious difficulty. Because housing was poor, wages low, and factory work plentiful, laborers refused to remain in any one factory very long. Seeking better conditions and higher wages, they practiced what the communists called "flitting," moving from job to job, never becoming experienced and skilled at any one task, and consequently frustrating efforts to increase labor productivity on a broad scale. For the year 1931 the turn-over rate was 90 percent, and in the following year it rose to 107 percent, a situation that meant that millions of workers were intermittently on the move between factories in search of tolerable wages and living conditions.

While the heads of industries and factories competed with one another for laborers by promising better housing, rations, and wages, the state was compelled to introduce a variety of economic and legal measures designed to provide workers with incentives to get the work done and to pin them to their factories. Such measures ranged from new emphasis upon piecework rates (that is, payment according to the amount of work achieved rather than for the time the worker spent in the plant) to a broad scale of wage levels for different skills. Severe penalties were levied for unexcused absence from work; an internal passport system was established in part as a means of controlling the workers' movements; and the Commissariat of Labor gained the right to assign workers to industries of special national importance or to order workers to new districts.

In addition, many techniques were devised for bringing ideological and social pressures to bear upon the laborer in order to get him to work harder and more responsibly. Thus, for example, the regime encouraged factory workers to form themselves into groups known as shock-brigades. The shock-brigade would publicly pledge itself to some extraordinary accomplishment—to fulfill its monthly plan in three weeks, to produce twice as much as the next shift, or to devote its holidays to work in another factory whose production might be lagging. Communists and Komsomols (enthusiastic young apprentice communists) would spark these shock-workers and attempt to involve as many others as possible in voluntary extra work. Another approach was to urge workers to practice "socialist emulation," that is, to strive to keep pace with the best producers. The term itself, of course, implied that the best worker was the one most dedicated to socialism and therefore most loyal and worthy of reward. On the reverse side of this coin, workers who refused to volunteer off-duty hours were considered guilty of unsocialist attitudes or disloyalty, and thus the moral pressure to work harder was made sharp and painful. Judging from the regime's strenuous efforts to recruit shock-workers—in 1931 and 1932 more than 65 percent of all workers were said to be participating in some form of "socialist emulation"—this device was evidently considered a fruitful method for squeezing greater productivity from the Soviet worker. Nevertheless, volunteer labor remained in short supply, and the state's labor costs continued to rise.

Construction costs, too, increased more rapidly than had been expected. Delays in the completion of expensive construction work tied up scarce investment funds for long periods of time; in particular, new gigantic projects, such as the tractor plants at Kharkhov and Stalingrad and the ambitious projects for huge steel-producing combines at Magnitogorsk and in the Kuznetsk Basin, all drove costs upward, compelling the planners to shift more and more money into heavy industry.

Because of the increased costs of labor and construction, the initial investment plan broke down very early. Stalin was forced to pursue the Left's alternative to extreme lengths, squeezing more and more money from the peasant by extracting his grain at ruinously low prices.

Ultimately, it has been estimated, 86 percent of all investments during the first plan period went to heavy industry. This increasing emphasis upon the heavy industries meant that the light industries (those producing such items as textiles and shoes, processing food, and making furniture) as well as the smaller industries (crafts, trades, and shops) were financially starved. Without many of the necessities of life—adequate housing, food, health services, and good clothing—the hard-pressed Soviet people were compelled simply to tighten their belts, patch their rags, and work ever harder in the factories and on the farms.

The nation's lopsided investment situation was aggravated still further by the world depression, which brought disastrous slumps in the level of agricultural prices, particularly in grain. From 1928 to 1931, the price of rye and wheat fell 60 percent. This catastrophic drop in world prices meant that more grain had to be exported for the much needed machine tools and capital that the Soviet Union required in order to satisfy Stalin's determination to push ahead industrially. Similarly, it meant that the planners had to prune further investments in consumer goods industries, suppress the import of items not vitally necessary to the economy, and dispatch new collection squads of disciplined communists to seize more grain and dairy products for export from villages where peasants starved and died before their eyes. During the very years of the great famine, the USSR gave up commodities bitterly needed by the Soviet people, exporting grain and other agricultural products for the materials so vital to the development of industry.

As the plan advanced in the face of these many difficulties, impelled by Stalin's ruthless desire to move forward, its functioning took on an unexpected frenetic quality. It operated as a vast railway system might if its director should cancel all regular schedules and order all trains to arrive at all stations as quickly as possible. While planners and managers at every level should be credited with accomplishing much, the degrees of chaos created by the feverish hurry and the intensity of force required to move ahead seemed to advance the whole system inevitably toward more and more coercion from the top. In other words, once the process of swift industrialization had begun, this process seemed to inject its own imperatives into the situation, commanding the men involved to stop at nothing to keep it going. The decision to achieve virtually instant industrialization committed the party to whatever measures were required to reach that goal. And once caught in the trap of its own resolve to industrialize, the party was uncompromisingly held to this resolve by a man who could not turn back or temper his passion for greater and greater speed. No matter how many Soviet citizens starved, Stalin meant to "overtake and outstrip the advanced capitalist countries."

Concerning the overall accomplishments of the first plan, both positive and negative aspects must be acknowledged. The very success of its great quantitative advances, for example, created many difficulties. The emphasis upon numerical quotas encouraged all industry, from workers up to directors, to stress numbers produced rather than the quality and usefulness of the goods produced. In addition, ineffective planning and management techniques, the influx of unskilled and irresponsible laborers, poor factory conditions and machine shortages, all combined to lower quality, to provide shoddy goods or products that could not be used. Similarly the irregular development of industries produced halts and bottlenecks in production. During the first plan, then, the industrialization process was confused and harassed, costly and chaotic; but *essentially, fundamentally,* and *all-importantly,* it worked. In four years the Soviet Union had taken "a great leap forward."

Strains on the Social System

The great social transformation involved in these efforts to industrialize and the social costs of this transformation have been briefly alluded to earlier. A closer assessment needs to be made of these aspects of Stalin's revolution. During the period of the First Five-Year Plan the number of nonagricultural workers increased from 15.5 million to 24.1 million, while the urban population grew from an estimated 27 million to 40 million. This great influx of people into the cities, as well as the effort to build new cities where open countryside had existed earlier, placed great strains upon every facet of urban life. The new urban dwellers needed food and housing, medical and hospital services, education, entertainment, and consumer goods of every kind.

Basically, however, the issue posed to the regime by this massive population movement was far more profound than the relatively simple problems of providing housing, goods, and services, even though these problems could not be solved adequately at this time. Stalin's more formidable task was to transform ignorant and often hostile peasants and their wives, enthusiastic but unskilled and untrained young men and women from the towns, and aging remnants from the ranks of prerevolutionary labor into a highly skilled, productive, and reliable work force. The need was to remodel this vast inchoate mass into something like the already existing German urban proletariat, to create a new kind of Soviet citizen accustomed to the rhythm and tedium of work in the factory, knowledgeable about machinery and technology, and driven by an inner urge to work productively for long hours. In a few years something like the West's "Protestant Ethic" had to be engrafted upon the minds of illiterate muzhiks, Kazakh shepherds, and unruly youths so that they would be motivated to work hard and to acquire the necessary skills to work effectively.

In the West the creation of productive urban labor forces took place over time in a variety of Catholic-Protestant and bourgeois environments, where it had been possible to argue with telling effect the godly virtues of productive work; the disciplining of workers had also included the decades of poverty, starvation, strikes, low wages, and legalized exploitation by factory owners, described by Karl Marx and many others as deadly warfare between classes. This disciplinary process, Stalin decreed, must take place virtually overnight in the backward Russia he so frenetically urged ahead.

Basic technical education for the ordinary worker was also a fundamental need. Schools were established in the factories themselves to train men and women first to read and then to master the special productive skills the state needed. Classes proceeded day and night, so that while some laborers were pulled away from their machines during workdays, other weary men and women attended evening classes after hours. During the First Five-Year Plan nearly half a million skilled laborers were trained in this fashion, but the needs of the economy were for many millions more.

Because of the grim conditions in the factories, which encouraged the workers' habits of flitting, training was much less effective than it might have been. Annually from 1928 through 1933, the number of workers who left one job for another significantly exceeded the total number of workers employed. Adverse effects upon the training of skills were only a relatively minor aspect of this problem, however. More important were the need to establish the disciplined functioning of these wandering millions and the consequent measures devised to do so. Restraints were sought: the development of efficient administrative machinery, powerful instruments of bureaucratic control, and harsh punishments that would compel the worker to report to work on time, to fulfill his quota, and to give at least minimal care to the machines with which he worked. Because of the inferior quality of the workers and the hurry to move along, agencies involved with the workers —from the OGPU (secret police) to the party and the trade unions—assumed ever more coercive postures, moving from encouragement and help to directives and commands. But despite the increasing momentum of such efforts to drive the worker to greater effort and efficiency, the workers, many of them former peasants who had escaped the collectivization campaigns, continued to talk back to their bosses, complained, struck, and walked out to search for the better job elsewhere.

To combat such negative responses and to enforce the state's wishes, the trade unions became an arm of government as a branch of the Commissariat of Labor. They now undertook to get the worker to perform more efficiently and stay on the job. Such a "betrayal" by the unions only intensified the workers' agonies. In his book *Smolensk under Soviet Rule,* Merle Fainsod, quoting documents from the Smolensk party archives, which were captured by the Germans early in World War II, has presented the following illustration which typifies the strife in the factories. It comes from an OGPU report of a factory meeting in 1929. The assistant director of a factory and the chairman of the factory trade union committee called this meeting with the workers to discuss how the latter should help to lower production costs. But as soon as the meeting opened, the workers began to leave in protest and anger. According to the OGPU report, as they walked out, they shouted:

"You well-fed devils have sucked the juices out of us enough. You hypocritical wall-eyes are pulling the wool over our eyes. For twelve years already you have driveled and agitated and stuffed our heads. Before, you shouted that the factory owners exploited us, but the factory owners did not force us to work in 4 shifts, and there was enough of everything in the shops. Now we work in 4 shifts. When before 4 men worked, now only one works. You are bloodsuckers, and that's not all, you still want to drain blood out of our veins. If you go to a shop now and want to buy something the shops are empty; there are no shoes, no clothing; there is nothing the worker needs."[12]

In the years of the first plan, such complaints were commonplace. But Stalin needed production and there was to be no escape or respite for the workers.

Not only were ordinary, well-disciplined industrial workers in short supply; it was also evident to everyone that if the factories were to function at all well, the state even more desperately required thousands of technical specialists, engineers, scientists, and managers. So great was this need that former bourgeois engineers and managers were put to work, some of them being released from prison or exile for this purpose. Although they appear to have served loyally on the whole, they were treated with suspicion and blamed for failures; intelligentsia baiting was a popular and vicious sport enjoyed by the party and the lower echelons of society, and many honest men were tried and condemned for their alleged efforts at sabotage.

Other technical and industrial experts were imported from America and the West European nations. Just as Peter the Great had gone to the West for educated specialists in an earlier century, so Stalin brought German, British, and Dutch experts into Russia to teach him how to modernize. These emergency measures, however, still could not satisfy the demand for skills, and in 1930 the nation's universities and technical schools were reorganized so that they might furnish more Soviet-trained specialists.

[12] Merle Fainsod, *Smolensk under Soviet Rule* (Harvard University Press, Cambridge, 1958), p. 311.

Such was the regime's grim determination to create specialists that technical and scientific departments in the universities were simply taken over by the government's economic commissariats, and as these departments came under the control of the industrial branches of the government, the latter used them to train the skills needed in specific industries. In short, so important did Stalin consider the economic struggle that he redirected the whole thrust of education. Its primary aim became the production of sufficient numbers of well-trained men and women who could be directed into production work. The effect upon education was to narrow and limit its function to the task of preparing vocational and professional specialists who could be fitted into the economy much as new gears are fitted into a machine. The humanities and arts could wait, the study of literature and philosophy and history became unnecessary luxuries, for in this society that believed its life depended upon swift economic growth, engineers and managers became generals at the front lines fighting for survival.

During the First Five-Year Plan the number of technical schools tripled and the number of their graduates rose from 200,000 to 754,000. Instructional units defined as universities increased from 129 to 645 through these years and the student body increased from 167,000 to 394,000. Students were assigned to schools according to the current needs of the nation's economy and they went to school without charge, their scholarships varying according to the priority the state placed upon their special knowledge. All parts of the educational system were thus revised to serve one end—to supply trained personnel for the economic machine—and every effort was made to shorten the courses, to concentrate upon narrow technical requirements, and to turn out more and more specialists as quickly as possible.

Unfortunately, the haste, the lack of adequate numbers of well-trained teachers, and the resulting poor preparation of many of the students had predictable consequences. By 1932, the Soviet press was complaining that the new technicians and engineers were ill-prepared to carry out their assigned duties. Their limited competence, in turn, made even more difficult the feat of producing assigned quotas in the factories, complicated efforts to achieve intelligent management of labor and materials for low-cost production, and thus slowed the progress of industrialization.

Inevitably, as the regime persisted in its attempt to control all things for the purpose of achieving economic growth, the state became almost the only employer. All workers, except the peasants on the collective farms, were employees of the state, paid from its coffers, and subject to its increasingly rigorous rules. For the managers and engineers who worked in production, this situation was particularly painful, because failure to perform properly in these chaotic times often meant facing trial in the criminal courts. Offenses a manager might be tried for included "excessive demands for manpower and engagement of workers above requirements as established in the productive-financial plan, failure to ensure a timely supply of manpower and to train skilled workers, infringements of wage standards established by collective contract or fixed by the State, failure to carry out decisions reached at production conferences, wrong utilization of raw or other materials, failure to uphold labour discipline through slackness, etc."[13]

Frequently in these years managers and engineers guilty only of trying to make impossible projects succeed were brought to trial, charged with sabotage and deliberate undermining of the plan objectives. In such conditions it was safest to avoid production work entirely. As a consequence, engineers and managers very early in the plan began a new kind of "flitting" by slipping out of their responsible management and production jobs into staff, research, or advisory positions. Unlike the "flitting" workers, they were not searching for better wages, rations, and living conditions, but for escape from conflict with party and OGPU officials, with workers, and with their colleagues—all of which could and all too frequently did end up in formal charges and trials. To hold a position of authority in production was almost too dangerous; thus despite all efforts to keep them in the responsible jobs, many well-trained men and women found ways to escape.

[13] Baykov, p. 216.

Finally, in addition to harsh penalties, legal actions, and other coercive measures, the government applied exhortation, harnessing the communications media to help in getting the important work done. Social pressures were brought to bear upon tired workers in a variety of ways. The press and radio incessantly prodded the workers to volunteer their free time for extra labor. Teams of workers or shifts in the factories were persuaded that it was socialistically moral to compete with one another to see which could work hardest, produce most, or add the most volunteer hours of extra-duty work in some lagging factory at night or on holidays. Tales of great feats of production by champion shock-workers and triumphant efforts by teams of volunteer workers filled the newspapers. Stalin, his lieutenants, his expanding police forces, and the tempered party cadres were learning how to drive the old society to work in the factories, no matter how loud the outcries of agony and weariness.

Yet it would be improper not to emphasize that during this first plan there was much genuine popular enthusiasm for the plan, for the additional effort and the volunteer work; undoubtedly on the part of many Soviet citizens there were both fervent support and sympathetic understanding of the need to tighten their belts, to deprive themselves of food and good lodging, so that the future lot of Soviet citizens might improve. Stalin's Five-Year Plan held out a fascinating promise of abundance and power. To the hungry, hardworking industrial laborers and their new managers, and even to some of the peasants in their collectives, the promise was profoundly moving. Paraphrased, the message repeated tens of millions of times by every form of communication available to the leader was: "Work hard now! Make the necessary sacrifices! Your children will be educated as you never were; they will live in good houses, enjoy the fruits of well-tilled fields and the products of powerful industries. Russia will rise from its thatched roofs and mud floors to become one of the great modern nations, and its socialist people will achieve happiness and prosperity. There is no other way."

Despite all the pain of those first years at the beginning of the Second Bolshevik Revolution, many Russian citizens of the Soviet Union believed in this dream and voluntarily dedicated minds and muscles to a future they longed for, for themselves and their children.

Strains on the Party

The decision to industrialize the Soviet Union by means of a series of centrally directed five-year plans had far-reaching implications for the evolution of the Soviet Union's Communist party that could not have been fully predicted by anyone when the decision was first made. This decision was, at least in part, a recognition that socialism in one country could not be built without a powerful and forceful party dictatorship. And it was a decision to abandon once and for all the old faith of the Left communists in democratic action, self-government, and equality, for it was solidly founded on a faith in the ability of a ruthlessly commanded paramilitary party machine to wage a successful social war against the people of the Soviet Union. Industrial revolution was the aim, and the people were to be compelled to do whatever was necessary to accomplish it.

Although the party had been largely transformed into Stalin's machine by 1928, it still had to be tempered and toughened before it could execute the leader's orders as well as he wished it to. A recurring question through the years from 1928 through 1932 was: "How tough must the party be?" And Stalin's answer, always, was: "Much tougher than it is." Moreover the party, under his leadership, was destined to control every facet of Soviet life—whether economic, political, cultural, or intellectual; all aspects were to be subject to party supervision; therefore, the party had to be prepared to rule on all problems almost like an omniscient and omnipotent god.

In 1928, the party was still not sufficiently unified under Stalin's leadership to play this role. Although Stalin had at this time defeated the Left Opposition, he now found his will opposed by the very men with whom he had allied to win his earlier victories. These allies on the Right, supporters of the NEP and of cautious cooperation with the peasants, who had proved so effective against the impetuous, revolutionary Trotsky and the bureaucratic Zinoviev and Kamenev, in 1928 became

Stalin's stubborn opponents, for they feared his growing dominance and his hardening determination to industrialize at the cost of the peasants' welfare. As always, Stalin refused to brook opposition.

The principal leaders of the Right inside the Politburo were the eminent theorist Nikolai Bukharin, the head of Soviet Trade Unions, Mikhail Tomsky, and Alexei Rykov, then Chairman of the Council of People's Commissars. In mid-July Bukharin clashed sharply with Stalin over the collectivization question and Bukharin subsequently published a penetrating criticism of Stalin's claim that the marketed grain shortages in 1927 and 1928 had been caused by the kulak's obdurate refusal to sell his grain. By early 1929 these members of the Right were trying in vain to remove Stalin's principal supporters from the Politburo. The struggle became the familiar one of men who had lost real power crying out against "bureaucratization" and "one-man rule."

In his struggle against the Right, Stalin used the same tactics he had already developed in the earlier party battles. In February 1929, the Party Control Commission called the rightist leaders to account, and Stalin accused them of being counterrevolutionary, anti-Marxist, and prokulak. His charges were accepted as true by a Central Committee meeting in April, which recommended that Bukharin and Tomsky be dismissed from their official positions.

At the end of April, with the First Five-Year Plan safely confirmed by the Sixteenth Party Conference, Stalin stepped up his political attack. In June Tomsky was removed from his office as the leader of the trade unions; in July Bukharin was deprived of his chairmanship of the Comintern. Even this did not fully satisfy Stalin, and in November the Right was formally required to recant its "dangerous views." Yet when the public and humiliating exercise of recantation was completed, the Central Committee found the performance wanting; Bukharin was accordingly expelled from the Politburo and the others were advised that any further struggle against the party line was prohibited. Although Stalin had won this battle, it should be noted that these men were not at this moment expelled from

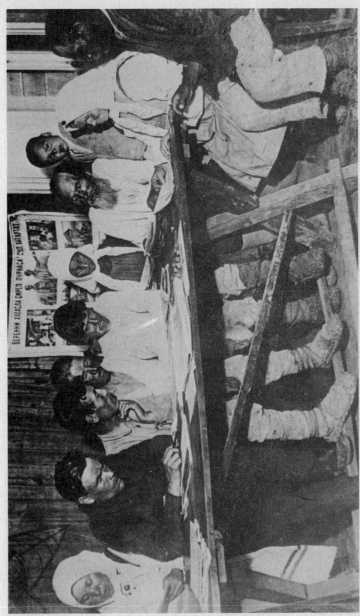

Peasants learning to read

the party and exiled as Trotsky had been. They were to remain in uneasy juxtaposition with the leader, assigned to a variety of influential tasks, hating Stalin, while representing views he despised, and anxiously searching for ways to prevent the consolidation of his power.

Thus, the dictatorship of Stalin in these years was exercised in an environment of stress and distrust, with the main center of power easily identifiable and with islands of partially repressed but stubborn opposition in many quarters. Men who wished to continue in the party could do so only by joining themselves totally with its destiny, losing themselves in the collectivity, "abandoning their own personalities," as the leftist Pyatakov put it. All were compelled to submit overtly to the will of the party—actually the will of one man. For many, this was no problem, for they genuinely willed what Stalin willed, but for the opposition, submission meant humiliating defeat and abandonment of the revolution.

At this time changes occurred within the party management that were not common knowledge. Theorists and intellectuals were being pressured to conform or were driven from the ranks of the leadership. Into their places went Stalin's bullyboys, ex-undergrounders, hardfisted Old Bolsheviks and old friends from the civil war, such men as Kliment Voroshilov, Lazar Kaganovich, and Sergei Ordzhonikidze. These years also revealed much about Stalin himself that had not been completely evident before.

Lenin had thought him too rude, but Lenin had not fathomed the profound significance of that rudeness. What he had perceived was but the tip of an iceberg indicating the inhuman coldness of Stalin's heart and mind. Stalin, in his effort to transform the fundamental character and culture of his nation, demonstrated an utter lack of restraint and moral scruples, an inability to suffer with other human beings. He may be credited with great courage, so to seize hold of a whole society and to hammer it into the form that his party had decided upon, but this was a frightening and insensate courage. Under his direction the first plan swiftly lost its rational character as an organized effort to make measured advances within the realm of the practical. Initial successes led him to increase the tempo, to raise the targets; then, almost like a madman, as some of his colleagues believed he had become, he sought to whip the Soviet Union forward in a race to do the impossible. Presuming that where a little force and terror had accomplished much, greater pressures would accomplish more, he lashed unceasingly at the whole society with his Herculean demands.

It appeared to outsiders that the race itself was beginning to demand all his attention. He acted like a man unaware of the sufferings of human beings as he pored over the machinery—the party, the Soviet government, the OGPU, the intelligentsia, the workers, the peasants—calculating how best to bring out more productive efforts from these combined elements. Observers concluded from his abstract concern with the efficiency of the total machine that he had no real feeling for the people involved. Years later, Trotsky was to say: "Principles never exerted any influence over Stalin. . . . The immediate administrative task always loomed before him as greater than all the laws of history."[14] Stalin's behavior through the years of the first plan, at least, appeared to bear out Trotsky's words.

Although he never forgot the goal of his endeavor—national and personal power based upon industry—Stalin seemed to disregard the human qualities of the ordinary men and women, the peasants, the workers and intellectuals, who were pursuing this goal with him. He worked to secure precise and immediate efficiency from the administrative machines he directed. He gave untiring attention to the tiniest administrative detail, watching here, influencing there, pressuring men and changing organizations so that they would more quickly respond to his touch. The party became a party of *apparatchiki*—officials and bureaucrats—who issued orders, shouted, and punished and thus drove factories and the society to an increasing crescendo of effort. Yet Stalin seemed almost unaware of the increasing resentment, dissension, agony, and suffering of the people—consequences that would sooner or later have to be faced.

[14] Leon Trotsky, *Stalin, An Appraisal of the Man and His Influence*, edited and translated by Charles Malamuth (Hollis and Carter, Ltd., London, 1947), p. 358.

Was he truly carrying out the will of Lenin? Was this work that he was doing revolutionary work, and was this brutal struggle against his own people the revolutionary struggle that Lenin's ideology and party were destined to bring about? While Stalin perhaps displayed a more insensitive ruthlessness than Lenin, certainly he *was* implementing the policies and ideas of Lenin to the best of his capacity to understand them. Too roughly perhaps, without the art and sophistication Lenin might have used, but he was nevertheless fleshing out Lenin's precepts and striving for Lenin's communist dream. Having begun the Second Revolution in 1928, he would not pause until its goals were achieved. But if he was a true disciple of Lenin, he was also, it must be noted, the follower of Ivan the Terrible and Peter the Great, and self-consciously so. Aware of the important roles these men had played in Russia's past, he made much of the comparison, proud to be emulating very awesome predecessors—two tsars who, like himself, had tried to reshape Russia drastically within a time span too short to permit peaceful evolutionary development.

CHAPTER THREE

The Consolidation of Totalitarianism

The Second and Third Five-Year Plans

DURING the Second Five-Year Plan (1933–1937), while the country's projected overall rate of industrial growth was slowed somewhat in comparison with the first plan, Stalin was clearly persisting in the great drive. Gross production of all industry at the end of the plan was to be 214 percent greater than its value in 1932 (calculated at 1926–1927 prices), with heavy industries increasing 197 percent, and light or consumer industries even more, by 233 percent. Coal production was to expand 237 percent, steel 289 percent, and smaller consumer items, such as footwear, 220 percent.

While new construction received continuing attention, the regime placed growing emphasis upon mastering techniques, developing new industries, increasing labor productivity, and lowering production costs. Most construction work during the first two years was designed to complete projects begun during the first plan or to improve the situation of industries already in operation, in the hope that by the end of the plan 80 percent of all production would be coming from plants built since 1928. Special efforts were to go to the very necessary improvement of railroads, which had been almost ignored during the first plan, and to the development of new metals industries.

The aim of "mastering techniques" became a predominant theme during the second plan because the first years had irrefutably proved the economy's desperate need for competence, efficiency, and responsibility at all levels. At the management level, skilled and responsible men who possessed the qualifications and the courage to make production decisions were especially scarce. Extensive reorganizations of industrial and governmental administrative agencies were carried out to make better use of available expertise, and managers were given increased personal responsibility. They were also compelled to take courses and to pass examinations in specific technical subjects needed for their work, with the result that many thousands of incompetent people who had worked as engineers and technicians during the first plan were weeded out and transferred back to shopwork.

To achieve increased labor productivity, the already familiar practices of socialist emulation were continued, and workers were urged to devise new ways to improve technological processes in order to produce more goods or to raise the quality of their work. Probably the most significant labor innovation of this period was the Stakhanovite movement, named after a coal miner, A. G. Stakhanov, who, on August 30, 1935, working with a well-organized team of his fellow miners, hewed a record 102 tons of coal in six hours. His achievement resulted from what may be termed a rationalization of the production process. That is, he introduced a division of labor in his work team that increased its efficiency; he arranged for the use of superior equipment; and he adapted the work to the peculiar conditions of his mine. To the party leaders, Stakhanov's

rationalization techniques appeared applicable to other industries. Accordingly, in December 1935, a Plenum of the Central
Committee resolved that all mining and many heavy industries
should institute "Stakhanovism."

This resolution soon burgeoned into a nationwide campaign. In individual factories and mines, the best workers were
selected to become Stakhanovites. Managers went out of their
way to provide these potential record breakers with assistants,
the best machines and other necessities. Once the Stakhanovite
had set a new record of increased production, his achievement
became the norm against which the work of the factory rank
and file was judged, for it was assumed that if the Stakhanovite
could increase his productivity, then others, using his methods,
could do almost as well. The old norms were raised 15 to 50
percent, even though the workers of the rank and file seldom
enjoyed the ideal conditions that were prepared for the Stakhanovite. When and if a factory's laborers fulfilled the new
norm, Stakhanovites began the process all over again. Piecework
rates, too, were affected by Stakhanovite achievements, being
lowered when a Stakhanovite set up higher norms. Workers
who could not speed up received decreasing wages. For inexperienced and older workers, and for those in poorly equipped
factories, the pressures to emulate Stakhanov simply meant
putting forth ever harder and harder efforts to produce.

To keep the Stakhanovite movement going, the regime
called upon the whole gamut of incentive systems available
to it. "Stakhanovite" became a term of honor, signifying a
dedicated socialist, a distinguished worker for society. The
special awards or decorations granted to these men and women
entitled them to higher pensions than ordinary workers received; at the same time their advanced piecework rates and
special money prizes enabled many Stakhanovites to make
better wages than their foremen. Thus the Stakhanovite could
expect his efforts to be crowned with high honor and high
wages; he was the hero of labor, the Stalinist crusader for
industrialization.

At least in part because of the Stakhanovite movement,
labor productivity actually overfulfilled the goals set for it by

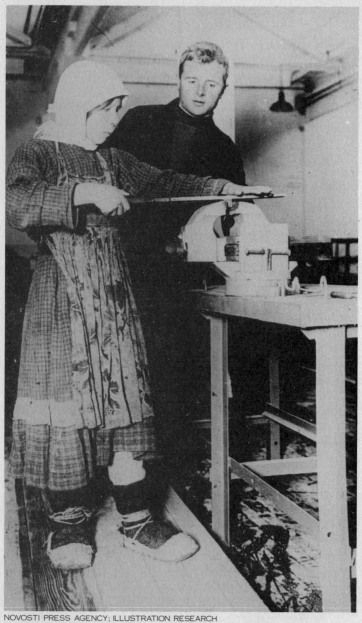

Peasant girl learning industrial work at Nizhni Novgorod's automobile plant, 1931

the second plan. Other factors helped. More and newer machines were produced for factory and farm, and disciplinary measures for ensuring better work were steadily tightened. As early as November 1932, for example, workers and employees absent from work for one day were ordered dismissed and deprived of their housing accommodations. In addition, new regulations intended to slow the swift turnover of labor required that a worker who applied for a new job must show a certificate signed by his last employer stating his reasons for leaving the last job. Meanwhile, factory technical schools, as well as the universities, were steadily improved by insistence upon high qualifications for teachers and by the introduction of compulsory lectures and entrance examinations for students. Factory training was widely encouraged, so that workers everywhere were continuously pressured to study on the job.

In agriculture inescapable pressures were maintained to persuade or compel the peasants to move into collective farms. The number of kolkhozy (collective farms) rose from 85,000 in 1930 to 243,700 in 1937, and the percentage of households collectivized, which rose very sharply in 1931, from 24 percent in January to 61 in October, thereafter rose more slowly until it reached a high of 93 in 1937. State farms were also multiplying. By 1938, there were almost 4,000 of them as compared with 1,400 in 1928, and these state farms were rich in capital, tractors, and other agricultural implements almost beyond earlier dreams. The sown area cultivated by collective and state farms increased from 33.6 to 99 percent of the arable land. Numbers of Machine Tractor Stations, serving both the collective and the state farms, rose from 150 in 1930 to 6,358 in 1938, and the number of tractors they employed increased from 72,000 to 483,500.

The immense quantitative success of the first two plans may be indicated by a few key statistics. According to Soviet calculations, engineering and metal industries production increased in value between 1929 and 1938 over ten times (calculated at 1926–1927 prices); in absolute figures, coal production rose from 40 to 132 million tons; oil rose from 13.8 million tons to 32.2 million tons; steel production went from 4.9 million tons to 18 million; and, indicative of what the two plans meant for the individual, the production of leather shoes rose from 48.4 million pairs in 1929, to 213 million in 1938. While these are scattered and brief figures, they clearly demonstrate that the industrial production drive had taken immense strides. In fact, the industrial base built since 1928 gave positive promise that continued planned growth might well accomplish all that Stalin hoped for.

Unfortunately, there were other influences at work in the world destined to complicate the Soviet Union's further progress. Indeed, it was an awkward time to begin the third plan, for the international situation in 1938 was in a perilous state and events were rapidly moving toward World War II. In July 1938 troops of the Soviet Union and the Empire of Japan clashed in full-scale battle on the borders of the People's Republic of Outer Mongolia, and during the last years of the Second Five-Year Plan, Soviet weapons and men sent by Stalin into Spain were supporting Republican and other forces fighting against Franco's Royalists, who were in turn armed and aided by Fascist Italy and Nazi Germany. Soviet participation in this latter struggle heightened tensions in Europe and increased the Western nations' fear of communism.

The most serious threat of all, however, was posed by Hitler, for he had made significant and dangerous expansionist moves in the West and had aggressively boasted of his intention to drive eastward into Russia. Therefore, while the Third Five-Year Plan began already heavily weighted with targets for heavy industry, new threats and events—such as Hitler's absorption of Austria, his occupation of Czechoslovakia, his invasion of Poland, and Stalin's war with Finland—were to compel successive upward revisions of these production goals. By 1940, allocations for defense industries were twice the amount planned earlier, and by 1941 they had risen to three times the planned figure of 1938. Finally, when war came to the Soviet Union in 1941, the third plan was abandoned, to be replaced by a series of shorter, crash plans as war flooded over the countryside.

In general, the last two years of the 1930s continued the already impressive accomplishments of the decade. Oil production, which stood at 13.8 million tons in 1929, had, by 1940, risen 250 percent to 34.2 million tons; coal production had risen 400 percent, from 40 million tons to 164 million tons; steel, 400 percent, from 4.9 million tons to an estimated 18.4 million. Such statistics could be listed at great length, but the figures given make the point that from 1928 to 1940, within the space of twelve years, Stalin had carried the industrialization of his country much further than anyone had thought would be possible. He had done it at great cost, with immense waste in material and human resources, but he had done it.

While these quantitative economic facts are of enormous significance, and while they form a necessary and irrefutable background of accomplishment against which all other developments of the 1930s must be studied, they represent only a small part of the story of Stalin's achievements during this decade. Of comparable significance are the political and social changes that accompanied his drive for industrialization. However, it is not possible to gain a clear understanding of the domestic atmosphere and the evolution of events in the social and political areas of Soviet life without first viewing these events in their world context. To understand better why Stalin conducted his domestic policies as he did, we need to know how he stood in his relations with the outside world. Therefore, we must note briefly the Soviet Union's international situation at this moment in history.

Foreign Policy in the 1920s and 1930s

The heritage of Lenin in foreign policy was confusion, buried deep in the contradictions of revolutionary ideology and historic national policies. The new state under both Lenin and Stalin sought to preserve and strengthen its security within the system of nations and, simultaneously, to advance the cause of world revolution by working (or seeming to work) for proletarian uprisings everywhere. To both Lenin and Stalin, national security was always the immediate goal, while world revolution was presumed to lie somewhere in the future; yet both aspects of the dual policy were actively pressed, with the result that by turns each frustrated the other. Stalin, indeed, often seemed to be striving for failure. While he attempted to gain diplomatic friends, the Comintern's revolutionary activities or his own fire-and-brimstone speeches terrified the very nations whose friendship he courted. Paradoxically, the Comintern was often used—and this more and more as the years went by—as an instrument for preserving Soviet security rather than for directing world revolution. Wearing now the mask of the conventional national state leader, now the mask of world revolutionary, Stalin found his foreign policies misunderstood by the noncommunist world. In the long run this fundamental dualism of Soviet relations repeatedly proved self-defeating.

Lenin's chief foreign policy aims after the civil war had been to secure trade relations, recognition, and a place for the Soviet Union at world diplomatic tables. Meanwhile, he had attempted to win as much support for the world revolution as possible, by establishing close relations with the workers of other nations through the Comintern's policy of a "united front" with workers no matter what their party affiliations might be. The triumvirate, and later Stalin alone, continued these same policies, although emphases and strategies were differently mixed. Stalin's preoccupation with domestic affairs and with his struggle for power during these years, as well as his blundering ineptness and lack of sympathy for revolutionaries in other countries, brought him little early success and much condemnation from his voluble critic of this date, Trotsky.

Most of the chief events of this period have already been touched upon, and need only to be set in perspective at this point. In Germany, which by the Treaty of Rapallo of 1922 had become the Soviet Republic's first anti-Versailles ally, Stalin refused to believe that German communists could possibly carry on a successful revolution. Consequently, when Heinrich Brandler, chief of the German Communist party, was given contradictory orders by Comintern leaders and attempted an insurrectionary movement that ended in failure late in 1923, Stalin actually seemed to be well pleased. Great Britain gave formal diplomatic recognition to the Soviet Union in 1924 and agreed to the establishment of an Anglo-Russian Trade Union in 1925. But when Soviet communists attempted to take advantage of the British General Strike of 1926 to plot revolution with British workers, workers and government alike cooled to the official friendship. In 1927 the British cut off both diplomatic ties and the Trade Union relationship.

Stalin's early relations with China were equally unsuccessful. Here he followed Lenin, both by supporting the Chinese nationalist movement and by accepting Lenin's diagnosis, which considered China ripe for a bourgeois-democratic and nationalist, rather than a proletarian, revolution. He therefore urged Chinese communists to join with Chiang Kai-shek's nationalist movement in its struggle to win predominance over several other self-appointed "governments," and he dispatched Soviet advisers to work with Chiang and train his soldiers to fight for a democratic political order. But as Chiang won victory after victory, the Chinese general grew restive in his alliance with the communists. Finally, in April 1927, Chiang carried out a bloody massacre of his erstwhile communist allies. By mid-1927, Stalin's advisers were forced to withdraw to the Soviet Union, Chinese communists were in chaos, and Stalin's foreign policy as well as his Comintern policy in China (for both were involved) had been clearly discredited by this catastrophe. Trotsky, railing openly at all these failures, charged Stalin with betraying world revolution.

From 1928 until late in 1939, Stalin's fundamental policy may be described as a search for peace and security. During these years, although he employed a variety of approaches to the problem, for he was living in a world seemingly bent on war and destruction, essentially his goals of peace and security did not change. Theoretically, this policy accorded with Leninist doctrine. New imperialist wars were to be anticipated and Stalin's task was to steer around them for the good of the Soviet state. Initially, therefore, he hopefully pursued the establishment of a number of diplomatic relationships, which would preserve his freedom to maneuver as he wished and to continue his anti-Versailles policies and his friendship with Germany. With his nation formally recognized by the great powers in Europe, Stalin charged his diplomats to seek the recognition of the United States, and in November 1933 this project was successful.

His relations with Germany at this time were to prove much more hazardous. In that nation, where economic depression and national pride at the start of the 1930s bred fierce pressures for political change, members of the German Communist party fought in the streets against the rising strength of Adolf Hitler's National Socialists. Stalin, however, refused to support the German communists' efforts to oppose Hitler, arguing that Hitler's party was not the major threat to communism in Germany; more dangerous enemies, he thought, were the Social Democrats and supporters of trade union legalism. At least in part because this stand weakened Hitler's opponents, the Nazi leader was enabled to come to power in early 1933, whereupon he swiftly made clear his determined antipathy toward communism by destroying the German communist movement. At this point Stalin was compelled to conclude that there had appeared on the continent a virulent and explosive new force profoundly committed to the destruction of bolshevism.

Stalin registered his awareness of the Nazi danger in his report to the Seventeenth Congress of the Party on January 26, 1934. "Quite clearly," he said, "things are heading for a new war," and he charged that the policy of the Nazi regime recalled "the policy of the former German Kaiser, who at one time occupied the Ukraine and marched against Leningrad, after converting the Baltic countries into a place d'armes for this march. . . ."[1] Then, after analyzing other dangers of the international situation, he summarized the position of his own government with the following words:

> Our foreign policy is clear. It is a policy of preserving peace and strengthening trade relations with all countries. The USSR does not think of threatening anybody—let alone of attacking anybody. We stand for peace and uphold the cause of peace. But we are not afraid of threats and are prepared to answer the instigators of war blow for blow. Those who want peace and seek business relations with us will always have our support. But those who try to attack our country will receive a crushing repulse to teach them in future not to poke their pig snouts into our Soviet garden.[2]

[1] J. V. Stalin, *Works* (Foreign Languages Publishing House, Moscow, 1953–1955), XIII, 309.
[2] Stalin, XIII, 312.

Such threats had no effect upon Hitler. He had ostentatiously withdrawn from the League of Nations in 1933, and in 1934 he organized a putsch against Austria, which only the threat of Italian military action halted. Through these years and after, he defied the Treaty of Versailles, first by rearming Germany and second by reestablishing military conscription, and he capped these moves in 1936 by sending troops into the demilitarized Rhineland. In the context of his times, each of these steps threatened world peace, while Hitler's Aryan fulminations, as well as the ambitious outpourings of his propaganda agencies, made it clear that he would not rest until he ruled the major portion of Europe. Stalin, in response to the Nazi menace, but still in pursuit of the peace and security he had to have if his five-year plans were to be completed, moved to a new policy position. He turned openly to the Western powers by joining the League of Nations in 1934 and by supporting collective security.

While it is seldom possible to know in any event exactly why Stalin behaved as he did, the reasons for certain decisions can occasionally be inferred from later acts. Sometime in 1934 he apparently resolved to persuade the Western democracies that bolshevism was not a danger to them, that indeed, the Soviet Union was one of the great bulwarks of democracy, and that they should, therefore, join the Soviet Union in an alliance against Hitler. For the Western powers, the abruptness of this about-face made it hard to accept. They had been frightened too often by the nightmare of world communist revolution; they were resentful of the Soviet pose of moral superiority that seemed to them both artificial and untenable. They were disturbed by reports of the authoritarian methods of the Soviet government. And they were in fact not at all persuaded that Hitler was as bad as Stalin, or as dangerous to themselves.

It should be added here that even while he went all out to win the friendship and support of the Western powers, Stalin, the devious, quietly played a parallel hand. Soviet-German relations had been good since the Treaty of Rapallo; in the late 1920s there had been mutually valuable exchanges of products—military equipment and manufactured goods from Germany in return for raw materials from the USSR. This old relationship was too important to throw away lightly, and in the spring of 1934 Stalin determined to achieve some kind of alliance or understanding with Hitler. He made several attempts to do so during the very years when he was wooing the Western powers, and of course these parallel policies, with the pro-Western tendency dominant, help to confuse further the question of Stalin's real preference during these years.

Stalin's sharp turnabout toward the West began to take concrete form with the establishment in France of the policy of the Popular Front. There, in July 1934, the French Communist party offered to ally itself with the other socialist parties of France in a common front "to save the democracy against rightist and fascist bullies." Subsequently, the parties of this Popular Front joined in the formation of Popular Front governments, which in theory at least suggested that French communists (and by implication all other communists) warmly supported the Western democracies. Meanwhile, in May 1935, a Franco-Soviet pact of mutual assistance was signed, and the same month a tripartite pact was signed with Czechoslovakia, pledging that the Soviet Union would aid Czechoslovakia if that state were attacked by a third party but that Soviet troops would move only after France did so.

When, at the Seventh Congress of the Comintern, July–August 1935, the Popular Front policy was proclaimed an international policy, communists around the world were officially pledged to join with the masses and leaders of any party that would resist European fascism and Japanese militarism. The communists, who had for so long denounced the capitalists and their ways, now asked to be accepted as the true friends of all democratic bourgeois states. The Western powers were supposed to forget the earlier threat of world communism as if it had been nothing more than the kind of bogeyman mothers use to frighten little children.

In Spain, one of the testing grounds of the new international Popular Front policy, that policy quickly became mired in new difficulties. There, in 1933, a rightist regime had actively suppressed parties favoring the Spanish Republic. In response, a Popular Front of leftist parties was organized in 1934 to protect the nation against the rise of Spanish fascism.

This front won a majority in the *Cortes* (parliament) in early 1936, thus strengthening the Republican regime in Spain, but a military revolt in Spanish Morocco, led by General Francisco Franco, began what quickly became a violent civil war.

Again, in the events that followed in Spain, Stalin's real purposes must remain in the realm of speculation. Perhaps, as some still believe, he wanted to establish a communist-dominated Spain. It is more likely, however, that he feared a fascist Spain which would flank his ally, democratic France, and prevent French armies from moving effectively against Nazi Germany should war come. Whatever his reasons, in late 1936 he decided to intervene in the Spanish Civil War by providing military equipment and Soviet advisers to the beleaguered Republican government.

In Spain Stalin came down hard for the preservation of democracy and the Republic, his envoys seeking to persuade France and Great Britain to do the same. But these powers, for domestic and political reasons too complex to elaborate here, chose to stand aside, even supporting a blockade against the Spanish Republic. Italian and German planes, tanks, and military personnel were sent in by the fascist powers to support Franco. Fighting against them were communist international formations, recruited from many nations, which defended the Republic.

To Stalin, defense of the Republic was defined in a surprisingly limited way that excluded cooperation with any groups (even communist sympathizers) that sought to undermine Republican power. Observers watched almost unbelievingly as NKVD agents (successors of the earlier OGPU) from the Soviet Union, following Stalin's orders, suppressed and dismantled native communist and anarchist factions striving for social revolution. Stalin's forces, in other words, supported the democratic Republic and prevented social revolution with chilling efficiency; unfortunately, the very ruthlessness of their methods in this theater of operations won the Russians few adherents among the Western powers.

While these disturbing events were taking place in Western Europe, problems at least as foreboding were developing in Asia. When in mid-1929 the Manchurian warlord, Chang

Hsueh-ling, seized the Chinese Eastern Railway, previously under Soviet-Manchurian control, the Soviet Union's General Blyukher countered by moving troops to recapture it. Northern Manchuria had long been an area of conflict between Russian and Chinese interests, but now an aggressively expanding and militaristic power challenged both. Japanese armies, invading the mainland in September 1931, drove Chang from power, spread through Manchuria, and by March 1932, signifying their control of this area, renamed it Manchukuo. Although the new regime was ostensibly an independent state, it became in fact a puppet of the Japanese; its northern borders extended from east to west along Soviet borders and its southwestern boundary pressed against the Soviet puppet state of Outer Mongolia.

In a series of humiliating negotiations, Stalin permitted the Japanese to force him to "sell" them the Chinese Eastern Railway at a price that was disgracefully low. He did it only because he could not afford war. In the years that followed, the Japanese pressed hard at the boundaries of the Mongolian People's Republic, which had been established under Soviet auspices in 1924 and which Stalin had no intention of yielding. Dangerous clashes of hostile patrols kept nerves tight. From 1937 into the summer of 1939, the forces of Japan and the Soviet Union fought pitched battles in this region. Although the armies were those of the puppet states, planes, guns, and other matériel belonged to the rival nations supporting them; in other words, the battles along the borders of Mongolia and the Soviet Far East, like those in Spain, were made more deadly by the open involvement of foreign armaments. The immediate threat to Soviet territory was very great in this eastern theater; obviously there could be no rest for Soviet workers and factories while Japan, a potential ally of Hitler and Mussolini, provoked successive attacks against Soviet territory.

The Japanese menace in China subsequently spread far beyond the Manchukuo conflict by provoking Chinese opposition. This led to the invasion of China in 1937, when the Japanese opened an undeclared war that was to last for eight years. Chiang Kai-shek's Popular Front with the communist leader, Mao Tse-tung, begun in 1936, was strengthened by this war, and Stalin could not help becoming involved, since thousands of miles of Soviet borders were threatened. From 1937 on he sent military aid to Chiang.

It is not at all strange that Stalin, feeling himself thus threatened from all sides, desperately sought to achieve collective security in alliance with other nations and in the League of Nations. To the misfortune of the whole world, his hopes were disappointed. Neville Chamberlain, who became Prime Minister in Great Britain in May 1937, was persuaded that Hitler was a thoroughly evil man who would have his own way or cause war, and Chamberlain was far more afraid of war than of dishonor. When Hitler demanded to have the German-populated Sudetenland of Czechoslovakia yielded up to him, Chamberlain and Daladier of France visited Hitler at Berchtesgaden in September 1938, and then went on to Munich, where they agreed to Hitler's demands for the sake of "peace in our time."

This shameful act of appeasement, coming after years of strenuous Soviet efforts to win trust in the West, apparently persuaded Stalin at last that his search for security through alliance with the West was a lost cause. Although his envoys at the League of Nations, and in formal conferences, had for years begged for resistance to the fascists, and although they urged the use of military force against Hitler in defense of Czechoslovakia, his government was unable to act at this juncture. According to the Soviet pact with France and Czechoslovakia, Russia could not move militarily until France did so.

The Soviet Union's own position was likewise threatened by this event. Chamberlain and Daladier, by insisting upon peace and sacrificing Czechoslovakia's Sudetenland in order to keep the peace, had now opened the way to Hitler's further expansion eastward. After Munich, Hitler, with Polish help, nibbled further at the boundaries of Czechoslovakia, and on March 15, 1939, his troops moved again. Occupying Bohemia and Moravia, Hitler set up a separate state of Slovakia. For the time being, with the assistance of Great Britain and France, he had destroyed Czechoslovakia as an independent nation, and he appeared to be turning his attention more and more to the East.

Stalin of course had never fully trusted the Western capitalists, for his ideology and his experience had demonstrated to him their implacable hatred of communism. After Munich, he was persuaded more than before of the deliberate intent of the capitalist nations to turn Hitler eastward and, while the communists and Nazis destroyed one another in a great holocaust, to stand on the sidelines anticipating their own future profits. He expressed these views forcefully on March 10, 1939, speaking to the Eighteenth Congress of the party. The Western powers, he said, were "egging the Germans on to march further east, promising them easy pickings, and prompting them: 'Just start war on the Bolsheviks, and everything will be all right.' " He charged that the Western nations were disappointed with the Germans for not marching against the Soviet Union, and expressed his frank opinion of those people whom he had been seeking for allies: "Far be it from me to moralize on the policy of non-intervention [the refusal to block the Germans from Czechoslovakia], to talk of treason, treachery, and so on. It would be naive to preach morals to people who recognize no human morality. Politics is politics, as the old, case-hardened bourgeois diplomats say. It must be remarked, however, that the big and dangerous political game started by the supporters of the policy of non-intervention may end in a serious fiasco for them."[3]

Announcing that the Soviet Union stood "for peaceful, close, and friendly relations with all the neighboring countries which have common frontiers with the USSR," Stalin once again altered his course and through the months from March until late August 1939, shifted away from the West, back toward friendship with Germany. As these months went by, inexorably leading to World War II, he negotiated in fact with both sides. "Our orientation in the past and our orientation at the present time," he had said in 1934, "is toward the USSR and toward the USSR alone."[4] The statement was just as true in 1939. While he undoubtedly believed that the Western powers were willing

[3] Alvin Z. Rubinstein (ed.), *The Foreign Policy of the Soviet Union* (Random House, New York, 1960), p. 141.
[4] Stalin, XIII, 309.

to betray him in order to preserve themselves, he left the door open through the first half of 1939, apparently hoping against hope that Western leaders would eventually recognize Hitler's malevolence and would steel themselves to do battle as allies of the Soviet Union. Meanwhile, he cautiously opened other doors; his foreign emissaries began making subtle but obvious approaches to the Germans that in August 1939 were to end in an alliance with Hitler.

The Onset of the Purges

As the decade of the 1930s ended, Stalin may have felt some temporary satisfaction that his diplomacy had fended off the many foreign dangers threatening the forward progress of Soviet industrialization. Trotsky could condemn him for abandoning world revolution, but he had saved the Second Bolshevik Revolution. If, however, Stalin felt some satisfaction with these results of his foreign policy, he was not content with the progress of the industrialization drive during the 1930s.

The economic administrative machinery developed during the First Five-Year Plan had not worked well enough to satisfy his incessant demands for greater production, improved quality and efficiency, lower costs, and more rapid tempo. Moreover, although the policy he directed for the swift growth of industrialization had the formal approval of the party and the profound commitment of millions of workers, no one worked well enough or fast enough to please him. To Stalin, it was obvious that the whole society needed to be driven harder; some powerful external force had to be applied if the economy was to function with the speed and efficiency he demanded.

The means of exercising extraordinary coercive influence was at hand in the form of the Unified State Political Department (OGPU)—the secret police. Leninist ideology had long since legitimized the use of terror against "enemies of the state," and Lenin's employment of Red Terror immediately after the October Revolution and into the 1920s had set precedents Stalin found invaluable. To whip the economy forward and compel the intellectual and social modernization needed to improve the functioning of the economic machine, he systematically expanded the use of terror until it became a routine but terrible feature of Soviet life.

It is not surprising, given the working of Stalin's mind and the kind of system he had devised for running the nation, that he interpreted any failure by others to fulfill his commands as deliberate opposition, sabotage, or evidence of potential rebellion. To crush out such failure (or opposition), he broadened and toughened long-used techniques of purging the party ranks of its dissenters, until he had created a system for purging the whole society of all whom he and his police suspected or feared. In so doing he set himself and his police above the law, opening the way for capricious terror and for the illegal arrest of millions of men and women. These victims, arrested without sufficient legal justification and usually sentenced without any formal judicial procedure, were locked up in labor camps and prisons where they worked at hard labor, dying in droves or managing to survive somehow through degrading, hopeless years.

It is still difficult if not impossible to explain why the purge system ran wild, why Stalin's police became inquisitors and persecutors of a whole society, until often enough they themselves fell victim to the persecution, and why millions upon millions of Soviet people had to be humiliated, disgraced, and literally worked to death in vast labor camps. Through all the stages of the purges that Stalin carried on during the late 1930s, few rational observers understood what was happening. Even today few scholars would say that they know why the purges of the late 1930s, like a devastating tornado, spiraled into an ever-widening vortex of destruction, creating scenes and events more suited to Dante's *Inferno* than to everyday life in the twentieth century. We can only circle around this terrible phenomenon, attempting to understand some of its discrete aspects.

Stalin did not invent the purge system of the 1930s, although there is considerable evidence that he personally elaborated some of the more brutal characteristics it displayed. Actually, long before 1930 the practice had grown up whereby the lower ranks of the party were periodically subjected to

Listening to *Pravda* being read—workers on the metro (subway) in Moscow, 1936

screening efforts of the Party Control Commission. Thus, as early as 1921, some 200,000 members of the postrevolutionary party (total 730,000) had already been expelled for various reasons. In line with this precedent, during the routine but painful screening of 1933, some 17 percent of the party members were purged, and in the successive checks of 1934 through 1936 thousands more were dropped from the rolls. Apparently, far too many people regularly joined the party for protection and privilege; some wanted simply to ride on the bandwagon of the ruling group, or to make a career of high office; obviously, to keep the party strong and loyal to its revolutionary objectives such members had to be identified and ejected.

Similarly, there were strong precedents by 1934 for harsh treatment of economic personnel. Since the state owned and directed all economic activities, production and management failures of many kinds could easily be interpreted as crimes against the state. From 1927 on, there had been a number of show trials of industrial technicians, foreign experts, and professional specialists, who were accused of sabotage, espionage, and antigovernment conspiracy. Even at lower levels, throughout the First Five-Year Plan, managers and technicians had been subjected to a constant barrage of criminal charges for their failures, many of which culminated in trials, fines, and imprisonment.

Finally, the machinery for the terror was already in existence. The Cheka of the first years had become the OGPU, the organization responsible during the collectivization campaign for dealing with the kulak victims. The OGPU established and ran the labor camps where millions of peasants were imprisoned, and thus became the possessor of an immense pool of labor which it assigned to construction projects like the Volga-Don Canal and to timber, mining, and road-building projects in Siberia. By July 1934, when the OGPU became the NKVD (The People's Commissariat of Internal Affairs), the organization was staffed by men and women calloused by long experience to treating their fellowmen with heartless, official brutality.

But while Stalin did not invent the purge system, it cannot be denied that he contributed directly to its immense expansion in the 1930s, and his personal character and ambition clearly influenced some of the most perplexing events of the purges. Consider, in particular, his attitude toward the Communist party. The master of the machine was displeased with its functioning. Although he had captured control of the party, and it had performed passably well through the First Five-Year Plan, there had been cries of agony from members and leaders, as well as many dissenting voices suggesting other, milder techniques for achieving the nation's industrial development. In 1933 important high party members, many of them prominent Old Bolsheviks, courageously demanded more patience, more humanity and less ruthlessness during the second plan. But the "Supreme Apparatchik" was convinced that he could achieve his ends only if he had a perfectly responsive party machine. His towering crimes of the middle and late 1930s, which were to include the murder of almost all of the Old Bolsheviks, can only be explained, if they can be explained at all, as Stalin's effort to break the party completely to his will, to transform it into an absolutely submissive and efficient instrument that would unquestioningly obey his orders.

During the years of the second plan, scattered clues left by close observers show Stalin to have been taut and resentful, suspicious of other party leaders—even of old and long-trusted friends—to the degree of paranoia. His habits of keeping his own counsel, of scheming in secret, of moving his pawns in the dark, and his deep distrust of the world, so characteristic of his years as an underground agent, dominated his thought and conduct during this period. Considering the pressures he felt regarding the industrialization drive, the encroaching dangers from Germany and Japan, and what he interpreted as the continuing deliberate betrayal of the West, one can well understand why he saw himself as a beleaguered warrior menaced by the whole world and why he believed himself justified in using any means to win his ends. He felt that other, weaker communists, as well as his enemies abroad, were deliberately undermining Soviet progress and security, forcing him to drive the nation forward for its own preservation. In addition, as the evidence certainly shows, he had only contempt for many of his colleagues, sure that he alone could save Russia.

But Stalin's aims and character cannot wholly explain the terrible phenomena of the purges. Unleashing the most widespread and systematic use of terror the world has ever known, he developed a kind of weapon that in any society would have effects not amenable to control. For when capriciously brutal, anonymous men in uniform are free to carry out beatings, illegal arrests, torture, imprisonment, exile without trial, and secret executions of citizens—whose ranks include many widely respected leaders—the results can only be irrational terror, alienation, disorientation, and the ultimate breakdown of many normally important social institutions. The instrument of coercion, if not perfectly controlled, becomes a madman's gun, shooting in all directions, encouraging confusion, inefficiency, and hysteria, as often as greater production or increased effort. Such was the case in the Soviet Union.

From 1933 until World War II, within a tortured, suffering Soviet society the terror developed its own life, growing and expanding as if by laws of its own. Presumably Stalin's initial assumption had been simply that if a little terror drove managers and laborers to work harder, intensified and expanded terror could make them work harder still. But when millions of honest workers were sent to labor camps without knowing the reason, when the secret police organization arrested by quota to replenish its stocks of slave labor, when NKVD interrogators earned Stakhanovite prizes for obtaining greater numbers of confessions, and when each police office was assigned a percentage of the local population to arrest each month, the system had run wild.

The Great Purges

Some effort must be made here to set in chronological order the events of the purging of party leaders. If we concern ourselves only with what actually occurred, the story is simple. In Leningrad, on December 1, 1934, a young communist named Nikolaev assassinated Sergei Kirov, Chairman of the Leningrad party organization and member of the Politburo. Stalin appeared to go berserk. He rushed to Leningrad, participated in the investigation, and ostensibly concluded from the evidence obtained that the assassin was a member of a still-existing Left

Oppositionist movement, who had been provoked to his deed, at least indirectly, by Zinoviev and Kamenev.

Stalin assigned a new man, Andrei Zhdanov, to replace Kirov and to investigate the assassination. Immediately thereafter thousands of people in Leningrad were arrested and exiled from the city. Zinoviev and Kamenev were themselves called to account, arrested, condemned to prison, and forced to accept moral responsibility for the assassination on the grounds that their earlier opposition had given encouragement to Nikolaev's dissent. The party-wide investigation to ferret out all the ramifications of the supposed conspiracy which then began was to end two years later in the first purge trial of former Old Bolshevik leaders.

Publicly mouthing imprecations against the spies, imperialist agents, and murderers, who he insisted were at the bottom of a great conspiracy, Stalin prepared a bloodbath for the party. The role he cast for himself was that of public defender of the purity of Lenin's party against native and foreign foes determined to destroy it.

Actually, the reasons for Kirov's assassination were not as simple as Stalin would have had them appear. It is still not clear whether the assassination was indeed the work of a vast conspiracy (as the published evidence from the subsequent trials seemed to prove) or whether, as later evidence indicates, Stalin himself organized or at least ordered the assassination of Kirov to rid himself of a dangerous and popular rival. Despite the testimony of the purge trials, the weight of the evidence supports the latter view. Stalin seems to have engineered Kirov's death and then attempted to use the event as an excuse for eliminating all other opponents, rivals, or personal enemies in the party.

Stalin's guilt is implied in part by the role Kirov was playing just before his death. The Leningrad leader, along with other members of the Politburo, had argued vehemently for a relaxation of Stalin's harsh policies and is believed to have opposed Stalin at the Seventeenth Party Congress in 1934; as a brave leader and one of the strong men of the party, he posed a serious threat to the fulfillment of Stalin's plans. Also important, in terms of highly credible evidence, is the indictment of Stalin by his most critical successor, Nikita Khrushchev, in the

Secret Speech presented in 1956 to the Twentieth Congress of the Communist Party. Khrushchev pointed out a strange series of events that followed the assassination. "After the murder of Kirov," he reported to the party's leaders, "top functionaries of the NKVD were given very light sentences, but in 1937 they were shot. We can assume that they were shot in order to cover the traces of the organizers of Kirov's killing."[5]

Khrushchev was much more explicit five years later in his concluding remarks at the Twenty-Second Party Congress, which took place in late October 1961. The long quotation that follows is a revealing illustration of the murderous milieu in which Stalin worked. According to Khrushchev:

> The mass repressions began after the murder of Kirov. A great deal of effort is still necessary to determine fully who was guilty of his death. The more deeply we study the materials relating to Kirov's death, the more questions arise. It is noteworthy that Kirov's assassin had previously been twice arrested by the Chekists near the Smolny [the Party headquarters in Leningrad], and that weapons had been found on him. But both times, upon someone's instruction, he had been released. And this man was in the Smolny, armed, in the very corridor along which Kirov usually passed. And for some reason or other it happened that at the moment of the murder the chief of Kirov's bodyguard had fallen far behind. . . .
>
> The following fact is also very strange. When the chief of Kirov's bodyguard was being driven to the interrogation—and he was to have been questioned by Stalin, Molotov, and Voroshilov—on the way, as the driver of the vehicle later said, an accident was deliberately staged by those who were to bring the chief of the bodyguard to the interrogation. They reported that the chief of the bodyguard had died in the accident, although actually he had been killed by the persons escorting him.
>
> Thus the man who guarded Kirov was killed. Then those who had killed him were shot. This was apparently not an accident but a premeditated crime. Who could have committed it?[6]

[5] Nikita Khrushchev, *The Crimes of the Stalin Era* (The New Leader, New York, 1962), p. S22.

[6] Charlotte Saikowski and Leo Gruliow, *Current Soviet Policies, IV: The Documentary Record of the 22nd Congress of the Communist Party of the Soviet Union* (Columbia University Press, New York and London, 1962), p. 197.

Somewhat rhetorically in a later paragraph Khrushchev again asked why the chief of the bodyguard was killed and why both the NKVD men who were escorting him were later shot. His answer pointed straight at Stalin: "This means that someone had to have them killed in order to cover up all traces."[7] Whatever the truth may be, and we seem destined to learn little more of it soon, Kirov's assassination gave Stalin the excuse he needed to mount a frontal assault against the Old Bolsheviks who had stood against him in the past as well as those who might conceivably resist him in the future.

Investigation of the wide conspiracy, supposedly brought to light by Kirov's assassination, continued all through 1935 and the first half of 1936. Then, on August 19 of the latter year, a show trial of sixteen Old Bolsheviks began. It was a public trial, under the military section of the Supreme Court. The charges were treason. Zinoviev and Kamenev and fourteen other Old Bolsheviks were charged with a leftist conspiracy to overthrow Stalin and other members of the Politburo. The court's proceedings moved as if following an unreal scenario. The accused duly acknowledged their guilt as charged; indeed, they literally fell over themselves in their eagerness to confess to the most heinous crimes, and the prosecutor, Andrei Vishinsky, completed his case with the words: "I demand that dogs gone mad should be shot—everyone of them!"[8] They were executed the following day.

No one had seriously believed that Stalin would kill his former colleagues. In so doing he had advanced one more step toward perfecting an obedient and efficient machine that would carry out his orders. With inhuman single-mindedness, he was ridding the machine of some of its "imperfect" human impedimenta.

A second trial was held during the last week of January 1937. This time the victims were described as the "Anti-Soviet Trotskyite Center," so called because they were accused of conspiring with Trotsky. The seventeen defendants included

[7] Saikowski and Gruliow, p. 197.
[8] People's Commissariat of Justice of the USSR, *The Case of the Trotskyite-Zinovievite Terrorist Centre, August 19–24, 1936* (Moscow, 1936), p. 164.

Yury Pyatakov, Leonid Serebryakov, and Karl Radek. All these men had long been staunch and eminent members of the party. It is impossible, therefore, to believe them guilty of the extravagant crimes with which they were now charged, especially since no evidence of their guilt except their own confessions has ever come to light. As part of their treachery, according to the official transcript of this trial, the accused had been united from 1933 on in a Trotskyite center whose "principal aim" was "to overthrow the Soviet Power in the USSR and to restore capitalism and the power of the bourgeoisie by means of wrecking, diversive action, espionage and terrorist activities designed to undermine the economic and military power of the Soviet Union, to expedite armed attack on the USSR, to assist foreign aggressors and to bring about the defeat of the USSR."[9]

In addition, the defendants at this trial were found guilty of "negotiations with certain representatives of Germany and Japan," "diversive and wrecking work in industry, chiefly in enterprises of importance for defense purposes, and also on the railways. . . on the instructions and with the direct participation of agents of the German and Japanese intelligence services." They were condemned, as well, for having spent their last years "disrupting plans of production, lowering the quality of products, organizing fires and explosions at factories and factory departments and mines, organizing train wrecks and damaging rolling stock and railway track."[10] The list of crimes perpetrated by men who had been the nation's leading citizens went on and on, becoming more and more unbelievable as it grew.

And once again, at this trial, as at the earlier one, men whom the tsar's police and prisons had never broken, rushed to confess complicity in every crime they were accused of. Subsequently, thirteen members of the group were shot, while the remainder received sentences of from eight to ten years.

[9] People's Commissariat of Justice of the USSR, *Report of Court Proceedings in the Case of the Anti-Soviet Trotskyite Center, Moscow, January 23–30, 1937* (Howard Fertig, New York, 1967), p. 574.
[10] People's Commissariat of Justice of the USSR, *Case of the Anti-Soviet Trotskyite Center,* p. 575.

For the outside world, as well as for thousands of members of the party, the confessions of the accused stretched all credulity. How could men so totally committed to communism and to the party for so long a time calmly confess to these unspeakable crimes against the party? Had they truly endured all the rigors of revolution, civil war, the New Economic Policy, the political struggles, and forced industrialization, while pocketing the gold of some hated foreign government? Had they indeed been traitors from the beginning, as some of the "evidence" argued? The mysteries were not then and have not yet been cleared away, although we know now that the confessions were secured by means of refined and prolonged torture, both physical and mental.

The trials continued, while men watched unbelievingly. In June 1937 came another chilling announcement. A secret military court had tried Mikhail Tukhachevsky, Commander of the Red Army and a hero of the civil war, along with seven other prominent generals, on charges of espionage. Specifically, these men were accused of conspiring with Germany to overthrow Stalin. All the defendants were found guilty and were immediately executed. Nineteen years later, Khrushchev was to reveal that neither Tukhachevsky nor the others had been guilty, that in fact there had been no evidence against them, and the Soviet government soon after announced their posthumous rehabilitation.

Finally, in March 1938, came the Trial of the Twenty-One. Almost as if he were replaying his personal nightmare of the 1920s, Stalin now turned from his purging of the Left Oppositionists and attacked the Right. This time the defendants were billed as the "Anti-Soviet Bloc of Rights and Trotskyites." Most prominent among the accused were Bukharin, Rykov, Rakovsky, and the former NKVD chief, Yagoda. These men were charged with planning to overthrow the Soviet government and to replace it with a bourgeois-capitalist regime. They were also accused of scheming to break up the nation by chipping away the Ukraine and Far Eastern territories. Finally, as if sure by now that the Soviet people would believe anything, Stalin's prosecutor declared that the defendants had been paid German agents since 1921, British agents since 1926, and agents of the Nazi terrorist police, the Gestapo, since 1933. Considering the characters and careers of the men involved, such charges were simply monstrous, and no supporting evidence has ever been discovered. Yet the propaganda machine and the terror worked so perfectly that no doubting or dissenting voices questioned the charges. No one challenged the verdict that some of the greatest men of the party had been vicious and deliberate traitors since the first days of the Bolshevik Revolution. During this trial the now familiar drone of lengthy and incredible confessions was heard again. Then the sentence: except for two men, death.

When Yezhov, the head of the NKVD who had masterminded the work of arresting and obtaining confessions, was finally removed from office in July 1938, to be replaced by Lavrenty Beria, the Old Bolsheviks had been almost totally liquidated. Not all had been tried in the great show trials. Many had been quietly arrested and exiled without notice of trial, often without explanation. Others died mysterious accidental deaths, or committed suicide. The mere statistics of the consequences of Stalin's purge of the high ranks of the party suggest an appalling carnage. According to Nikita Khrushchev, of the 139 members of the party's Central Committee at the party's Seventeenth Congress (1934), 98, that is, 70 percent, were arrested and shot. Khrushchev went on to say: "The only reason why 70 percent of Central Committee members and candidates . . . were branded as enemies of the party and of the people was because honest communists were slandered, accusations against them were fabricated, and revolutionary legality was gravely undermined."[11]

While Khrushchev placed almost exclusive emphasis upon the arbitrary destruction of the party's leadership, it must be noted that the purges of the party leaders were accompanied by simultaneous and widespread purging at all levels of the party and of the society as a whole. Waves of arrests flooded across the nation in these years. Many were stimulated in part

[11] Khrushchev, p. S20.

by confessions tortured from innocent people who were then forced to implicate others as their co-conspirators. But guilt was easy for the police to assign. Former members of the bourgeoisie, of anarchist, Social Revolutionary, or Menshevik parties, former supporters of Trotsky or Bukharin, relatives, friends, or even distant associates of an accused or condemned man—all were tarred by the mere guilt of association. Men and women who had been abroad, who had studied foreign languages or read foreign books, were automatically suspect. Even worse, NKVD agencies were assigned quotas and ordered to arrest a fixed percentage of the community in which they worked. As a result, the interrogation rooms of the NKVD, as well as prisons and labor camps, were packed with engineers, lawyers, professors, party members of the rank and file, condemned NKVD officers, and military men, as well as innocent workers and peasants and confused members of national minority groups. One had only to be accused by the NKVD to be on one's way to Siberia.

Stalin's purge had passed far beyond the limits of sanity or sense. While the nation sought for labor, millions of able-bodied men and women languished and died in concentration camps. And while the nation struggled valiantly to build schools and educate the professional people so vital to its development, thousands of skilled engineers, economists, scientists, and scholars worked with shovels and picks in forced labor gangs. Police raided private homes and apartments nightly, driving their victims away in "Black Maria's," while families wept in terror and neighbors packed their own bags in anticipation of the punishment that might come to them because the victims had been their friends or acquaintances. The terror touched almost everyone.

What happened to the Red Army officers' corps well illustrates how devastating was the impact of the widening circles of arrests set off by the Great Purges. Japanese intelligence estimates place army losses at three-quarters of the members of the Supreme War Council, 2 of the nation's 5 marshals, 13 of its 15 generals, 62 of its 85 corps commanders, 110 of its 195 divisional commanders, and 220 of its 406 brigade commanders—all of whom were executed. Some 90 percent of the army's generals and 80 percent of the colonels were arrested along with 30,000 officers of lower rank. The army was paralyzed. One cannot help but wonder: to what purpose?[12]

Whatever else Stalin's purges accomplished, there can be little doubt that they gave him the kind of control over the party that he wanted. Trotsky perceptively commented that "in order to establish the regime that is justly called Stalinist, what was necessary was not a Bolshevik Party, but the extermination of the Bolshevik Party."[13] In this judgment he was right, for from 1934 through 1938, Stalin exterminated the party as an independent band of elite revolutionaries or bureaucrats sharing in the decision making that determined Soviet destinies. The old elite was simply wiped out and in its place went men and women who had learned to fear the pathological suspiciousness of the leader, the man who, as Khrushchev was to say, saw "everywhere an in everything, enemies, two-facers, and spies." This man, who "choked a person morally and physically,"[14] had tolerance only for those who efficiently executed his orders. By his purges he had taught the party that the only correct line was his, that to deviate from his commands meant ruin or death.

In sum, this new Ivan the Terrible had made himself an absolute tsar. The party, henceforth, was to be little more than his first servant, abject, terrorized, and brutalized by its master. The fate of the Soviet people was even more tragic, for they were helpless under the terror; it was too awesome and incomprehensible to oppose, too irrational to analyze and destroy, too omniscient even to discuss out loud with impunity. Men and women held their peace and dreaded the night because no one could hope to know when or where the capricious arm of the NKVD would strike next.

[12] Leonard Schapiro, *The Communist Party of the Soviet Union* (Random House, New York, 1960), p. 420.
[13] Leon Trotsky, *Stalin, An Appraisal of the Man and His Influence,* edited and translated by Charles Malamuth (Hollis and Carter, Ltd., London, 1947), p. 403.
[14] Khrushchev, p. S34.

Totalitarianism as a Social System

As Carl Friedrich has suggested, the totalitarian regime is an autocratic one using "organization and methods developed and employed with the aid of modern technical devices in an effort to exercise as much control as possible in the service of an ideologically motivated movement dedicated to the total reconstruction of an allegedly moribund mass society." Or more simply, totalitarian dictatorship may be defined as "a system of autocratic rule for realizing totalist intentions under modern technical and political conditions."[15] In an analysis that has stood the test of time with slight changes, Friedrich considers the distinguishing characteristics of the totalitarian form of autocracy to be: "(1) a totalist ideology; (2) a single party committed to this ideology and usually led by one man, the dictator; (3) a fully developed secret police; and (4) monopolistic control over (a) mass communications; (b) operational weapons; and (c) all organizations, including economic ones, thus involving a centrally-planned economy."[16]

While there has been and will continue to be much discussion whether this kind of government is a new phenomenon or simply a familiar form of government—autocracy—making use of modern control techniques, the term *totalitarian* is useful here to describe the social system developed under Stalin in the late 1930s. As we examine more closely the peculiar governing system that evolved under Stalin, two points should be underlined. The first is that Stalin himself exerted a unique impact upon the system due to his own obsessive and continuing personal need to achieve total control, not just of the Soviet political system but of *all* aspects of the society—economic, cultural, intellectual, and psychological. Second, it seems quite obvious, his autocracy could never have achieved such a high degree of effectiveness but for the fact that in the twentieth century important new communication techniques, organiza-

---

[15] Carl J. Friedrich, Michael Curtis, and Benjamin R. Barber, *Totalitarianism in Perspective* (Frederick A. Praeger, New York, 1969), pp. 135–136.
[16] Friedrich et al., p. 126.

tional and administrative devices, and new kinds of weapons have made attainable far more extensive or "total" control of a whole society by a central government than has ever before been possible.

Stalin's effort to secure total control was concentrated basically in his struggles to establish absolute personal domination over party and state. In the years of the purges, he advanced steadily toward this objective. Through his personal secretariat, directed after 1930 by a little known servitor, A. N. Poskrebyshev, Stalin ruled the party, bypassing both the Politburo and the Central Committee whenever he wished. This personal secretariat, or *Special Sector* as it is sometimes called, appears to have dealt directly with the secret police, with the Comintern, with the Commissariat of Foreign Affairs and, when Stalin chose to have it do so, with all other agencies of party and state in such a way that Stalin could personally order and institute his policies in every field.

Together with the personal secretariat, Stalin was also served by an amorphous, informal advisory group, which might elsewhere be termed a "kitchen cabinet." His "cabinet" consisted of a loose and ever-changing set of old cronies and drinking companions who held high offices in both party and government. His friends of the civil war, Kliment Voroshilov, Marshal S. Budenny, Vyacheslav Molotov, and others, frequently sat with him for hours around a long table piled high with food and the different kinds of wines Stalin liked to sample. They met in the evening in his simple Kremlin apartment or at his villa outside Moscow, and they mixed stories, rude jokes, and official business through the nights and into the early morning hours.

Stalin was a nocturnal man, who apparently felt most at home gathering reports from these old friends and plotting political moves in his own mind as he picked at the roast suckling pig and sipped his Georgian wines. We have only three or four detailed reports of the way business was carried on at these sessions, but they are sufficient to show that Stalin rudely and personally decided the most important affairs of state during these informal midnight banquets among men who dared not question his absolute authority.

Exercising dictatorial command over all aspects of policy, domestic and foreign, Stalin made his party officers and the NKVD responsible for the proper functioning of the state bureaucracies. His ever-present demands for greater efficiency, along with the expanded educational system and widespread terror, had the positive effect of raising the competence of both bureaucrats and bureaucracies. The purges, spreading through the ranks of administrative and economic officials, educators and party members, served to remove those who were old, tired, incompetent, or for any reason deemed untrustworthy. And the threat of the purge acted as a goad for those who remained.

Into the places left empty by execution and exile rose thousands of young, well-trained men and women, steeped in the values of Stalinism, tempered in the struggle to succeed by the ferocious conflicts of the industrialization campaign, owing their careers and their futures to the man who was now publicly call the *Vozhd,* the leader. Government offices and factory management staffs alike were wrapped round by over-lapping control agencies designed to catch up the laggard and unmask the saboteur. Party cells in each office, institute, and factory vied with special sections of the secret police to inspect and examine and report, in relentless efforts to force the bureaucracies to work efficiently.

The NKVD, responsible since 1934 for all internal security, for penal institutions, police, frontier guards, highway adminis-tration, fire departments, and civil registry offices, became in the late 1930s perhaps the most complicated and extensive terrorist police organization the world has ever seen. And by the end of the great purges, it had also become a gigantic eco-nomic empire, employing millions of slave laborers at starva-tion levels, and by means of their efforts performing over 17 percent of the nation's total economic work. Deeply involved in timber and mining, in highway building and other construc-tion projects, this vast police empire had become a kind of

Frankenstein's monster, terrorizing the Soviet people in all areas of political, economic, and social life. Meanwhile, it informed not only upon others, but upon itself, frequently purging its own hierarchy of even its highest as well as its middle-level officials, in a manner carefully calculated by Stalin to preserve his ultimate control. In other words, moving the levers of power quietly within his own Special Section and at his Kremlin dining parties, Stalin created the same atmosphere of insecurity in the NKVD that purges, arbitrary punishments, and frequent personnel changes maintained in party and state organizations.

In the army, the purges of Tukhachevsky and the other generals set off organizational reforms designed to strengthen both party and NKVD controls. A devoted Stalinist, L. Mekhlis, was appointed to the Political Administration of the army, and young, newly trained communist officers were promoted to fill the gaps left by purges. In late 1937 communist commissars became coequals of the commanding staff, another step forward in tightening party controls. In addition, the introduction of NKVD agents, operating systematically in well-organized sections, permitted Stalin to divide power in the army between the party, the state, and the NKVD, manipulating each element as he chose. So long as he dominated the army, there could be no serious armed effort at rebellion or resistance, for in the context of our century, and of Stalin's totalitarian system, the weapons of combat—heavy artillery, planes, and tanks—were simply not available to the common man or the conspiratorial group. In the late 1930s, his multiple control systems, greased by terror and powered by his willful capriciousness, functioned with surprising effectiveness.

At the lower levels of the society the totalitarian system of rule could not be resisted easily, if at all. Millions of industrial laborers were caught within an iron cage of rules that compelled them to work and punished them harshly for unexcused absences and incompetence. Almost every facet of their economic lives was open to state regulation. In October 1940, the publication of a government decree on state labor reserves resulted literally in the conscripting of young people for training and labor. And in the countryside where the great majority of the population (67 percent in 1940) was tied to the collective and state farms and rural villages, escape was almost impossible, unless a person were fortunate enough to be included in a levy of young peasants needed for factory work. In the physical sense, then, Stalin's political-economic control was virtually total.

But this was not enough for the dictator. He wanted the Soviet people to *think* and *feel* correctly. Accordingly he demanded that the intelligentsia, whether young or old, labor to strengthen the dictatorship and prepare for the future by acting as "engineers of the human soul." Their mission was to teach Leninist-Stalinist doctrines and to preach the ethic of obedience to the state and sacrifice for the future.

All formal communications media in the nation were subject to party control. All newspapers, journals, magazines, books, and even the wall newspapers tacked up at factories and clubs were wholly committed to thundering out the party line. Billions of words daily, in the press, on the radio, in countless meetings of party agitators, in public and social organizations and in the schools, reiterated identical arguments acclaiming the undying truths of the Leninist-Stalinist doctrine. Over and over was sounded the imperative that every good citizen should dedicate himself to working for socialism under Stalin's great leadership. And in the late 1930s a new note, the greatness of the Russian nation, became a major theme, for war was looming on the horizons to east and west. It was time to stimulate Soviet patriotism and to portray Stalin and the party as the true defenders of Russia.

Artists and literary men were also dragooned or bludgeoned into helping achieve perfect thought control. Ordered to practice "socialist realism," they attempted to describe in their creative works the positive aspects of the Five-Year Plans, to glorify the heroism of workers and kolkhoz peasants, and to extol the tractor drivers and lathe operators whose "voluntary" extra toil was saving the motherland. Poets, novelists, and artists who could not thus tailor their art to the economic and propaganda aims of the *Vozhd* learned to keep quiet, or if they wrote and could not say the right things, they soon found their sorrowful ways to the prisons and the labor camps.

Other writers, especially those adept at composing panegyrics, ensured the success of their careers by writing eulogies to Stalin, who increasingly encouraged tasteless obeisance to himself. More and more frequently he was referred to as the Genius, the Omniscient Leader of the People, the One Source of True Marxism, the Great Economist, and so on. Perhaps he had been corrupted by the heady wine of absolute power. Or perhaps he realized that Russia's suffering masses needed a Giant-Tsar Symbol, an Omnipotent-Myth Figure, a Great Father, to quote, to reflect upon, and to worship as peasants were still wont to worship the icons in the religious corners of their huts. At any rate, the cult of Stalin took root and flourished. In press and radio, in novels and every public address, and in the essays of school children and the exhortations of every factory agitator, the sacred image of the *Vozhd* was invoked constantly. Stalin could do no wrong. If by chance a worker or peasant should curse him, strike his picture, or make some idle joke about him, and have the misfortune to be observed by an informer of the NKVD, the culprit could be (and often was) sentenced to hard labor lasting for many years.

The nation's scholars were also placed under many constraints during these years. Soviet scientists were ordered to set their research within the Marxist-Leninist philosophical framework, to think according to the rules of the dialectic, and they were obliged to focus their attention primarily upon demonstrating the validity of the Marxist approach to life or developing new ways to push Soviet modernization forward more rapidly. The humanities and social sciences became in effect branches of Marxism-Leninism. Historians were ordered to rewrite history in ways that would serve the industrialization campaign, the need for more patriots, or other varied purposes of the *Vozhd.*

The *Vozhd* himself helped his scholars prepare a new *History of the Communist Party,* which patiently and obsessively rewrote the past to suppress and vilify his enemies and to present him as the one true successor of Lenin. The section authored by Stalin, "Dialectical and Historical Materialism," set forth his peculiarly mechanistic and simplistic view of the theories of Marx and the history of man. Like any scholastic drillmaster he reduced the philosophical bases of Marxism to a set of numbered, categorial rules, set forth in primitively positive terms. Presented thus simply, the principles could be grasped by any common laborer, while anyone who had learned to read could, by memorizing the numbered statements, easily master Stalin's picture of past and future and the laws governing history.

If it had been his purpose thus to simplify and vulgarize the more sophisticated complexities of Marxist thought so that even the poorest and most ignorant of his people could fathom the reasons for their struggle and their suffering, Stalin's rigid laws might have been justified, but, in fact, he was not intentionally oversimplifying. He apparently believed that his interpretation of the laws determining historical change and of the way these laws functioned was scientifically and absolutely true. And he used his overwhelming authority to compel other men—philosophers, scientists, and artists—to fit their work within the rigid constraints of his philosophical model.

In addition to purging the party of Old Bolsheviks, who could remember his origins and mistakes, Stalin also suppressed those books, records, and documents out of the communist past that did not match the vision of history he wanted his people to have. Dangerous books—for example, anything written by Trotsky, Radek, or Bukharin—were banned; others that did not show Stalin as a hero from the turn of the century onward were suppressed or rewritten. Russia's classics were rigorously scanned, and writers like Dostoevsky were blacklisted. The dictator's intention was to condition his nation to think as he wished it to; his basic technique for achieving this end was to censure and limit the ideas and information available to it. For the same reason Stalin carefully and systematically isolated the land and its people from the West and from the West's books, newspapers, and evil ideas. The citizen who betrayed even a casual interest in foreign objects—books, radio broadcasts, languages, or clothing—was instantly suspect and in danger of losing his freedom.

Education, too, functioned as an instrument of Stalin's

physical dictatorship and of his thought control. For him education was a means of training men and women for slots in the economic, social, political, or cultural machinery of the society. The mission of the educator was to provide the requisite numbers of technicians, professional specialists, managers, teachers, and doctors, and to make certain that they had been subjected to enough political indoctrination to ensure their proper attitudes on the job. Men and women were becoming replaceable parts in Stalin's machine, cogs that could be slipped into the production system wherever needed. And the schools did well, turning out growing numbers of engineers, agronomists, administrators, and technicians, all of them well exposed to the one truth of Stalinism.

By 1936, Stalin felt so secure in his dictatorship and so convinced of the full support of his people, that he presented his nation with a constitution, proclaiming it the most "democratic" in the world. In fact it preserved the perfect authority of the party, although in so doing it mentioned the party only twice and the role of the *Vozhd* not at all. The audacious mockery of its articles can only be appreciated when one pauses to wonder why no massive denunciation went up repudiating a document that blatantly offered so fraudulent a democracy.

But there were no public denunciations, only joyful acceptance of the constitution and widespread enthusiasm for the election campaign that followed during 1937 (at the height of the Great Purges). In fact, the grateful response of the Soviet public to the 1936 Constitution was in itself a massive demonstration of the overwhelming success of Stalin's thought control. He had achieved such a degree of acceptance and had so thoroughly cut the Soviet Union away from the rest of the world that many millions had no choice but to believe what his press and radio told them. If some secretly doubted or dissented, they had learned the lesson of the purges—silence or approval were essential if one wanted to remain outside the prisons and the camps.

But even his highly successful thought control was not enough for this man who sought the perfect administrative machine. Stalin wanted a New Soviet Man. He wanted a quiet, puritanical, hardworking man whose mind was programmed to accept the self-righteous line of the *Vozhd* no matter how that line might twist and turn, whether it demanded work, war, sacrifice, or mindless approval. With his machinery of political-economic administration and his instruments of terror, Stalin had won effective physical control. And with his dictatorship over the press, the schools, the teachers, the Soviet borders, and all radio channels, he at last possessed the environmental controls needed to assure success in determining the information inputs and the thoughts of the guinea-pig humans he was experimenting with for the sake of totalitarianism. But all these were not enough. He longed for total victory—a New Soviet Man who would think and respond automatically in the prescribed ways; and to achieve this, much more was needed than terror, thought control, and technical education. Creation of such a man would require careful socialization from the cradle upward.

Accordingly, child and youth organizations were expanded. Young Octobrists became Pioneers, Pioneers became Komsomols, and Komsomols (there were nine million young people between the ages of fourteen and twenty-eight in this organization in 1939) were expected to become good Communist party members. Starting then with the children, appealing to their enthusiasm, idealism, and hopes for the future, Stalin attempted to imbue them with the total values of the new system that were to replace all other values and loyalties. This kind of training created, as it was intended to do, the notorious Pavlik Morozov and many other young Pioneers who earned praise for betraying their parents to the state for a variety of minor defections. Such training was further intended to mold young Soviet citizens and soldiers who would stand ready to serve any cause unquestioningly—to organize agricultural enterprises, to build new cities in the Far East, to work on the toughest construction projects in northern Siberia, or to die in battle in Spain or Manchuria—anxious to sacrifice themselves for the nation and its omniscient, kindly, and paternal leader.

The nation's public organizations were enlisted to reinforce the state's application of the carrot and the stick. All public organizations were, according to the Constitution of 1936 (and in actual fact), sparked by communists; that is, all public organizations were controlled by the *Vozhd* for the purposes of the *Vozhd*. The Trade Unions, serving as "transmission belts" of state policy, encouraged shock-workers and socialist competitions, awarded banners and titles for outstanding labor successes, and provided paid vacations to Black Sea resorts for feats of valor in factory and field. Sports and paramilitary organizations developed the muscles, health, courage, and special skills needed for defense. And the *Vozhd* himself gave special awards and honors to those who excelled in fulfilling his goals.

Finally, the pressures for conformity and the penalties for dissent combined to influence behavior even within the family. Terrorist police and the arbitrary punishment they meted out to individuals made men fear to confide their misgivings about the Soviet system even to their wives. Parents were reluctant to admit to their children that they did not share all of the *Vozhd's* values, and brothers or lovers hesitated to discuss their dissenting opinions, fearing they would thus "contaminate" the loved one who might subsequently be found guilty of listening and not reporting.

Tortured by the NKVD myth that its informers were everywhere—and they were undoubtedly present in many different social settings, in factories, taverns, clubs, and families —men and women learned not to discuss politics, not to criticize, not to possess or read the wrong books, not to be too ambitious. Society in a sense became atomized, each atom avoiding and distrusting its neighbor. Only in the worst of the labor camps, it seems, was a certain sort of freedom and fearlessness permissible, for there the individual had already lost all that could be taken away from him except his life, and that was often too miserable to be held very dear.

If even this totalitarian system did not work well enough to satisfy Stalin, it was because men grow accustomed to terror, and there is a limit to how much terror can be applied before it destroys both victim and master. Then, too, no matter what environment surrounds them, men will spend some of their effort and intelligence trying to care for their loved ones or struggling for more food, security, or power. And in the end, some men and women simply cannot be broken, no matter how great the threat. If the totalitarian system did not work as efficiently as Stalin willed it to, it was because the human spirit and mind cannot be totally controlled or programmed, even by the fearsome technological apparatus and the oppressive bureaucratic instruments that the twentieth century placed in Stalin's hands. If the system fell short of his desires, it was because there was too much inefficiency, error, waste, and hurry in the way the system was thrown together; there was too much incompetence among its officials, and too much inhumanity in it. But it did not fail because Stalin himself lacked persistence and determination. Indeed no man has ever tried harder to build the perfect autocracy.

Above the confusion, agony, and bloodshed, the Supreme Apparatchik applied his brutal pressures systematically—terror and rewards, indoctrination, organization, ruthless and capricious punishment, the falsification of history, the perversion of art and literature and education, and the corruption of human souls. His purpose, as he had said in 1931, was to catch up. He would catch up or destroy his human materials on the way. The ultimate human cost of his objective was very great—many would say, too great, but on the economic side the truly jarring fact is that *in terms of production Stalin had attained his chief goals, even before the war.* He had very successfully modernized those aspects of Soviet society essential for the political and military strength he and his party had decided were imperative. It is a tragic commentary on man's destiny that in the process of trying to save his nation and build a socialist utopia, Stalin created a totalitarian society of monstrous proportions—a political and social system in which all aspects of human life were so regimented and brutalized that life itself became virtually intolerable for millions of its citizens.

CHAPTER FOUR

World War II and Its Consequences

From Munich to the Invasion

As the decade of the 1930s drew to a close, the international situation posed serious threats for Russia's dictator. The peace and security so necessary to the successful building of socialism in one country were proving more and more difficult to maintain. Through 1939, the acts and postures of other nations increasingly drew Stalin's attention from domestic to foreign affairs. However, the primacy that he gave to domestic objectives was still evident in the diplomatic efforts he put forth then and later to keep his country from becoming involved in a major war. Such primacy was evident both during and after the tense months between the Munich crisis and Hitler's final engulfment of Czechoslovakia on March 15, 1939, when Stalin was finally forced to accept the failure of his efforts to achieve collective security in the West. Seeking alternatives, from March through July he pursued a new policy, walking on the tightrope between the Western powers and Hitler's Germany and negotiating with both. As the months passed, however, and it became clear that the Western powers did not seriously contemplate entering into an effective alliance with him, he swung over to the only hope that remained—alliance with Hitler. Such an alliance, as it happened, was facilitated by Hitler's need for Russian neutrality when German troops invaded Poland, a campaign the Nazi leader was determined to begin in the late summer of 1939.

Stalin's intelligence services apparently advised him well about German plans and needs, for Stalin's wooing of the German Fuehrer was systematic, cool, and self-assured, though always cautious. Deeply distrustful of the German leader, Stalin at first permitted only the slightest hints of his interest in rapprochement to slip out to Nazi foreign officials; with equal distrust, Hitler and his colleagues studied the portents and countered with their own subtle feelers, at the same time following closely the negotiations Stalin continued to carry on with Britain and France and undoubtedly wondering which party was being deceived.

Stalin's speech on March 10, indicating a desire for friendship with his neighbors and a reluctance to rake others' chestnuts out of the fire, was his first overt move in the new diplomatic game. Then, on April 17, he set out his bait in another form. The Soviet ambassador to Berlin, Alexei Merekalov, sought out the state secretary of the German Foreign Office, Baron Ernst von Weizsacker, and in the course of a long conversation made a statement that aroused considerable interest on the part of the Germans. According to Weizsacker's official report, Merekalov said: "There exists for Russia no reason why she should not live with us on a normal footing. And from normal, the relations might become better and better."[1] German officials pored over these words carefully, wondering how far they might go in making known their own interests.

[1] Raymond James Sontag and James Stuart Beddie (eds.), *Nazi-Soviet Relations, 1939–1941* (Department of State, Washington, D.C., 1948), p. 2.

A few weeks later, in early May, Vyacheslav Molotov, one of Stalin's closest associates, became Commissar of Foreign Affairs in place of the Jew, Maxim Litvinov, who had so strongly argued the case for friendship with the Western powers and for collective security within the League of Nations. By this change Stalin seemed to be signaling his rejection of the pro-Western policy. Again German officials pondered long on the significance of Stalin's move, seeking to distinguish intent from accident. By late May, Weizsacker, cautiously probing for a clearer picture of Soviet intentions, turned to the German ambassador at Moscow, Friedrich Schulenburg, for advice, admitting his concern that "a very open [German] statement in Moscow, instead of being beneficial, might not rather be harmful and perhaps produce a peal of Tartar laughter."[2]

Meanwhile, Stalin and Molotov, without tipping their hands in any definite way, nonetheless managed to keep the dangerous game going. Typical of their circuitous maneuvering at this time was an enigmatic conversation in mid-June, when the Bulgarian minister, Draganoff, talked with an undersecretary of the German Foreign Office, Ernst Woermann. The Bulgarian minister related to Herr Woermann the substance of a talk he had had the previous day with the Soviet chargé d'affaires in Berlin. It seemed the latter had visited him and, while talking of many things, had explained the alternatives then open to the Soviet Union, possibly as he saw them himself, or possibly as they were viewed by the Soviet government. This intimation of what Russian officials might be thinking, made through a third person, the Bulgarian minister, in such a way that no one could know what weight to give it, was such a minor masterpiece of Machiavellian diplomacy that it deserves quotation in full. According to the Bulgarian minister, the chargé had said that the Soviet Union:

> . . . was vacillating between three possibilities, namely the conclusion of the pact with England and France, a further dilatory treatment of the pact negotiations, and a rapprochement with Germany. This last possibility, with which ideological considera-

[2] Sontag and Beddie, p. 9.

tions would not have to become involved, was closest to the desires of the Soviet Union. In addition, there were other points,
for instance that the Soviet Union did not recognize the Rumanian possession of Bessarabia. The fear of a German attack,
however, either via the Baltic countries or via Rumania was an
obstacle. In this connection the Chargé had also referred to
Mein Kampf. If Germany would declare that she would not
attack the Soviet Union or that she would conclude a nonaggression pact with her, the Soviet Union would probably refrain
from concluding a treaty with England. However, the Soviet
Union did not know what Germany really wanted, aside from
certain very vague allusions.[3]

To Hitler and his aides, such hints repeated many times
by a variety of sources were too tantalizing to ignore. A pact
with Russia would protect the flank of the German armies as
they went into Poland, and Hitler could not but be frantically
aware that the end-of-summer campaign his generals had
planned demanded the swiftest possible completion of such a
pact. While Stalin, through Molotov, pressed for economic,
geographic, and political concessions, always distrustful and
slow to accept German promises, Hitler's officials persuaded
themselves that an alliance was possible. They pressed more
and more openly for a working out of a detailed agreement.

In mid-August, the German foreign minister, Joachim
von Ribbentrop, directed his ambassador in Moscow to assure
Molotov that there were "no real conflicts of interest between
Germany and the USSR." The ambassador was instructed to
argue that there was indeed "a natural sympathy of the Germans
for the Russians," which had "never disappeared"; and he was
to emphasize that it was in the "compelling interest of both
countries to avoid for all future times the destruction of Germany and of the USSR, which would profit only the Western
democracies." Finally, he was to inform the Russians of von
Ribbentrop's own eagerness to make a personal visit to Moscow
"to set forth the Fuehrer's views to Herr Stalin."[4]

---

[3] Sontag and Beddie, p. 21.
[4] Sontag and Beddie, pp. 51–52.

Despite this urging, Molotov and Stalin continued to hesitate until the precise wording of an agreement had been actually worked out with von Ribbentrop. By this time Polish-Nazi relations had reached the breaking point, Hitler's forces were poised for invasion, and the wily Stalin made the most of the situation to obtain his own objectives. At last on August 20, Hitler personally dispatched a telegram to Stalin declaring his acceptance of the draft agreement and begging Stalin to accept a visit from von Ribbentrop for the purpose of finalizing the pact.

Stalin had what he wanted. Amid photographers and toasts, the Nazi-Soviet Pact was signed at Moscow on August 23, 1939. Stalin had changed sides, with a sudden reversal of position that caught most foreign observers by surprise. In a toast that night, he told the German envoys: "I know how much the German nation loves its Fuehrer; I should therefore like to drink to his health." Molotov, according to a German official who was present, "raised his glass to Stalin, remarking that it had been Stalin who—through his speech of March . . . which had been well understood in Germany—had brought about the reversal in political relations." And when von Ribbentrop was taking his leave, Stalin assured the Nazi leader that "he could guarantee on his word of honor that the Soviet Union would not betray its partner."[5] Thus a new friendship was pledged between two leaders who had seemed to outside observers to be irreconcilable and incompatible. Winston Churchill dubbed it the "Unholy Alliance."

The terms of the pact were simple. Each signatory agreed to refrain from "any act of violence, any aggressive action, and any attack" upon the other. Should either be attacked by a third power, the other would not aid that third power. To cement their friendship, each of the two governments agreed to consult and exchange information, to refrain from collaboration with groups hostile to the other, and to work out disputes "through friendly exchange of opinion or . . . arbitration commissions." The pact was intended to endure for ten years.

[5] Sontag and Beddie, pp. 75–76.

In a secret protocol, Stalin and Hitler set down the details of the agreements they had reached over their "respective shares of influence in Eastern Europe." In the Baltic region the dividing line between them would follow the northern boundary of Lithuania. Should there be a revision of the boundaries of the Polish state—and all knew that such revision would occur immediately—the area of Poland east of the rivers Narew, Vistula, and San was to be placed under Soviet influence. The question of whether an independent Polish state should be maintained was to be determined by future political developments. Finally, the protocol affirmed the Soviet Union's "interest in Bessarabia," a reference to Russian territories lost to the Rumanians in November 1918, and Germany specifically avowed its "complete political disinterestedness in these areas.[6]

With his flank thus protected, Hitler launched the invasion of Poland on September 1, 1939. The event marked as well the beginning of World War II, for on September 3, Great Britain and France responded by declaring war on Hitler, even though they had little hope of getting material aid to Poland.

During the first week of September the Nazi blitzkrieg in Poland advanced even more rapidly than the Germans themselves had hoped. Their success in fact presented Stalin suddenly with the possibility that the armies of his erstwhile friend Hitler might well flood throughout Poland, ignoring the line of influence drawn by the secret protocol and positioning German forces all along the eastern boundary of Poland, at Russia's border. This threat, however, did not materialize, owing to Hitler's anxiety to share with Stalin the guilt for Poland's demise. As early as September 3, von Ribbentrop advised Schulenburg at Moscow that the Polish forces would be defeated "in a few weeks," and asked him to suggest to the Russians that they prepare to move troops into their agreed sphere of influence in Poland. Molotov had to reply that it was not yet opportune for Soviet forces to move. On September 9, von Ribbentrop tried again, and on the following day, Molotov admitted that the "Soviet Government was taken com-

[6] Sontag and Beddie, pp. 76–78.

pletely by surprise by the unexpectedly rapid German military successes."[7] The Soviet Union needed more time.

During these hectic days the diplomatic personnel of Germany bickered with Molotov and Stalin over what sort of published statement should be given to the world to explain the Nazi-Soviet military occupation of Poland. At first Stalin proposed to announce that Soviet armies were moving into eastern Poland to protect the Ukrainians and White Russians of Poland who were "threatened" by the Germans. Naturally, the Germans objected to this kind of rationalization. When von Ribbentrop countered on September 15, with a suggestion that the two powers should issue a joint statement, Molotov in his turn archly replied that a joint statement was "no longer needed." Finally, with Soviet troops ready to move into Poland at six o'clock on the morning of September 17, Stalin conferred with Schulenburg and read him the note that had been prepared for the Polish ambassador at Moscow. When Schulenburg objected to several discrete points, Stalin, without consulting Molotov, who was at his side, revised the draft on the spot. This revision the Germans found exactly to their liking and much more diplomatically worded than before. According to Gustav Hilger, the counselor of the legation at the German embassy in Moscow, Stalin said: "The old Romans did not go into battle naked, but covered themselves with shields. Today correctly worded political communiques play the role of such shields. . . ."[8] In this case, however, the diplomatic shield he prepared very poorly concealed Stalin's moral nakedness. Asserting that the occupation by German and Soviet troops was taking place in full accord with the Nazi-Soviet Pact (as if that fact alone justified the invasion of Poland), he cynically explained that "the aim of these forces is to restore peace and order in Poland, which has been destroyed by the collapse of the Polish state, and to help the Polish population to reconstruct the conditions of its political existence."[9]

Red Army troops met little resistance, captured 180,000

[7] Sontag and Beddie, p. 91.
[8] Gustav Hilger and Alfred G. Meyer, *The Incompatible Allies* (The Macmillan Company, New York, 1953), p. 302.
[9] Sontag and Beddie, p. 100.

Polish soldiers, and occupied those eastern portions of Poland allotted to Soviet control by Stalin's and Hitler's secret accord. With the Nazi seizure of Warsaw on September 27, Poland was defeated. The USSR, as a result of this brief campaign, gained 13,000,000 people and 80,000 square miles of territory, and Poland for the moment ceased to exist as an independent state. Following immediately upon these events, Stalin signed a new protocol with the Germans, expanding Soviet influence in Lithuania. In addition, he moved to absorb the newly seized portions of Poland into his Ukrainian and White Russian Republics and to establish mutual assistance pacts with the Baltic nations, Estonia, Latvia, and Lithuania.

If Stalin took momentary satisfaction from his territorial acquisitions, through the year that followed this fourth partition of Poland, he could only have viewed with mounting concern an international situation that worsened far more rapidly than anyone could have anticipated. It is reasonable to assume that he had signed the pact with Hitler hoping to remain aloof and observe from the sidelines while the German war leader involved Germany in a grim war of attrition with the Western powers, as had happened in World War I. Had Stalin's gamble worked, he might indeed have won peace and security for the Soviet Union. However, during the nineteen months after the collapse of Poland, Hitler's star was in the ascendant. Despite all Stalin's hopes, Hitler's domination of Europe was to be swiftly won. And Stalin, at least aware that events might not accord with his wishes, clearly felt a growing need to shore up his western boundaries and strengthen his control of buffer zones in Eastern Europe. These might afford the USSR some protection, if trouble were to come from the west. Stalin's efforts in this direction, however, repeatedly irritated Hitler and ultimately convinced the Nazi leader that only a war with the Soviet Union could remove the threat and annoyance this nation presented to Germany.

Stalin's efforts to bolster his western defenses also involved him in late 1939 in fateful negotiations with Finland. To protect his boundaries, he attempted to persuade Finland, whose border ran just a few miles north of Leningrad, to exchange territory in this region for Soviet land in the Murmansk area, and thus to move the Finnish boundary back toward Viborg. When the Finns refused his request, Stalin resorted to force. At the end of November 1939 the Red Army invaded Finland, beginning a grotesque and tragic struggle that cast the Russian Bear in the role of a clumsy villain savagely assaulting a small nation of helpless but courageous people who were defending their homes. In point of fact, Stalin's concern for his second city was well founded, for the Finns were dangerously friendly to the Germans. Yet the sight of Red Army forces invading Finland stirred the West to indignant action. British and French leaders rushed military material to the Finns, and the French began preparations to attack Russia along its Caucasian border. In fact, the image of the Russian Communist Bear fighting tiny Finland appeared so to incense the Western nations that they tended even to forget their own war with Hitler and prepared to fight the Russians. In December the League of Nations, condemning Russian aggression in Finland, expelled the Soviet Union from its circle of member nations.

March 1940 brought a halt to the Winter War with Finland, but there was to be little calm for Stalin. Hitler's armies were now on the move again in Europe. In April the Germans occupied Denmark and invaded Norway, and on May 10, they attacked the Low Countries of Europe, and France. Their swift drive through Belgium compelled a desperate evacuation of British forces at Dunkirk that began on May 26, and shortly thereafter Belgium surrendered. By the middle of June, France was beaten, and Hitler's empire had reached the Atlantic, his southern flank protected by fascist Italy, which had also declared war against Britain and France. Thus virtually all of Western Europe had fallen under the rule of the Aryan madman. Stalin's gamble that Hitler might be destroyed by the Western powers had failed. Only Great Britain remained to resist, and now Hitler's attention turned toward the English Channel.

As Hitler went about efforts to mount an invasion of Britain, Stalin moved more forcefully to strengthen Russia's European frontiers. In mid-June, he sent his trusted lieutenants, Andrei Zhdanov, Andrei Vishinsky, and Paul Dekanozov into the Baltic nations of Estonia, Latvia, and Lithuania, to incorporate these small nations into the Soviet Union; the three states were officially recognized as new Soviet Republics in July. Stalin also moved in June to cash the blank check concerning Bessarabia that Hitler had signed over to him in the secret protocol of the Nazi-Soviet Pact. After a period of strained diplomatic exchanges with the Germans, the Soviet Union proceeded unilaterally to take back this territory it had lost in 1918. On June 27, Molotov informed Ambassador Schulenburg that the Soviet government had delivered an ultimatum to Rumania "regarding the accession of Bessarabia and the northern part of Bukovina," and had demanded a reply within one day.[10]

Hitler, furious with his Soviet "ally" for thus taking action behind his back, but precariously locked in the air war with Britain, reluctantly instructed the Rumanian government to give up its territories in order to avoid war. Undoubtedly, Stalin's aggressiveness in the Balkans and his obvious effort to get as much as possible on all fronts while he could reinforced Hitler's distrust. The latter, balked by his inability to drive British aviators out of the skies, began to consider more seriously the need to expand eastward. On July 31 he ordered that plans be started for an invasion of the Soviet Union.

In August, Hitler's efforts to bring down Great Britain without an invasion by sea (which he was unable to implement) proved no more effective than before. In September, worried about Stalin's ambitions in the Balkan area, Hitler moved to counter the earlier Russian advances by sending German troops into Rumania, breaking off major areas of this little nation for Hungary and Bulgaria. That same month he also signed a tripartite pact with Italy and Japan. And on December 18, 1940, Hitler gave his official approval to the German plan for the forthcoming invasion of the Soviet Union, "Operation Barbarossa," scheduled to begin in May 1941.

Throughout these months Stalin's policy was one of painfully devious maneuvering, continued public protestations of friendship and loyalty to the Nazis, and earnest examination of the signs that pointed to a Nazi invasion of Russia. One especially bizarre aspect of the devious game Stalin played was the

[10] Sontag and Beddie, p. 163.

continuing exchange of goods between the two countries. The USSR furnished sizable quantities of grain fodder, timber, base metals, and oil, and Germany paid for these with ships, naval supplies, munitions, and other manufactured goods. The Soviet Union also made its transportation facilities available for transit trade from the Middle and the Far East, aiding Hitler to obtain vitally needed quantities of rubber. Thus Stalin, by helping his ally against the Western powers, simultaneously helped Hitler to build up the German war machine for its attack on Russia.

Stalin himself, from all reports that we have of him during the months before the invasion, refused to hear of war with Germany. It was almost as if having worked so hard to avoid war and to preserve his power, he found the very idea of a conflict unthinkable. His newspapers dared not print rumors of war except to denounce foreign "provocative" statements that it was coming. And when, near the end of March 1941, Yugoslavia followed Bulgaria in signing the tripartite pact, Stalin remained quiet, apparently fearing to make any overt move that could be interpreted by the Germans as hostile. Yet this inaction must also have seemed dangerous to him, for when a revolution occurred in Yugoslavia and the new ruler rejected the signing of the pact, Stalin came out in full support of the Yugoslavs. On April 3, Molotov signed a five-year nonaggression pact with Yugoslavia. But only a few days later the fecklessness of this move was revealed, when Hitler's Luftwaffe attacked Belgrade on April 6, and his land forces entered Yugoslavia and Greece. Within three weeks both nations were under the German heel. Like a child who had been spanked, Stalin obsequiously ordered the ambassador of the now defunct Yugoslavia out of the Soviet Union. He seemed to be trying to persuade Hitler that he had meant no harm. Only in the Far East during these weeks did Stalin move forcefully to shore up his defenses, obtaining a treaty of neutrality with the Japanese on April 13. By this agreement he freed himself for the moment from the worry that Japan might attack him from the rear should he be forced to face the German conqueror.

Up to the last moments in May and June, Stalin never ceased to protest his friendliness toward Hitler. While German

troops were being shifted to the Soviet borders, Stalin's newspapers continued to deny rumors of such movements. While
German planes flew hundreds of reconnaissance sorties over
Soviet territories, Molotov made only self-contained, formal
protests to the German ambassador. In the middle of June,
Tass, the Soviet Press Agency, denied rumors about "an im-
pending war between the USSR and Germany" circulated by
"forces arrayed against the Soviet Union and Germany, which
are interested in the spread and intensification of the war."[11]

Stalin, warned by other governments that an invasion was
coming, refused to listen. Even the date of the intended invasion
was reported to him, but he had gone deaf. He would not or
could not believe that his diplomacy had failed. His actions in
these last days before the war make one wonder at the strength
of his willfulness: so often had he been able to implement his
designs within the Soviet Union that perhaps he was simply incapable of acknowledging that all his efforts to outmaneuver the
German Fuehrer could meet with failure in the end. Up to the
very last minute, then, he would not believe that the German
attack was coming because he did not wish it to. Later, in August
1942, when Churchill recalled to Stalin his last telegraphed
warning of the imminent attack, Stalin explained his conduct
by saying: "I remember it. I did not need any warnings. I knew
war would come, but I thought I might gain another six months
or so."[12]

Yet even after the invasion had begun, according to the
assertions of Khrushchev in his Secret Speech of 1956: "Moscow
ordered that the German fire was not to be returned." And
Khrushchev rhetorically asks, "Why?" His answer: "It was because Stalin, despite evident facts, thought that the war had not
yet started . . . and that our reaction might serve as a reason
for the Germans to begin the war."[13] Even after the event, it
seems, Stalin's determination not to have a war with Germany
may have been more real to him than the war itself. At this

[11] Sontag and Beddie, p. 345.
[12] Winston Churchill, *The Hinge of Fate* (Houghton Mifflin Company, Boston,
1950), p. 493.
[13] Nikita Khrushchev, *The Crimes of the Stalin Era* (The New Leader, New York,
1962), p. S39.

incredibly late date he would not accept the evidence that his policies had failed. Once again his refusal to accept reality at this moment surely underscores the immense power of his will.

At 9:30 on the evening of June 21, 1941, Molotov summoned Ambassador Schulenburg to his office, requesting him to explain why the German government was dissatisfied with the Soviet government, and "the reasons that had caused the present state of affairs."[14] Thus confronted, the German ambassador had no reply. Early on the morning of June 22, however, Schulenburg returned, this time with orders just received from Berlin. The message he delivered was von Ribbentrop's announcement that Hitler's troops were attacking. Molotov heard the ambassador out, then furiously denounced the German action, ending finally with the plaintive words: "Surely we have not deserved that?"[15]

Whether deserved or not, Operation Barbarossa, the Nazi invasion of Russia, had begun, and when Hitler's 181 divisions crossed into Russia, they found the Soviet Union with some 150 divisions along its 1,600-mile western border in various states of unpreparedness. Essentially, the German plan was to mount three great armored spearheads, each of them heading for a vital Soviet target and each commanded by a Prussian field marshal. In the north, Wilhelm von Leeb's forces advanced on Leningrad; in the center, Fedor von Bock's armies raced toward Smolensk and Moscow; and in the south, Gerd von Rundstedt's armies advanced toward Kiev and the Ukraine's wheatlands. The initial goal of Operation Barbarossa was the quick capture of these major targets. Complete victory was expected to follow later in the year.

The War, Allied Negotiations, and Stalingrad

The armies of Hitler and his allies numbered some 181 divisions, with approximately three million men. Fully ready for battle were 3,350 tanks, 7,000 artillery pieces, 2,700 planes, and 600,000 motor vehicles. Along the Soviet line, while Stalin had

[14] Hilger and Meyer, p. 335.
[15] Hilger and Meyer, p. 336.

at least 40 divisions on the frontier and others behind it, all were unwarned and unprepared. An example of the shocking degree of unpreparedness on the Soviet side is described by General Heinz Guderian, the famous master of the blitzkrieg who had been assigned the task of spearheading the German's central thrust. Just before the attack on June 22, when he looked into the fortress at Brest-Litovsk from an observation post across the Bug River, he saw the Soviet soldiers there carrying on routine drill exercises, apparently oblivious of any likelihood of war. Guderian considered canceling a preattack artillery barrage he had ordered, since there was no visible need for it, but the order for the barrage had been given and he let it stand. His forces advanced without serious opposition.

Within two weeks, the troops thrusting toward Moscow had captured 300,000 Red Army men. In the north and the south, the armored blitz moved with similar rapidity, advancing far into its assigned regions of operation, capturing masses of Soviet troops and finding all in confusion.

Stalin, reportedly, was paralyzed with fear. Permitting Molotov to announce to the country on June 22 that the Germans had invaded, he personally kept silent until early in July. In later years Khrushchev, building up his own reputation for valor, found it easy to denigrate Stalin's. According to him, Stalin, believing that "this was the end," that "all that Lenin had created" had been lost forever, simply ceased to exercise his usual direct control over events.[16] In part, at least, this might explain why there was so much chaos at the front, for men trained to obey only the orders sent down from the leader were slow to act on their own initiative when the leader did not speak.

On the other hand, Khrushchev's allegations may not have been completely accurate, for important developments were taking place in Moscow. In May, even before the invasion, Stalin had assumed new guiding roles in the government. Previously occupying only his party position, the General Secretary for the first time had assumed the leadership of the government, as Chairman of the Council of Commissars. On June 30, he also stepped into the post of Chief of the State Defense Committee,

[16] Khrushchev, p. S40.

the organization responsible for directing the war, and finally in July, he named himself Commander-in-Chief. If he had indeed panicked during the first moments of the German onslaught, his panic passed quickly, and the familiar indomitable determination to preserve his power and his nation had recovered its force.

In his first wartime speech, broadcast to the Soviet people on July 3, Stalin boldly set forth the dangers facing the nation and explained the kind of leadership with which he meant to pursue the struggle to save the Soviet Union. He called upon his people to "understand the full measure of the danger that threatens our country and abandon all complacency, all heedlessness." In order to drive these points home, he described in harsh phrases the enemy and the issues. The German, he said, "is cruel and implacable. He is out to seize our lands watered with our sweat, to seize our grain and oil secured by our labor." He is "out to restore the rule of the landlords, to restore Tsarism, to destroy the national culture," and he would convert the free peoples of the Soviet Union "into slaves of the German princes and barons. Thus the issue is one of life or death for the Soviet State, of life or death for the peoples of the USSR. . . ."[17]

In order to save the nation Stalin ordered an all-out effort to withdraw from the western provinces and to destroy all goods and equipment that might help the invader. "In case of forced retreat of Red Army units," he said, "all rolling stock must be evacuated, the enemy must not be left a single engine, a single railway car, not a single pound of grain or a gallon of fuel." He ordered collective farmers to drive off their cattle; grain, fuel, and metals were all to be destroyed if they could not be withdrawn. Guerilla forces were directed "to blow up bridges and roads, to damage telephone and telegraph lines, to set fire to forests, stores and transports," and to hound and annihilate the enemy "at every step."[18] Stalin had gone to war with the same blood-chilling determination to win that he had shown in constructing his totalitarian regime.

[17] Alvin Z. Rubinstein (ed.), *The Foreign Policy of the Soviet Union* (Random House, New York, 1960), p. 175.
[18] Rubinstein, pp. 175–176.

Soviet soldiers on a roof in Stalingrad, 1942

The dead at Stalingrad

While armored spearheads drove toward Leningrad, Moscow, and deep into the Ukraine, Stalin discovered that he had gained enthusiastic allies abroad. Winston Churchill, on the evening of June 22, pledged the Soviet Union every material assistance his nation could give, and on July 12, Sir Stafford Cripps, the British ambassador to the Soviet Union, signed an Anglo-Soviet pact of mutual assistance in which each side promised it would never negotiate a separate peace with Hitler. At the end of July, Harry Hopkins, President Roosevelt's special deputy, visited Moscow to work out Lend-Lease arrangements, which during the war were destined to deliver some eleven billion dollars' worth of food, fuel, military equipment, and clothing to the Red Armies. In August, with the aim of making possible the transport of supplies from the Persian Gulf to the Soviet Union, Great Britain and the Soviet Union occupied Iran. And in October, the American, Averill Harriman, and the Britisher, Lord Beaverbrook, promised in Moscow to supply a billion dollars' worth of Lend-Lease aid during 1942.

In the first terrible months, when German victory seemed almost assured, Stalin desperately sought help of every sort, even suggesting that allied troops might be brought in via Iran or Archangelsk and thrown into his front lines. As he calmed, however, and as the Soviet armies began to function more effectively, he was quick to reject with more characteristic distrust every subsequent proposal that foreign troops serve in Russia.

In meetings with representatives of the West, Stalin and his deputies exhibited what was to remain throughout the war an almost stereotyped aloofness. Stalin himself displayed an impressive mastery of grand strategy and minute detail touching on a range of subjects from an exact knowledge of foreign politics to the precise characteristics of the weapons he wanted from his allies. At each of these meetings, as reported by Westerners who participated, it was obvious that he alone was the Soviet decision maker, for frequently he accepted, or refused to accept, new plans without conferring with his subordinates, many times without so much as a glance at his own technical specialists who were seated nearby. Throughout the war, negotiating by correspondence or in person with representatives and leaders of the allied nations, he acted with a cool and sophisticated aplomb edged with cruel arguments and merciless logic—always in defense of his nation.

He was at times querulous, at others peremptory, adamant, and even insulting in his demands that other powers fulfill their obligations as he and his nation were fulfilling theirs. On the other hand, he was capable often of showing cordial and heart-felt appreciation for the aid and understanding of his allies, even to the extent of confiding to Churchill or Roosevelt how painful was the burden of fighting Hitler's warriors. But always, in greater or lesser degree, Stalin revealed his permanent and profound suspiciousness of the Western allies. The deep-rooted xenophobia shown by the Marxist-Leninist toward the capitalist West, the paranoid fear of the undergrounder, the hard skepticism born of his disappointing experience in the 1930s, when it had appeared to him that Britain and France were trying to turn Hitler in his direction—all these seemed to sustain in him the feeling that he must move warily in a jungle where the Western tigers might at any moment betray or destroy him.

During the first months of battle, Stalin's thoughts had already turned to the future; he began very early to plan the territorial settlements he wanted when the war had been won. In fact, even during his first meetings with British representatives he spoke hopefully of guarantees for the restoration of his country's boundaries to the positions they had occupied just prior to Hitler's attack. For example he emphasized to the British foreign minister, Anthony Eden, who visited Moscow in December 1941, that any Anglo-Soviet agreements would depend upon British acceptance of these preinvasion frontiers. At that time he also presented to Eden a full list of his plans for the postwar settlement. According to the notes Eden made, Stalin proposed:

> the restoration of Austria as an independent state; the detachment of the Rhineland from Germany as an independent state or a protectorate; possibly the constitution of an independent state of Bavaria; the transfer of East Prussia to Poland; the return of the Sudetenland to Czechoslovakia; Yugoslavia should be restored and receive certain additional territory from Italy; Albania

should be reconstituted as an independent state; Turkey should receive the Dodecanese Islands with possible readjustments of Aegean Islands in favor of Greece; Turkey might also receive some territory from Bulgaria and in Northern Syria; Germany should pay reparations in kind, particularly in machine tools, but not in money.[19]

Offering a trade—concession for concession—Stalin added that he "was willing to support any [postwar] arrangements Britain might make for securing bases in the Western European countries, France, Belgium, The Netherlands, Norway, and Denmark."[20] Here, the former revolutionary who had developed a nationalities' policy for his own country designed at least in theory to permit each national group to determine its own destiny, had become a man of power, willing to trade other nations and peoples for the interests of his own state. Somewhat taken aback by his blunt effort to reach agreements intended to reshape the European state system, the representatives of the allied countries replied that it would be best to win the war before dividing up the spoils. Stalin was put off for the moment, but he was to return again and again to the question of the postwar settlement.

The second, and certainly the most important, issue that arose between Stalin and his allies in the early years of the war concerned Stalin's demand that the allies establish a second front in Western Europe, specifically in northern France, in order to draw off a fair share of the German divisions from the Eastern Front. On July 18, 1941, Stalin wrote Churchill that such a front should be established, "not only for the sake of our common cause, but also in Britain's own interest."[21] In early September, he returned to the question. After outlining the grim situation in the Ukraine and admitting that the Soviet Union was in "mortal danger," he went on to say: "I think the only way is to

[19] Cordell Hull, *The Memoirs of Cordell Hull* (The Macmillan Company, New York, 1948), II, 1167.
[20] Hull, II, 1167.
[21] Ministry of Foreign Affairs of the USSR, *Correspondence between the Chairman of the Council of Ministers of the USSR and the Presidents of the USA and the Prime Ministers of Great Britain during the Great Patriotic War of 1941–1945* (Foreign Languages Publishing House, Moscow, 1957), I, 13.

open a second front this year in the Balkans or in France, one that would divert 30 to 40 German divisions from the Eastern Front. . . ."[22] This kind of request soon turned into a series of nagging complaints when the second front did not materialize, and still later, into a succession of imperious and insulting demands. It was one of the rocks on which the mutual trust of what Churchill called the "Grand Alliance" was eventually to founder.

Fortunately for the Soviet Union and its allies, the Germans did not win their war in the first months. Although they surrounded Leningrad and placed it under a siege that was to last 900 days and claim a million Russian lives from battle, cold, and starvation, the city continued to resist. In the Ukraine, German and Rumanian forces took Kiev and Kharkov by October, but on the outskirts of Moscow, the German advance bogged down. On December 5, this German Center Group, totally unprepared for a winter war and having reached the end of its ability to advance, halted and prepared for the winter. Just one day later, with devastating timing, the Soviet *untermenschen,* the Slavs who, according to Hitler's theory, should by now have been totally defeated, counterattacked before Moscow and drove the Germans back. The temperature was forty degrees below zero.

As victory for the Germans proved progressively more elusive here than it had been in Poland and France, troubles began to mount in the Nazi camp. In November, Hitler's chief of staff, Walter von Brauchitsch, worn out with Hitler's contemptuous abuse, suffered a heart attack and was forced to retire. Hitler, living in the Wolf's Lair, his command post in East Prussia, quarreled with von Rundstedt and dismissed him. Von Bock, commanding the central front, reported sick and withdrew from active service; Guderian, too, was dismissed. The brittle Prussians, so arrogant from easy past victories, were breaking up against the rock of a Soviet military force that intended to fight forever if need be to defend the motherland. On December 18, Hitler named himself Commander-in-Chief.

By mid-January 1942, it had become clear to Hitler that the Soviets were not only continuing their attack on the troops

---

[22] Ministry of Foreign Affairs of the USSR, I, 21.

before Moscow, but were actually attempting to encircle those troops. He was compelled to order a withdrawal to safer positions and to reconsider his battle plans. The Soviet Union had by this time suffered immense losses. By the end of 1941, over three million men had been taken prisoner by the Germans, and the German-occupied territories held what had previously constituted 40 percent of the nation's population. With these territories, the Soviet Union had lost over 60 percent of its coal, steel, and aluminum production and nearly 40 percent of its grain. Nevertheless, the slowdown and the protracted fighting before Moscow clearly indicated, if earlier events had not done so, that the war would continue for a long time.

In the grim campaigns of 1942, Hitler gave up his effort to fight decisively along the entire length of his front. While holding his forces around Leningrad and before Moscow he pushed his southern armies through the Ukraine, hoping to reach the oil fields in the Caucasus regions. His units completed the siege at Sevastopol on July 3, and went on to take Rostov at the end of the month. At this point Field Marshal von Kleist was ordered to advance southeastward toward Grozny, in the oil fields, while another force under General Paulus drove across the Don River in the direction of the Volga city of Stalingrad. While the battles fought during these months were bloody and costly, Soviet military leaders were gaining experience. Not only were they learning how to fight Germans; they were learning, too, that they could win.

Meanwhile, Stalin persistently sought to persuade or shame his allies, Britain and the United States (for the latter had declared war on December 8, 1941), into mounting a second front. In May 1942, he sent Molotov to London and Washington, where the Russians wrung out a tentative and hesitant statement that Britain and the United States had reached a "full understanding with regard to the urgent tasks of creating a second front in Europe."[23] The words were interpreted by Molotov and Stalin as a promise that a second front would be opened in 1942, but such was not to be the case. The United States, tooling up to become the "Arsenal of Democracy" and to win back its place in

[23] Churchill, *The Hinge of Fate,* pp. 341–342.

the Pacific, had a long way to go. Facing the hard facts of logistics, the country found itself simply without enough ships to move troops and personnel throughout the Pacific, to send convoys to Murmansk, and simultaneously to mount an invasion of France that could be successful. By late July, Stalin, having sensed the delay in the West, was stressing the need for immediate action: "I state most emphatically that the Soviet Government cannot tolerate the second front being postponed till 1943."[24]

Despite his urgings, Western military advisers declared that a second front could not be mounted. In late July, therefore, Roosevelt and Churchill decided that the latter must visit Stalin personally to explain their position. That meeting, as Churchill has described it, was memorable and painful, with Stalin pointedly asking why the British were afraid of the Germans and Churchill trying to explain the special problems of a major amphibious landing on a well-defended shore. Churchill's efforts to interest Stalin in a smaller second front, the proposed allied landing in North Africa, only partially mollified the Russian leader. On the second day of this visit, August 13, Stalin handed Churchill the conclusions he and his advisers had reached in response to the announced postponement of the "promised" second front. It was a sullen, angry statement that flatly contradicted all of Churchill's arguments concerning the inadvisability of the second front in 1942: "It appears to me and to my colleagues that the year 1942 offers the most favorable conditions for a second front in Europe, seeing that nearly all the German forces—and their crack troops, too—are tied down on the Eastern Front, while only negligible forces, and the poorest, too, are left in Europe."[25]

Subsequent discussions in the following days were equally painful, but, as Churchill recalls in his memoirs, when he at last prepared to say good-bye to Stalin on the evening of the sixteenth, "Stalin suddenly seemed embarrassed and said in a more cordial tone than he had yet used with me, 'you are leaving at daybreak. Why should we not go to my house and have some drinks?'" To that Churchill replied that he was "in princi-

[24] Ministry of Foreign Affairs of the USSR, I, 56.
[25] Ministry of Foreign Affairs of the USSR, I, 61.

ple always in favor of such a policy," and they walked through long corridors of the Kremlin until they finally came to Stalin's modest apartment.[26] There they met Stalin's sixteen-year-old daughter, Alliluyeva, who in her more mature years fled the Soviet Union to settle in the United States.

Late that night and well into the morning, Churchill and Stalin sat at Stalin's dining table, picking "at a long succession of choice dishes," sipping wine, and exchanging jokes with Molotov. Lord Cadogan came in to help draft a communiqué to the world about the previous days' discussions, and at about 2 A.M. Stalin drifted off into another room to receive reports from the front lines. He returned later to approve the communiqué.

Similar glimpses of this nocturnal man, carrying on his work of supervising the nation and the war from his simple rooms in the Kremlin, have been recorded by Milovan Djilas in his *Conversations with Stalin*, by Stalin's daughter in her *Twenty Letters to a Friend*, and by Khrushchev in the book *Khrushchev Remembers*. A complex portrait emerges of a shrewd, patient, lonely, and totally committed man, goaded by a profound distrust of others and by his conviction that he alone could effectively oversee the machinery of government and war. Such a view also provides us with one of the rare indications that the man was humanly in need of friendship and aware of the suffering of others.

The battle for Stalingrad, beginning on September 15, 1942, became for Hitler an obsessive and manic effort to destroy a city bearing the name of his intractable opponent. In October, the Germans, throwing all that they had against the city, bombed it to rubble, without securing it. General Chuikov, the Soviet commander of the defense, had received orders to hold the city to the last man.

Inexorably, one of the most terrible battles of all time continued to build up, fired on the one hand by the German Fuehrer's fanatical determination to break through at this particular point, and on the other by the Soviet military decision to gain victory here at all costs. On November 19, Red

[26] Churchill, *The Hinge of Fate*, p. 496.

armies began to march against the flanks of the German forces attacking Stalingrad, swiftly completing a gigantic pincer movement and catching 330,000 Germans in a trap. Hitler would not permit General Paulus to surrender his doomed forces until artillery had literally pounded most of them to death. When Paulus surrendered at last, on January 31, 1943, only 90,000 Germans remained alive.

Six months later a second great struggle was to develop around the city of Kursk. Here Marshal Georgi Zhukov prepared carefully for the German attack, meeting it in early July with a force so overwhelming and terrible that the Germans were never again able to recapture the initiative. In a battle that lasted fifty days, the Nazi forces lost half a million men and thousands of tanks and heavy guns. Soviet forces, too, suffered high casualties, but the Russians could pay the price and still forge westward, while the Germans could only withdraw, hoping for some miracle to save them.

Stalingrad marked the decisive turn of fighting on the Eastern Front. After this battle, Soviet armies were to move steadily westward, crushing the still dangerous Wehrmacht in innumerable bloody battles fought through areas that had been devastated by military action only a few months before. And Stalingrad also brought a massive change in Soviet political influence, for whereas earlier Stalin had been cast in the role of a suppliant, begging for assistance from his allies, in 1943 his armies were victorious. They had met and halted Germany's best; they had turned the German menace back toward its homeland and were grinding its retreating ranks to bits. The Soviet Union through the remainder of the war possessed an international political authority that Russian emperors had only dreamed of, and Stalin in his relations with his allies, who had not helped him as much as he thought they should have, was quick to display his awareness of the new role and power of his nation.

Westward from Stalingrad

As Stalin's troops fought their way back across Russia, his tone with his allies grew more peremptory, his moves to achieve his own political ends less circumspect. He had long been seeking some good excuse for breaking with the Polish exile government at London, primarily because its leaders vociferously refused to accept as legitimate the Polish boundaries established by the Nazi-Soviet Pact and because he intended to ensure the existence of a friendly Polish government on his western boundary when the war was over. His opportunity came in early 1943, when the Germans revealed that they had uncovered the mass graves of some 3,000 Polish officers in the Katyn forest, near Smolensk. The Germans charged the Russians with having massacred these officers (even now the evidence that exists seems to corroborate this charge), and the Polish exile government immediately demanded an investigation by the International Red Cross.

In a letter to Churchill dated April 21, 1943, Stalin blamed the Germans, who, he said, had themselves "perpetrated a monstrous crime against the Polish officers," and he complained that the London exile government led by Wladyslaw Sikorski in demanding an investigation was actually cooperating with Hitler. This "treacherous blow at the Soviet Union to help the [Nazi] tyranny," was exactly the excuse he had been looking for. He hastened to assert that the Polish government at London, "having descended to collusion with the Hitler Government, has, in practice, severed its relations of alliance with the USSR," and he broke off relations with the London Poles.[27] No mention was made of his real reasons for forcing this issue, which, as already noted, were undoubtedly the exile government's refusal to accept the post-August 1939 location of Polish boundaries and its determination to restore a democratic government in Poland when it assumed power. Soon after this rupture of relations a "Union of Polish Patriots in the USSR" appeared, and it was evident that Stalin expected this group to serve as a procommunist exile government under his patronage.

To the Western powers these developments were profoundly disturbing for a number of reasons. Above all, Great Britain had entered the war to defend Poland's sovereignty. Subsequently some 150,000 Polish troops under the London

[27] Ministry of Foreign Affairs of the USSR, I, 120–121.

exile government had taken up the fight against fascist forces in the Middle East, while others led fighter plane skirmishes from England, and still others maintained a strong home army of guerilla fighters inside Poland itself. To withdraw support from these brave Poles could only be interpreted by Churchill and Roosevelt as a conscious betrayal of their friends. Thus Stalin pressed them sorely on an issue that could only be resolved by compromise. But in the months that followed, despite repeated efforts by both Churchill and Roosevelt to get him to reconsider, Stalin remained intractable—the London exile government of Poland was his enemy.

While the conflict over Poland and the confrontation of the allies that it provoked built up anger on both sides, the issue of the delayed second front caused that anger to explode into hot verbal exchanges. On June 24 Stalin, informed by his allies that the second front, promised in May 1943, must be postponed, and infuriated over the continuing delay, curtly rejected this latest postponement, pointing out that the decision had been adopted without his participation. Replying to Churchill's effort to explain and justify the decision, Stalin frankly announced that he suspected the motives of his allies: "I must tell you that the point here is not just the disappointment of the Soviet Government, but the preservation of its confidence in the allies, a confidence which is being subjected to severe stress." And he harshly declared that the second front was "a question of saving millions of lives in the occupied areas of Western Europe and Russia and of reducing the enormous sacrifices of the Soviet armies, compared with which the sacrifices of the Anglo-American armies are insignificant."[28]

As time went on, he found more and more reasons to feel resentful toward his allies. Later in the year he railed at the way Churchill and Roosevelt continued to make important decisions between themselves without bothering to consult with him. After the collapse of Mussolini's regime in Italy (July 25), he complained that he was not being given all the facts about the ensuing negotiations with the Italians. For example, a message written to both Churchill and Roosevelt on August 22,

[28] Ministry of Foreign Affairs of the USSR, I, 138.

put the point succinctly: "To date it has been like this: the USA and Britain reach agreement between themselves while the USSR is informed of the agreement between the two Powers as a third party looking on passively. I must say this situation cannot be tolerated any longer."[29] The relationship steadily grew more difficult.

Through the middle of 1943 it became more and more evident to all concerned that the Big Three needed to meet in order to work out differences and prepare for the postwar settlement. After long preparations, Stalin, Churchill, and Roosevelt met at Teheran from November 22 to December 1, 1943, for the first of the wartime conferences. At this meeting the problem of the second front ranked high on the agenda, and Churchill labored mightily to sell the idea of a small invasion in the Balkans; Stalin, however, pressed relentlessly for the landing in France. Ultimately, all agreed that the second front in France would be launched in May of 1944, and Stalin, wanting to be certain that his allies meant this promise, pushed hard to force Roosevelt to name the commander of the invasion.

A number of other matters were discussed at Teheran, among them the probable disposal of Germany after the war, the role of Turkey and, as always, the irritating Polish question. To understand the position taken by the Western allies in November 1943 regarding the postwar disposition of Poland, one must view their thinking against the background of contemporary military events. Until that moment Soviet armies had carried the overwhelming weight of fighting in Europe; Soviet soldiers had died by the millions in this struggle against Hitler's invaders, but now their comrades were more steadily winning battles and surging westward, reclaiming Russian territory and driving the Nazis before them. In November 1943, as they pushed westward, it was obvious that the Germans could not stop them and that the waves of Soviet armies would soon lap over Poland and into Germany itself. Although the British and Americans had provided the Soviet Union with considerable amounts of military and industrial supplies and had themselves fought on many fronts—in Africa, in Italy, and in raids inside

[29] Ministry of Foreign Affairs of the USSR, I, 149.

German-held lands, both Churchill and Roosevelt were painfully aware that their contribution was dwarfed by that of the Soviet Union. Moreover, despite all their promises to Stalin, they had been unable to open a second front in the west; the terrible costs of a coastal invasion in France, combined with critical military weaknesses created by the vast dispersal of their forces in the Asian war, had seemed to justify repeated delays but did not ease the burden of their consciences.

Thus, the British and American leaders went to Teheran awed by the courage and suffering of the Soviet armies and aware that these armies had paid the price in blood for their great victories. The Western representatives could not escape a strong feeling of guilt, a feeling that they had not done enough themselves to deserve the moral right to deny the Soviet heroes boundaries the latter demanded for their future security. Sheer *realpolitik,* too, suggested that when the war was over, Stalin would have his way in Eastern Europe no matter what the British and the Americans agreed to. All these elements entered into the thoughts and conduct of the Big Three at Teheran when talk came around to Poland, for Stalin, too, fully understood his new power and meant to make the most of it.

Churchill opened the Polish discussion in a private tête-à-tête with Stalin, suggesting that the eastern boundary of Poland be the so-called Curzon Line (devised after World War I), which more or less traced the boundary drawn by Stalin's pact with Hitler. Stalin, of course, was agreeable. Churchill then went on to suggest that Poland as a whole might simply be moved westward; that is, the new Poland might be recompensed for its losses to the east by moving its western boundaries further westward and absorbing German territory. He showed Stalin what he meant by moving three matches across the table, and Stalin was delighted. Subsequently, at a formal conference session, the Curzon Line with several revisions was accepted by Stalin as Poland's eastern boundary. Then maps were brought out and possible western Polish boundaries were studied by everyone present, the general feeling being that the Oder River in Germany would be ideal. Churchill, still doing his best to please the Soviet dictator, ultimately declared that he found the Oder line satisfactory, and he told the conference, "I would say to the Poles that if they did not accept it they would be foolish, and I would remind them that but for the Red Army they would have been utterly destroyed."[30]

Throughout these discussions Stalin was genial and courteous yet firm about what the others considered minor details, such as the way the Curzon Line should be bent to his advantage at its northern and southern ends. The role his allies assigned for him was scarcely a demanding one; he was not asked to fight for the Polish boundaries he preferred; the allies seemed to ask him simply to accept their concessions. He had only to smile and nod his head. In this manner, at Teheran, he gained the right to dominate Poland and to expand his influence into neighboring East European states; this was a victory voluntarily placed in his hands by a shrewd and realistic Churchill and a somewhat befuddled Roosevelt. The latter, it seems, came away from these parleys still somewhat puzzled. He had found Stalin "correct, stiff, solemn, not smiling, nothing human to get hold of."[31]

On January 1, 1944, the siege at Leningrad was lifted and Red Army forces moved westward toward Pskov. In the south, Kiev was recaptured, an almost empty rubble of destroyed buildings, and Soviet troops advanced toward the Bug and Dniester Rivers. The Germans were driven out of the Crimea and Odessa in the early spring, and with the coming of summer Finland sued for peace. Meanwhile behind the scenes, as Soviet troops moved steadily toward the Polish borders, Stalin and Churchill continued to quarrel bitterly about the future Polish government, Churchill supporting his exile, anti-Soviet government, and Stalin denouncing the London-based organization and supporting his own Poles.

Stalin now was playing the role of a belligerent national leader, sensitive and touchy about Soviet national honor, bullying in his manner. Churchill fought back as best he could.

[30] Winston Churchill, *Closing the Ring* (Houghton Mifflin Company, Boston, 1951), p. 396; cf. pp. 362, 394, and 403–404.
[31] Frances Perkins, *The Roosevelt I Knew* (The Viking Press, New York, 1946), pp. 70–71.

In March, thoroughly exasperated by Stalin's intransigence, the British leader advised Stalin of his intentions to report to the House of Commons, "that attempts to make an arrangement between the Soviet and Polish Governments have broken down; that we continue to recognize the Polish Government, with whom we have been in continuous relations since the invasion of Poland in 1939; that we now consider all questions of territorial change must await the armistice of peace conferences of the victorious powers; and that in the meantime we can recognize no forcible transferences of territory."[32]

Stalin immediately struck back, implying to Churchill that he was willfully violating the Teheran agreement. He went on to say: "As I see it, you make the Soviet Union appear as being hostile to Poland, and virtually deny the liberation nature of the war waged by the Soviet Union against German aggression. That is tantamount to attributing to the Soviet Union something which is non-existent, and thereby, discrediting it. I have no doubt that the peoples of the Soviet Union and world public opinion will evaluate your statement as a gratuitous insult to the Soviet Union."[33]

Despite these differences, when the second front in France finally began, on June 6, 1944, Stalin graciously sent the following telegram, which in some ways seems almost an implicit acceptance of many of Churchill's explanations previously rejected by the Russian leader. "My colleagues and I," Stalin wrote, "cannot but recognize that this is an enterprise unprecedented in military history as to scale, breadth of conception and masterly execution. As is known, Napoleon's plan for crossing the Channel failed disgracefully. Hitler the hysteric, who for two years had boasted that he would cross the Channel, did not venture even an attempt to carry out his threat. None but our allies have been able to fulfill with flying colors the grand plan for crossing the Channel."[34]

In June, Stalin went ahead with his own plans for Poland, recognizing the Polish National Committee of Liberation (the Lublin Committee), his own carefully selected communist Poles, as the legitimate exile government. The controversy

[32] Ministry of Foreign Affairs of the USSR, I, 211.
[33] Ministry of Foreign Affairs of the USSR, I, 213.
[34] Ministry of Foreign Affairs of the USSR, I, 227–228.

about which Poles should rule had by now grown into a major issue of conflict between East and West, and in August it took on even more serious proportions. When Soviet troops under General Konstantin Rokossovsky reached and occupied Praga, across the Vistula River from Warsaw, on August 15, Polish resistance forces inside Warsaw, loyal to the exile government in London, rose and began to attack the Germans inside the city. By this daring act they hoped to secure a place for themselves and their government in the postwar nation. But while Soviet forces continued active operations in the Danube area, their Baltic front suddenly came to a halt. In fact, the Russian troops made no attempt to cross the Vistula into Warsaw. Rokossovsky's forces did not move from August until January. Meanwhile, the Germans within the city viciously leveled it, block by block and street by street, in fierce fighting that wiped out the resistance force of some 300,000 men and reduced the city of Warsaw to rubble.

During this murderous fight Churchill and Roosevelt repeatedly begged Stalin to take some step to save the Poles in Warsaw, but nothing was done to accede to their requests. In order to drop airborne supplies to the fighters in Warsaw, they also asked for permission to land planes in the Soviet Union, but were refused. Stalin, in short, cold-bloodedly permitted the Polish Home Army to be destroyed, presumably to guarantee the destruction of the London-based government and the success of his own Lublin Poles. This act of ruthlessness sent a chill of apprehension through many people in the West who had earlier developed a feeling of friendliness toward the heroic conqueror of Hitler; certainly, it demonstrated to Churchill and Roosevelt that they were faced by a man who had no qualms whatever about using his new position of strength to gain his objectives.

Rumania and Bulgaria collapsed at the end of August. Churchill, struggling courageously to maintain the influence of the empire he represented, again flew off to visit Stalin, arriving in Moscow on October 9 to see if he could work out spheres of influence in the Balkans where Britain had long had friends. At the first meeting of this series, Churchill, reflecting the traditions of the British Empire, suggested stark and primitively simplistic numerical proportions for the sharing of influence. Writing on a piece of paper while his words were being translated, Churchill set down the names of the Balkan states and briefly indicated the proportions of influence he thought proper for Russia and Britain: Rumania 90:10, Greece 10:90, Yugoslavia and Hungary 50:50, Bulgaria 75:25.[35] He then slid the paper across the table to Stalin, who studied it a moment, put a large check on it with a blue pencil, and pushed it back to Churchill.

The British prime minister was not used to such swift and wordless decision making, and very possibly, he was a little taken aback by his own and Stalin's callous approach to the destinies of other sovereign states. In Churchill's own words: "At length I said, 'Might it not be thought rather cynical if it seemed we had disposed of these issues, so fateful to millions of people, in such an offhand manner? Let us burn the paper.' 'No, you keep it,' said Stalin."[36] Thus was completed another "deal" that would bring endless headaches to East and West through the following decades, for though there were to be other formal decisions about the Balkans at the Yalta and Potsdam Conferences in 1945, Stalin proceeded to act as if he regarded his arrangement with Churchill as both legitimate and binding.

During this same visit, Churchill and Stalin struggled again over the Polish question. Churchill persuaded Stalin to meet with Stanislas Mikolajczyk, premier of the London exile government, to talk over terms of a mutually acceptable postwar settlement. But to Mikolajczyk the terms of the agreement at Teheran were intolerable; even in Moscow he would not agree to the Curzon Line. Certainly the London Poles, by their intransigent insistence upon Poland's pre-1939 boundaries and their grim opposition to Soviet communism, did much to bring down their own house, and Stalin's insistence that in any Polish government his Lublin Poles must hold the preponderant majority of official posts also went far to eliminate any real possibility of agreement. In December 1944, the Lublin Committee declared itself the Provisional Government of Poland, and on January 5, 1945, the Soviet Union granted official recognition

[35] Winston Churchill, *Triumph and Tragedy* (Houghton Mifflin Company, Boston, 1953), p. 227.

[36] Churchill, *Triumph and Tragedy*, pp. 227–228.

to this Provisional Government. Both the British and the Americans continued to recognize the London Poles. Thus the stage was set for further controversy at the new meeting of the Big Three at Yalta, the little resort town on the southern coast of the Crimea, in early February.

Yalta, Potsdam, and Victory

At the Yalta Conference of the Big Three, which met from February 3 to 11, 1945, the three principals, Stalin, Roosevelt, and Churchill, met to bargain with one another for the type of world each wanted in the future. Ideally, these comrades-in-arms, close to the end of a devastating European war and professing the desire for permanent peace and goodwill among men, should have leaped at the task of conciliating one another. But such is not the role assigned to the leader of the nation state. These allies, coming out of long battles, were each anticipating the future with more or less realism, maneuvering for positions that would give their countries power and security during the coming years of peace, and calculating how to bargain for their own national interests most effectively.

The military situation had changed significantly since Teheran (November 1943), for the Second Front, launched on June 6, 1944, had successfully beaten back Germany's divisions in France and Belgium. The Western allies had kept their pledge; they had made the sacrifice of blood Stalin demanded; therefore, they came to Yalta with fewer feelings of guilt than before. As at Teheran, however, they were still inclined to treat the Soviet leader with excessive attentiveness, this time because they were concerned about the Pacific war, which Stalin had not yet entered. No matter how the war with Germany ended—and victory now seemed assured—they still had to turn their strength to the effort to defeat Japan.

The Chiefs of Staff of the Armies of the United States calculated (as late as July 1945) that victory in the Far East would require an invasion of the main Japanese islands by an armed force of five million men, which would find itself facing "the enormous task of destroying an armed force of five million men and five thousand suicide aircraft belonging to a race which had already amply demonstrated its ability to fight literally to the death."[37] According to the estimates of the American military experts, the final struggle would cost "over a million casualties, to American forces alone."[38] For these reasons both Roosevelt and Churchill went to Yalta eager to please the dictator and to obtain his active intervention in the Far East.

At the site of the meeting, Yalta, on the southern coast of the Crimea, Roosevelt was assigned quarters in the Lividia Palace, once a vacation home of the tsars. Churchill was lodged five miles away at the Voronstov Palace, built by an imperial ambassador to England, and Soviet headquarters were located in another luxurious remnant of the past, the Yusupov Palace. Between these palatial centers almost everything else lay in ruins. In preparation for the conference the Russians had done everything possible to achieve the dignity and pomp that ought to accompany the establishment of a new world order. And while there were no gala balls or similar dazzling social events, there were dinners in the evenings and just a touch of the magic of Scheherazade in the awesome power of the totalitarian Russian host. Churchill, for example, notes that after someone in his delegation remarked on the absence of lemon peel in the cocktails, "The next day a lemon tree loaded with fruit was growing in the hall."[39]

In the struggle to influence the decisions of the conference the relative strengths of the participants were in many ways unequal. Stalin's victorious armies were already in place, holding lands where he had determined that Soviet influence would predominate. Churchill's empire was collapsing; in terms of simple power, Britain had exhausted itself helping to win the war and had lost its former position of leadership to the two new superpowers, Russia and the United States. Churchill's florid and passionate arguments were beginning to bore both Stalin and Roosevelt and were no match for Stalin's divisions. And Roosevelt at Yalta confided to the others that the United

[37] Henry L. Stimson and McGeorge Bundy, *On Active Service in Peace and War* (Harper & Row, New York, 1948), p. 618.
[38] Stimson and Bundy, p. 619.
[39] Churchill, *Triumph and Tragedy*, p. 347.

Churchill, Roosevelt, and Stalin at Yalta, February 1945

States could keep troops in Europe no more than two years. To Stalin, then, went the spoils, for he and the Soviet Union intended to stay in Europe and had the power to do so.

Stalin came to Yalta determined to have his way with respect to certain issues. In order to achieve these objectives he willingly made a number of concessions about matters that were of little or no concern to him but of great importance to Roosevelt and Churchill. This gracious series of concessions persuaded the Western allies by the time they left the conference that they had won much by securing Stalin's agreement to their verbal formulas. Yet almost immediately afterward they were to find that the agreements and guarantees negotiated at Yalta had little or no meaning in those regions where Red troops bivouacked and where Stalin meant to prevail.

Because Yalta came nearer than any subsequent meeting to constituting the definitive peace settlement of World War II, its achievements and failures deserve to be examined in some detail. In the communiqués and secret protocols of this conference and in the subjects set aside for future decision were embedded many of the international problems the world has since struggled to solve.

Concerning the fate of a defeated Germany, it was decided that the country would be occupied by the Three Powers and by France, with a Central Control Commission of the Three Powers to be located in Berlin. France would also be given an option to participate on the Control Commission as a fourth member. A Reparations Commission was to be established, and Germany was to pay for the damages of war by giving up a portion of its industrial plants, machines, rolling stock, and other goods; in addition, Germany was expected to provide part of its future production and its labor force to its debtors. In this connection it was agreed that the Allied Reparations Commission, sitting in Moscow, should take as a basis for discussion of reparations the figure of twenty billion dollars, of which 50 percent should go to the Soviet Union.[40]

[40] U.S. Department of State, *Foreign Relations of The United States. Diplomatic Papers. The Conferences of Malta and Yalta, 1945* (Department of State, Washington, D.C., 1955), pp. 808–809, 971, 983.

Bitter and prolonged discussion brought about an agreement looking toward the eventual reorganization of the Lublin Committee's Provisional Government "on a broader democratic basis with the inclusion of democratic leaders from Poland itself and from Poles abroad."[41] From this statement, which appeared in the joint communiqué issued after the conference, it seemed that Churchill had finally made his point. The second paragraph of the communiqué read equally well, for it established a commission of ministers of the three governments to consult with the Polish Provisional Government on its reorganization. The communiqué further stated: "This Polish Provisional Government of National Unity shall be pledged to the holding of free and unfettered elections as soon as possible on the basis of universal suffrage and secret ballot. In these elections all democratic and anti-Nazi parties shall have the right to take part and put forward candidates."[42] While the wording seemed to bode well for the democratic evolution of Poland's postwar government, Stalin's determination to have a friendly, pro-Soviet government in Poland made the words meaningless. Something like the promised reorganization of the government did occur, but the "free" elections pledged by the participants at the Yalta Conference were never permitted.

The second major Polish question, concerning where to locate Poland's boundaries, was only partially settled. The Curzon Line with some small "digressions" was accepted for the eastern border, and it was stipulated that Poland "must receive substantial accessions of territory in the north (East Prussia) and west. . . . But the final delimitation of the western frontier of Poland," it was decided, "should . . . await the Peace Conference."[43]

That peace conference never came. Nor was such a conference necessary so far as Stalin was concerned, for immediately after Yalta, he sent Poles into Germany as far as the Oder and (Western) Neisse Rivers, unilaterally disposing of the matter. He thus arbitrarily delivered over to the Poles territory that

[41] U.S. Department of State, p. 973.
[42] U.S. Department of State, p. 973.
[43] U.S. Department of State, p. 974.

had been German for roughly three hundred years, compelling some six or seven million Germans to flee westward into what remained of Germany.

Another of the documents emerging from these joint deliberations was the "Declaration on Liberated Europe," which contained the pledge of the three Great Powers to work in concert to assist liberated peoples "to solve by democratic means their pressing political and economic problems." This "Declaration" formally upheld a principle of the Atlantic Charter—"the right of all peoples to choose the form of government under which they will live. . . ." And it promised that after the war the three governments would consult together on the "measures necessary to discharge the joint responsibilities set forth in this declaration."[44] Here again, so far as the destinies of the peoples of Eastern Europe were concerned, the promises were empty. Stalin was to hold the ground his armies occupied and to demand the establishment of pro-Soviet or communist governments.

A number of other communiqués were issued, dealing with such matters as the composition of the Yugoslav government, the Security Council veto of the United Nations, and territorial trusteeships. There were also several secret agreements not published at the time, one of which was of utmost immediate significance. This was the protocol on "The USSR and the Pacific War." After discussions between Stalin and Roosevelt so secret that neither Churchill nor the United States secretary of state, Edward Stettinius, was a party to them, this document was drawn up and signed by the leaders of the three Great Powers. Stalin agreed that "in two or three months after Germany has surrendered . . . the Soviet Union shall enter into the war against Japan. . . ."[45] For thus coming to the rescue of the allies in the Far East, Stalin was promised the preservation of the Mongolian People's Republic. Moreover, "the former rights of Russia violated by the treacherous attack of Japan in 1904" were to be "restored."[46] Thus, Stalin became avowedly im-

[44] U.S. Department of State, pp. 977–978.
[45] U.S. Department of State, p. 984.
[46] U.S. Department of State, p. 984.

perialistic, harking back to Russia's prerevolutionary past and acquiring or gaining control over properties once dominated by the tsars. Southern Sakhalin would revert to the USSR outright, the commercial port of Dairen was to be internationalized, and Port Arthur was to be leased to the Russians for use as a naval base. Both ports named are in China. A joint Soviet-Chinese Company was to be established to operate the Chinese Eastern Railway (sold under duress to Japan in the 1930s), and the Chinese Southern Railway and the Kurile Islands were to be handed over to the Soviet Union. President Roosevelt agreed to pressure Chiang Kai-shek of Nationalist China into making the very considerable "concessions" demanded from China.

Immediately after the Yalta Conference, Stalin embarked on a policy in Eastern Europe blatantly contradicting the agreements that had been made, but based on the presence of his Red divisions in Eastern Europe and on his imperative desire to have governments in these regions friendly to the Soviet Union. What had appeared to be the mutual accord of the conference was thus shattered. Events in Rumania immediately after Yalta well illustrate Soviet unilateral actions. There, on February 27, Andrei Vishinsky delivered an ultimatum to King Michael of Rumania, ordering him to dismiss his prime minister and to hand over that high office to Peter Groza, a communist; the ultimatum was made irresistible by the presence of Soviet tanks in Bucharest, and the new cabinet was accepted on March 6. While Stalin could claim as justification for this act, the "deal" he and Churchill had made dividing spheres of influence in the Balkans, in fact the Yalta "Declaration on Liberated Europe" had formally superseded their deal. Scarcely two weeks had passed since the Yalta conference when Vishinsky appeared at Bucharest; thus within this short space of time, naked force, acting in the interests of the Soviet Union, had superseded the Grand Alliance.

Events in Poland provide a second illustration of the change of attitude after Yalta. In Warsaw, despite the Yalta accord, Stalin blocked every effort of the Commission of Allied Foreign Ministers to form a genuinely democratic government. The words of high principle in the Yalta communiqué on that subject and the previously quoted statement that "all democratic and anti-Nazi parties shall have the right to take part and put forward candidates," were interpreted by the Lublin government and Stalin to mean that only pro-Soviet or Communist parties could offer candidates. Representatives from the London exile government briefly accepted in the government were harassed, persecuted, rendered politically impotent, and ultimately disgraced or driven out of the country. As for Poland's western boundaries, Stalin's action has already been discussed. The new Polish government moved its western boundaries to the Oder-Western Neisse line, arbitrarily annexing territory from Germany and displacing former German citizens.

The reparations issue had been left open at Yalta with the agreement that a Reparations Commission would sit at Moscow and decide what should be done, using as a "basis for discussion" the twenty-billion-dollar formula. But reality outran intent. Before the commission could act, factories, machines, transport facilities, and property of all kinds—down to furniture and bathtubs—had begun to pour from Soviet-occupied portions of Germany into the Soviet Union. The effort to negotiate a peace settlement for Europe had foundered and begun to break apart on national interests.

Meanwhile, after Yalta, Red armies continued to advance westward. Vienna was occupied by the Russians on April 15. An agreement with the Western allies left Prague and Berlin to the Soviets; then, late in April, Marshals Georgi Zhukov and Ivan Konev encircled Berlin, opening the final mass artillery barrages that drove Hitler to suicide and Germany to the final defeat. On May 7 the German admiral, Karl Doenitz, who for a moment in history played the role of Hitler's successor, ordered his representative at General Eisenhower's headquarters to sign the Act of Unconditional Surrender. Fighting in Europe stopped on May 8 at midnight.

With the war in Europe at an end, but with Japan still to be defeated, a new meeting of the Big Three was imperative. A number of matters needed discussion. There were, for example, the irritations built up in Great Britain and the United States over Soviet activities in Eastern Europe. Among other specific pressing issues were the settlements to be made about sharing the captured German navy, reparations payments, the election of new and democratic governments in the Balkans, and the final arrangements for Soviet participation in the war with Japan. In addition, Harry Truman, who had succeeded to the U.S. presidency after Franklin Roosevelt's death on April 12, fervently wished to get acquainted with the Russians and to administer the rebukes he and his advisers thought Stalin deserved for treating the Yalta agreements with cavalier contempt.

The conference at Potsdam opened on July 17. Truman was made chairman at the first meeting, and, as if to cover his uneasiness before the more experienced leaders of Great Britain and the Soviet Union, he quickly launched into forthright criticisms of Soviet policies after Yalta. But his attack upon Stalin's lack of faith accomplished little, for Russian armies held the ground Stalin wanted to influence; moreover, desiring Stalin's support against Japan, Truman could not press too harshly. Nor was his hand greatly strengthened by his British colleagues. On July 25, Churchill and Eden, having lost the elections at home, were replaced by the new prime minister, Clement Atlee, and his foreign secretary, Aneurin Bevin, and the new representatives were not prepared to play the vigorous role of the old warrior, Churchill.

A general agreement was reached by the now unfriendly allies at the Potsdam Conference that a Council of Ministers would draw up peace treaties for the defeated states. A Four-Power Allied Control Council was confirmed and although the Western powers refused to recognize Poland's western boundary as it then stood, this boundary, protected by Soviet divisions, became the *de facto* border of Poland. On the Polish boundary question, as always, tempers flared and a quarrel built up that lasted through two hours, until Truman decided that there was little purpose in continuing it. In his words:

> I could not agree to separation of the eastern part of Germany.
> Stalin, too, apparently had decided there was nothing to be gained by continuing this discussion.
> "Are we through?" he asked abruptly.

Churchill suggested that we were hardly through but that we should now turn to more agreeable things.

I announced that the conference had apparently reached an impasse on this matter and that the session was adjourned.[47]

Subsequently, although they returned to the issue again, no new decision was reached. Stalin had his way.

The objections raised by the secretary of state, James Byrnes, to the Soviet plundering of Germany before the Potsdam Conference, drew a suave suggestion from Molotov that they decrease the twenty-billion reparations bill by one billion. In other matters, Stalin was steady, stubborn, and determined to keep what he had won. Poland and Rumania were his; his troops were in Bulgaria, Yugoslavia, and Hungary, and what was done in these nations, henceforth, was his business and his alone.

The allies agreed to assign 10 percent of the industrial equipment from their three zones of occupation to the Soviet Union, along with an additional 15 percent in exchange for food and raw materials from Russia. Further boundary settlements on Russia's western regions were spelled out. Japan was summoned to surrender and the terms of an acceptable peace settlement with Japan were established. Agreeing to disagree on many issues, but to cooperate long enough to accomplish the one hard task yet before them, the Big Three left Potsdam on August 2. The Grand Alliance was coming to an end; the Great Powers were reverting to the jungle of international politics ruled by the struggle of each leader to secure the separate interests of his nation.

Some sense of the bitterness and personal disillusionment produced by the quarrels and frustrations of Potsdam were reflected in Truman's thoughts as he returned to the United States:

Anxious as we were to have Russia in the war against Japan, the experience at Potsdam now made me determined that I would not allow the Russians any part in the control of Japan. Our experience with them in Germany, and in Bulgaria, Rumania,

[47] Harry S Truman, *Memoirs,* Vol. I, *Year of Decisions* (Doubleday & Company, New York, 1955–1956), p. 370.

Hungary, and Poland was such that I decided to take no chances in a joint setup with the Russians. As I reflected on the situation during my trip home, I made up my mind that General Mac-Arthur would be given complete command and control after victory in Japan. We were not going to be disturbed by Russian tactics in the Pacific.

Force is the only thing the Russians understand. And while I was hopeful that Russia might someday be persuaded to work in cooperation for peace, I knew that the Russians should not be allowed to get any control of Japan.[48]

During the meeting, on July 24, when Truman had walked around the conference table to tell Stalin that the United States had just tested a new weapon of immense destructive force, Stalin showed only casual interest. On August 6, an American bomber dropped the first atomic bomb on Hiroshima. On August 8, Soviet armies under Vasilevsky advanced into Manchuria against the Japanese. Just a day following, the second atomic bomb was dropped at Nagasaki, and the Japanese sued for peace in a note sent on August 15. World War II came suddenly to an end, formalized two weeks later by a pompous ceremony of surrender staged by General Douglas MacArthur aboard the battleship *Missouri,* lying off Tokyo. Most of the world cele-brated this event, awed by the monstrous destructive force that had forced Japan's sudden capitulation and perturbed by the years of trouble and strife that obviously lay ahead.

The New Power Position

At the end of the war, Stalin was sixty-six. Victory had made the Soviet Union the second most powerful state in the world, a superpower rivaling the United States. Other great nations that had formerly ruled the world had either been destroyed by battle or were tottering toward ruin brought on by the long and exhausting struggle. Germany was no more than a set of regions occupied by foreign armies. Italy, too, had failed to realize Mussolini's dreams of Roman grandeur; France had suffered too much to contemplate great power for a number of years at least; and while the British Empire still called up

[48] Truman, p. 412.

nostalgia in the hearts of many dedicated servitors, the Empire was breaking up. Britain had become a second-rate power. In the Far East, Japan's emperor soon began to encourage the development of democratic institutions under the watchful eyes of an American occupation force. The world as a whole had become bipolar, with a new giant, the Soviet Union, obviously destined to play a dominant role in international decision making.

The Soviet predominance Stalin had so long schemed for in Eastern Europe was achieved. Finnish borders and possessions were established as he wished them to be. Latvia, Lithuania, and Estonia continued as Soviet Republics; the Curzon Line was Russia's western boundary with Poland, and a portion of East Prussia had been absorbed into the Soviet Union. The Carpatho-Ukrainian eastern tip of Czechoslovakia also became a part of the Soviet Union, along with Bessarabia and Bukovina. Red Army units occupied Poland, Rumania, Bulgaria, Hungary, and Czechoslovakia, and communists held positions of power in all these lands as well as in Yugoslavia and Albania. Finally, Soviet troops occupied eastern Austria and eastern Germany.

In Western Europe nations were in chaos, their ability to reestablish old democratic institutions in doubt. In France and Italy, strong communist resistance movements had won popular support by their wartime forays against the Germans. Thus, there seemed to be a possibility that Soviet ambitions for proletarian states as far as the Atlantic might well be realized.

But while heady vistas were opened by victory, and all the world recognized that the Soviet Union had become the predominant power on the continent, Stalin was deeply aware of the difficulties and dangers of his own position. At home, the war had taken an incredible toll. Appallingly, seventeen million people had lost their lives, while another three million had been disabled. The destruction of villages and cities had left some twenty-five million people homeless. Tens of thousands of industrial plants, hospitals, and schools lay in ruins; and in agriculture, livestock had suffered tragically, with only 15 percent of the prewar numbers of cattle, 60 percent of the hogs, and 50 percent of the horses, remaining.

There were, moreover, numerous troublesome political and psychological problems to be solved at home. During the war, Stalin had assumed for himself and for the party the role of the patriot fighting for Mother Russia. A Patriarch had been named for the Russian Orthodox Church in 1943, and anti-religious practices had been relaxed. National minorities had been encouraged to support the war, although several ethnic groups showing a special recalcitrance had been broken up and scattered across the land. All through the fighting, the Soviet press had implied that when the struggle ended, life would be easier: collective farms would be more relaxed, the terror would be ended, shops would have more goods for sale. Victory meant that now something must be done about all these promises and the expectations they had created. Another problem concerned the fate and state of mind of those millions of captives trans-ported westward by the Germans. These Soviet citizens would have to be repatriated and somehow the poisonous taint of Western ideas would have to be purged from them. Peace, then, brought the Russian dictator major challenges and problems at home.

Finally, at the very height of his euphoria over victory, Stalin, the suspicious communist and fanatic nationalist, could not have ignored the most worrisome problem of all. In the new world of peace the Soviet Union, its people and its material resources exhausted, now faced a relatively unjaded opponent. With the war's end the great behemoth across the Atlantic was hurrying to return its troops to shores untouched by battle. The arsenal of democracy, the capitalist United States, was more powerful economically than it had ever been before. Moreover, it possessed an incredibly dangerous new weapon, the atom bomb. For Stalin and for the Soviet people, while so great a potential threat existed in the world, there could be no rest even after victory.

CHAPTER FIVE

Postwar, Cold War, and the End of an Era

Problems of Economic Reconstruction

IN many ways Stalin's conduct after 1945 was even more compulsive than it had been in earlier years. Perhaps this was simply because he was older, less ready to innovate, and slower to comprehend unique problems. Conditioned like any other man by his earlier years, now, at sixty-six and in poor health, he grew increasingly conservative and vulnerably incapable of adapting to situations that were totally new or rapidly evolving. Typically, old men resent and criticize new ways, refuse to adapt to changing conditions, and eventually are pushed aside or discarded while younger men rush forward, confident of their own ability to solve any problem. In Stalin's case, however, the elderly Great Leader, with his indomitable will, retained power, and his exercise of that power was to influence profoundly the character of the postwar Soviet world.

He was deeply concerned by the Soviet Union's economic exhaustion at the end of the war, especially when compared with the tremendous new productive power acquired by the United States and the latter's ominous control over a new nuclear explosive force. Given the distrust of the capitalist world embedded in his mind by his ideological faith as well as by his character and experience, he reacted compulsively to drive his scientists and his economy toward the swiftest possible development of a Soviet atomic bomb. Obsessed, too, by his will to achieve the perfectly managed society, and persuaded as before that he alone could direct such a society, he attempted to pick up where the war had interrupted him; he went back in time to the last moments of peace to reestablish his system as it had been functioning then.

To Stalin, it did not appear to matter that the Soviet people were spiritually and physically exhausted, that they longed for a few moments' respite from the struggle to forge ahead, that they direly needed a touch of happiness in their lives. Indeed, refusing to concern himself with the people's immediate needs, he hastened instead to proclaim that there would be no pause, no relaxation. In his speech to the voters of the Stalin Electoral District on February 9, 1946, he outlined a new and tremendously ambitious economic program. Boasting about the way the system he had built had succeeded in driving off the Germans, he then summarized for his audience the levels tsarist production had reached before World War I.[1] "In 1913 there were produced in our country 4,220,000 tons of pig iron, 4,230,000 tons of steel, 29,000,000 tons of coal, 9,000,000 tons of oil, 21,600,000 tons of market grain and 740,000 tons of raw cotton."

Against these figures, in his repetitive, priestly style, he set the accomplishments achieved by 1940: "15,000,000 tons of pig iron; i.e., nearly four times as much as in 1913; 18,300,000 tons of steel; i.e., four-and-a-half times as much as in 1913;

[1] J. V. Stalin, *Works,* edited by Robert H. McNeal (The Hoover Institution on War, Revolution, and Peace, Stanford, Calif., 1967), III (XVI, 1946–1953), 11–12, 19–20.

166,000,000 tons of coal; i.e., five-and-a-half times as much as in 1913; 31,000,000 tons of oil; i.e., three-and-a-half times as much as in 1913; 38,300,000 tons of market grain; i.e., 17,000,000 tons more than in 1913; 2,700,000 tons of raw cotton; i.e., three-and-a-half times as much as in 1913."

And for the future? His announced intention was "to raise our industry to a level, say, twice as high as that of prewar industry." He predicted that the task would require at least "three more five-year plans." Specifically, he called for the annual production of 60 million tons of steel, 500 million tons of coal, and 60 million tons of oil. Once these levels of production were reached, he promised, the nation would "be guaranteed against all possible contingencies."

The nation responded neither with shouts of enthusiasm nor with cries for mercy. Apathy, indifference, weariness, and fear kept the people silent. The Fourth Five-Year Plan, announced later in the year, made even clearer to Soviet workers the perpetual treadmill on which they were trapped, for its emphasis was upon an immense increase in the production of heavy equipment and machine tools; by 1950 the output of producer goods was to exceed 1940 levels by 48 percent. Stalin's aim was clear—industrial growth, in addition to repairing all the damages of war, was to be whipped forward as ruthlessly as before.

Because the populace either could not or would not rise to the new challenge voluntarily, Stalin intensified old techniques—government fiat, coercion by the party, and police terror. Yet he was unable in any significant way to move his people to the kind of intense effort he demanded. Perhaps they were simply worn out; perhaps the returning soldiers and the exhausted wives and mothers who had kept the factories and fields producing during the war were determined at last to take some pleasure from life before it was over; or perhaps, because they had made money during the war and there had been nothing to buy, savings they had accumulated gave them a feeling of security and kept them from hurrying immediately back into the labor market. To correct the latter situation Stalin instituted a currency reform. In late 1947, citizens were directed to exchange their money—one new ruble for ten of their old rubles. For those who kept their money in Soviet savings banks exchange was one-to-one, but for the millions of peasants and others who kept their money at home savings were cut by nine tenths. This move effectively destroyed excess buying power and forced the Soviet "helots" to return to work in order to keep alive. It also compelled them to go without the consumer goods they had been dreaming of.

At the same time, Stalin mounted a massive campaign of propaganda and thought control designed to lift the people to new heights of obedience, loyalty, and industriousness. Trying to maintain the high levels of patriotism and sacrifice displayed so magnificently during the war, his communications media spoke endlessly of the danger of renewed attack from foreign capitalists and from spies and enemies within. In part, these efforts were aimed at destroying or suppressing the admiration for the West and for Western ideas and accomplishments, that had grown out of the wartime experience of millions of Soviet citizens who had worked or fought beyond Russian borders. In part, Stalin was attempting to reinstitute the kind of rigid control system he had perfected before the war. And, in part, he was simply trying to frighten tired men and women back into the factories and furrows.

Under the harsh direction of Stalin's favorite, Andrei Zhdanov, who enjoyed immense power from 1945 to 1948, the relaxations of the war period were furiously attacked; old truths were restated in their Marxist-Leninist dress with a special nationalist flavor, emphasizing the role of the Russians as liberators and leaders of the other national groups. Everything, Stalin seemed to insist in the first postwar years, must become as it was before. Unfortunately for him, however, the world had changed; his system of rule was already creaking with age; no longer could it satisfy Soviet needs, because these very needs had altered in countless ways. For Stalin the times were out of joint, and while he could not and certainly would not admit this truth, he had already outlived his usefulness as revolutionist and modernizer.

Development of the Cold War

During the first years of the postwar era the Soviet Union's expansion into the nations of Eastern Europe, Stalin's probing for influence elsewhere, and his intransigence in diplomatic relations with the West provoked the uneasy balance of political tensions called the *Cold War*. It will be obvious to the reader that the Cold War has deep and complex roots. The historian might choose to go all the way back to Russia's beginning as a state and trace the long course of conflicts between an Orthodox and autocratic Russia on the one hand and a Catholic-Protestant and rationalistic West on the other, for these conflicts created bitter and long-lived differences. Or, to begin much later, one might trace the Cold War back to Leninist ideology, with its aggressive, uncompromising, and devastating criticisms of Western capitalism and democracy. Along with the Western response to this ideology and to the new communist state's evolution, this approach would do much to explain the mutual hatreds and paranoid suspicions that characterized relations long before World War II. However, although the roots of this phenomenon go deep and the old scars are unforgotten, the Cold War that is to be discussed in these pages may be said to have begun when Stalin's postwar policies, whatever their motivation, shocked Western political leaders into the realization that it was time to forget their wartime euphoria about the brotherly Russians.

Why Stalin acted as he did cannot be answered precisely. In the eyes of many Western observers Stalin was the aggressor, deliberately pursuing a belligerent, expansionist policy based upon a calculating Marxist appraisal of international political opportunities. But in his own explanations and those of his colleagues, his policies were described as "peaceful and defensive." Stalin appeared to see himself as the embattled but courageous defender of the Socialist Motherland, doing only what had to be done to protect its security. While the exact measure of truth contained in these antagonistic viewpoints still cannot be determined, it is possible nonetheless to identify with reasonable certainty at least some of Stalin's motives.

The most obvious explanation of postwar Soviet diplomatic actions is based upon Stalin's belief in Marxist-Leninist-Stalinist ideology. We know that despite his wartime cooperation with the Western powers, he ardently adhered to the doctrine that conflict between "capitalist" and "socialist" worlds was inevitable; in his view, dialectical and historical materialism ordained a final, mortal combat between the classless society and the class society, which would end in the ultimate destruction of the latter. Stalin expressed his faith in this doctrine with startling force to the Yugoslav communist, Milovan Djilas, at one of Stalin's all-night dinners in April 1945. Djilas tells how during a discussion of the future, Stalin suddenly jumped up, crouching like a boxer, and "cried out almost in a transport. 'The war will soon be over. We shall recover in fifteen or twenty years, and then we'll have another go at it.' " Djilas found "something terrible in his words, yet there was something impressive, too, about his cognizance of the paths he had to take, the inevitability that faced the world in which he lived and the movement that he headed. . . ."[2] Clearly the ideology provided the built-in philosophical support that Stalin's experience and fundamental distrustfulness required. His deep-seated suspiciousness of the Western powers was intensified and systematized by the paranoid dogmas of Marx and Lenin.

Given his fundamental belief in the West's hostility and in the inevitability of conflict, it was quite natural that Stalin would fear the West. He could not believe its leaders' protestations of friendship; he could not breathe freely while the Soviet Union lay wounded and helpless; he could not sleep peacefully while his nation lived under the terrifying shadow of the American atomic bomb and within range of United States bombers. Nor could he countenance the establishment of hostile—that is, noncommunist—governments on his western boundaries, or anywhere else if this could be prevented.

In addition to Stalin's orthodox ideological perspective, his views were influenced by his role as supreme interpreter of the doctrine, and here practical considerations were of utmost

[2] Milovan Djilas, *Conversations with Stalin* (Harcourt Brace Jovanovich, New York, 1962), pp. 114–115.

importance. Always a canny judge of situation and timing, he was quick to recognize in the years immediately after the war the fluid nature of international political, social, and economic conditions. United States troops were returning home from the continent; old and discredited governments were attempting to reestablish order; prewar institutions of many of Europe's nations were ruined and in chaos. It appeared to be a time ripe with opportunity, a time to move swiftly in preparation for the conflicts he was sure would come.

Soviet western boundaries were particularly worrisome. Stalin wanted a buffer zone, a belt of nations, along his western border that would be not only friendly but also absolutely loyal to Soviet interests. In the three years from early 1945 to 1948, utilizing the presence of his troops in these countries, he did his best to guarantee that the new states would establish communist governments controlled by Moscow.

In general, the process of setting up the East European communist regimes followed a readily distinguishable pattern, albeit with several significant variations. During the first phase of the process, each Soviet-occupied state installed a coalition government, composed of the several parties already existing in the prewar period, along with Moscow-supported communist parties. Usually, the most powerful prewar political organizations were agrarian or peasant parties devoted to the upholding of democratic principles and to protecting the property rights of the peasants. Invariably, however, the communist parties in these coalition governments were recipients of special favors from the Soviet occupation forces, whose presence helped to secure for communist leaders the ministerial and military posts most essential for the control of the nation, in the Interior, Police, Justice, Commerce, and Defense ministries and the military services. With these functions of government in their hands, the communists held dominant control.

During the second phase of the communist takeover, elections were held. At this time the communists' struggle against the other parties became ferocious. Noncommunist candidates encountered many difficulties when they traveled into the countryside to campaign; their newspapers were suppressed and their rallies were heckled by communist toughs, transported to the meeting places in state-owned trucks, who frequently administered beatings to the noncommunist political leaders and their followers. Communist-directed police found it "impossible" to provide protection to noncommunist candidates, and in 1947 and 1948, there were instances when important political figures were beaten or even assassinated by the police themselves. Stubborn patriots and their followers tried vainly to alert the rest of the world to the mockery of these election campaigns, and the Western powers responded by sending protests to Moscow about the violence reported, but Stalin, having determined on a course of action, was not to be deterred. By the end of the second phase, the leading opponents of a country's communist regime either accepted the leadership of the communists, left the country, or were silenced by death, jail, or the prison camp.

During the third phase of takeover, the ruling communist party stopped pretending to be a subordinate part of a coalition; other parties were allowed to exist only as puppets of the communist leadership. The process of creating a Soviet-like governmental system, complete with secret police terror, party dictatorship, and highly centralized administration, moved into high gear, and during this phase loyal party members who had helped in the initial stages but who displayed too much independence or balked at the Sovietization of their nations were soon subjected to the swift and deadly purge system imported from Russia. As these "nationalists" were removed, tough "Stalinists" moved into the highest positions of power.

A brief listing of names, dates, and events can serve to flesh out and, while pointing up differences, underline as well the basic similarity of the process of Sovietization as it took place in East European nations after the war. In Poland, Stalin's Polish Provisional Government was recognized by the Great Powers in July 1945; by October 1947 this government had crushed the leadership of the massive Polish People's Party and had driven that party's leader, Stanislaw Mikolajczyk, out of the country. In Hungary, Marshal Voroshilov, the Soviet Chief of the Control Commission and an old crony of Stalin's, strongly supported the communists' attack on the Small Farmers' Party, which included the murder of its leader, Bela Kovacs, by Soviet soldiers, in February 1947. By the end of 1948, communists dominated that nation. In Rumania it was late February 1945 when the former prosecutor at the purge trials, Andrei Vyshinsky, arrived at a Bucharest controlled by Soviet troops and ordered the king to dismiss his prime minister and appoint the communist, Petru Groza, to that post. With the installation of the new prime minister, and with communist ministers of the Interior (police), Education, Information, and Agriculture, as well as communists in control of the National Security Corps and the army, there could be little doubt thereafter about who would rule Rumania.

Czechoslovakia was a case apart in the sense that the Soviet Union and its communism enjoyed a remarkable popularity, Czechoslovaks regarding friendship with the Soviet Union as their best protection against Germany. In the elections of May 1946, the Communist party won 38 percent of the votes, expanding its influence and placing its leader, Klement Gottwald, in office as premier. The coalition government he led lasted into mid-1947. Then the Communist party began pressing intransigently for radical social reforms, the minister of the interior packed the police force with Communist party members, and party leaders opposing the communists were denounced for conspiracy and subversion. By June 1948 the republic had become a communist dictatorship.

Yugoslavia was exceptional in another way, having won its own independence under Tito's leadership. From the first, therefore, its National Liberation Front was communist-dominated, and the romantic and incompetent representatives of prewar parties who joined the Liberation Front found that they had little chance of winning any real influence in Yugoslav politics. Renamed "The People's Front," this "coalition" was simply a bogus façade behind which the communists controlled Yugoslavia. The same was true in Albania, where a "Democratic Front" ran its slate for election with *no* opposition candidates. King Zog left the country, and power went to the communist leader, Enver Hoxha.

To Western observers and heads of state, Stalin's tough policies in Eastern Europe were cause for consternation. Difficult as it was for them to believe that he could deliberately throw away the friendship he had won in the West by his valiant struggle against Hitler, it was even more difficult to fathom his motives. Very soon, however, all the old fears of "bolshevism" and "communism" were revived, heightened to hysterical levels by the aggressive and violent actions of East European communist leaders, which were given attentive and detailed coverage in Western newspapers. Atrocities against private citizens and whole classes vied for space with accounts of purge trials that were in effect little more than formal systems of accomplishing the judicial murder of anticommunists. The murder of the internationally known Czech leader, Jan Masaryk, on March 10, 1947, convinced many in the West that the new communist regimes were being run by inhuman tyrants who competed for Stalin's approval by destroying all traces of democratic government within their respective countries.

The Western journalists and statesmen who freely interpreted Stalin's intentions from these events were literally terrified by what they saw. To these observers, who had hoped that a peaceful world might follow the war, it seemed evident that Stalin had set out on a new path of imperialism. According to their analysis of the news from Eastern Europe, world communist revolution was now being exported through puppet communist parties supported by the bayonets of the Red Army, and they assumed that Stalin intended to expand his authority as far as possible. Subsequent events seemed to confirm this analysis. Before the end of the decade Stalin's probing extended into North Korea, China, and Greece; in Western Europe powerful communist parties influenced by the Soviet party were active in Italy and France. To the Western powers, all these signs pointed to an aggressive Bolshevik armed power, intent upon maintaining a prolonged and steady campaign to extend its influence around the world.

Today it seems probable that this response to Stalin's expansion and probing was panicky and premature. However, given the brutal tactics of Stalin and the East European communists and the evangelical fervor of their revolutionary propaganda, it is difficult in retrospect to see how the Western powers could have responded otherwise. They were faced with what appeared to them to be irrefutable evidence that Stalin had reneged on his wartime agreements, defied the treaties and agreements of the wartime conferences, and unilaterally taken over many nations; not surprisingly, therefore, they responded by taking action to defend themselves against the frightening "communist menace."

The Cold War began in earnest in March 1947 when President Truman announced the United States policy subsequently known as the "Truman Doctrine." In effect the President officially declared that the United States considered itself obligated "to support free peoples who are resisting attempted subjugation by pressures."[3] At that moment Truman was thinking specifically of Greece and Turkey and of what he and his advisers considered to be threats posed by communist partisan forces acting against the government in Greece and by Soviet pressures on Turkey.

The Truman Doctrine was soon followed (June 5, 1947) by the Marshall Plan. Concerned with the weakness of the governments in France and Italy, one by-product of war-scarred economies, General Marshall, then secretary of state, proposed that the United States should offer financial aid to these nations to help bring their tottering economies back to good health and new growth. Otherwise, it was feared, the communists in these countries might gain control. By this time the United States Congress was sufficiently frightened by the "Red bogey" to appropriate the sum of twelve-and-one-half billion dollars to be spent in Europe during the next three-and-one-half years. During these same months other steps were taken to strengthen the positions of the Western democracies. American and British zones of occupation in Germany were fused in March, and a year later, France, Belgium, and Great Britain entered a new military alliance.

Each step taken by the Western powers called forth in turn responses from the Soviet side. And each step by either side added new passion to the Cold War, which now steadily mounted in intensity. Responding to the financial and military intervention of the United States in Europe, the Soviet Union established the Cominform (the Communist Information

[3] Richard F. Rosser, *An Introduction to Soviet Foreign Policy* (Prentice-Hall, Inc., Englewood Cliffs, N.J., 1969), p. 242.

Agency), a somewhat crude but submissive substitute for the Comintern, which Stalin had abolished in late 1943. The limited purpose of the Cominform was to coordinate the policies of communist parties in other nations with those of the Soviet Union. A more precise aim was to make certain that the Soviet Union and its East European satellites should speak with one voice in Stalin's struggle with the West.

Andrei Zhdanov, one of Stalin's principal lieutenants, and probably Stalin's chief assistant in the formulation of Soviet Cold-War policies at this moment, enunciated the new party line at the founding meeting of the Cominform, in September 1947. According to Zhdanov, the postwar world was split into two distinct camps: "the imperialist and anti-democratic camp, on the one hand, and the anti-imperialist and democratic camp, on the other."[4] The principal representative of the imperialist and anti-democratic camp, Zhdanov identified as the United States. "The cardinal purpose of the imperialist camp," he said, "is to strengthen imperialism, to hatch a new imperialist war, to combat socialism and democracy, and to support reactionary and anti-democratic pro-fascist regimes and movements everywhere." The purpose of his own camp, the anti-imperialist and democratic camp, Zhdanov declared to be "to resist the threat of new wars and imperialist expansion, to strengthen democracy and to extirpate the vestiges of fascism." Naturally the leading role within this camp was played by the Soviet Union. "This follows," Zhdanov said, "from the very nature of the Soviet socialist state, to which motives of aggression and exploitation are utterly alien, and which is interested in creating the most favorable conditions for the building of a communist society."

Zhdanov's analysis presented the international struggle as being sharply defined and unavoidable. There was a good world and a bad world. The Soviet Union, "staunch supporter of the liberty and independence of all nations and a foe of

[4] The following extracts are from the speech of Andrei Zhdanov, "The International Situation," translated in U.S. Representatives Committee on Foreign Affairs, *The Strategy and Tactics of World Communism,* Document No. 619 (U.S. Government Printing Office, Washington, D.C., 1948), pp. 216–217, 220, 229–230.

national and racial oppression and colonial exploitation in any shape or form" was throwing itself into the breach to block "America's aspirations to world supremacy. . . ." Zhdanov called for the French and Italian communist parties to defend their nations against the "American plan for the enthrallment of Europe," and in succeeding months communist-led strikes in both nations aimed at paralyzing their governments.

Western nations, having observed the Soviet Union's virtual assumption of control over seven East European nations and its apparent involvement in the struggle for more, could not accept Zhdanov's description of his country as a "supporter of the liberty and independence of all nations." Accordingly, they drew their own conclusions from these words and deeds, and proceeded with the Marshall Plan, offering aid widely to the war-ravaged nations of Europe. Poland and Czechoslovakia each expressed interest in receiving Western aid, but were sharply rebuked by Stalin. Molotov, who had gone to Paris to see what help Russia itself might receive, subsequently denounced the whole idea of American aid, and set up a countervailing "Molotov Plan." So the Cold War spiraled upward.

While the communist press attempted to create division between the Western powers, charging that the United States was deliberately undermining France and Great Britain, new and significant strains were developing within the socialist camp, specifically in the relations between Stalin and Marshal Tito, of Yugoslavia. Tito's position after the war was unique among communists, for he alone had led the defense of his country and could claim that his partisans had freed Yugoslavia from the Nazi scourge. A devoted communist, deeply committed to Stalin, he was also the national leader of the Yugoslav people, a brave and stubborn hero, absolutely sure that he and his partisan followers knew best what was good for Yugoslavia. Even more reprehensible than this nationalist pride and independence, in Stalin's eyes, were Tito's ambitions to play a predominant role among the Balkan nations and his desire to absorb the tiny state of Albania. Such initiative in a satellite was not to be permitted.

Zhdanov in his Cominform speech of September 1947 had promised a fair and equitable basis for future relations between socialist states. In his words, "the Soviet Union unswervingly holds the position that political and economic relations between states must be built exclusively on the basis of equality of the parties and mutual respect for their sovereign rights."[5] Soviet actions, however, fell short of this ideal, for in truth Stalin could not understand that another communist state could have interests other than those he chose to grant it; indeed he may have had in mind a plan to absorb all the satellite states into the Soviet Union. The contradiction between principle and practice, therefore, soon led to strife. When Stalin's joint-stock companies exploited Yugoslavia, Tito's representatives protested. When Soviet recruiters tried to enlist Yugoslav officials into Soviet espionage work in Yugoslavia, Tito plaintively remonstrated. When the Soviet ambassador, Anatoly Lavrentiev, developed his own spy system for the collection of information in Yugoslavia, meanwhile bypassing official Yugoslav channels, Tito's Central Committee forcefully objected.

In each case, the replies that Tito's complaints elicited from Stalin were uncomprehending and furious. In reference to the complaint about Ambassador Lavrentiev, for example, the letter from Stalin's Central Committee (that is, from Stalin) charged that Tito and Kardelj, his chief assistant, were acting as if Lavrentiev were no more than an ambassador from a bourgeois nation: "Do they realize that the Soviet Ambassador, a responsible Communist, the representative of a friendly country which liberated Yugoslavia from the German occupation, has not only the right but also the duty to discuss from time to time with the Communists of Yugoslavia all the questions they might be interested in?" The attitude of the Yugoslavs, this letter went on to say, "cannot be considered accidental. It derives from the general attitude of the Yugoslav Government owing to which the Yugoslav leaders often do not see the difference between the foreign policy of the USSR and the foreign policy of the Anglo-Americans. . . ."[6] This charge was true; Tito re-

---

[5] Zhdanov, p. 227.

[6] Ministry of Foreign Affairs of The Federal People's Republic of Yugoslavia, *White Book on Aggressive Activities by the Governments of the USSR, Poland, Czechoslovakia, Hungary, Rumania, Bulgaria, and Albania towards Yugoslavia* (Belgrade, 1951), p. 64.

garded himself as the leader of a sovereign state; he did not agree that Stalin and his emissaries could ignore Yugoslavia's sovereignty. In sum, neither he nor his most trusted colleagues were prepared to accept Stalin's assumption that Yugoslavia was simply one more Soviet Republic, subject to instructions from Moscow.

Apparently Stalin had long since forgotten what it was like to be opposed within the communist world. In all things, he believed, he had merely to whisper to have his will executed, and, indeed, at his whisper the Cominform met in June 1948 and formally excommunicated Tito and his party. Charging The Yugoslav leaders with holding "an anti-Soviet attitude . . . incompatible with Marxism-Leninism and only appropriate to nationalists," the official rescript of the Cominform declared: "the Central Committee of the Communist Party of Yugoslavia has placed itself and the Yugoslav party outside the family of the fraternal Communist Parties, outside the United Communist Front and consequently outside the ranks of the Information Bureau."[7]

In the years that followed Tito's excommunication, the declarations of obedient communists everywhere joined the chorus of statements by the Soviet press and radio urging loyal Yugoslav communists to rise against Tito and his "clique," and either to bring him around or drive him from power. A single illustration that well typifies the great flood of vituperation heaped upon the willful Tito is a Cominform Resolution of November 1949, which declared Yugoslavia to be in the "power of murderers and spies." Tito was accused of having set up a "fascist, anti-communist, police state" based on "kulaks in the countryside and capitalist elements in the towns." He and his cohorts, it was said, had "turned the country into a military camp, wiped out all democratic rights of the working people, and [they] trample on any free expression of opinion." Correction of this situation, the resolution declared, was the "international duty of all Communist and Workers' Parties"; more specifically, loyal communists in Yugoslavia were summoned

[7] Ministry of Foreign Affairs of Yugoslavia, pp. 73–74.

to struggle against the "fascists . . . for the regeneration of the revolutionary, genuine Communist Party of Yugoslavia. . . ."[8]

Presumably, in the aftermath of this kind of verbal barrage multiplied many times, the insubordinate Tito was expected to collapse in disgrace, but when he did not do so, the propaganda campaign was expanded to include economic, political, and military action. Members of the Cominform nations cut off established trade agreements with Yugoslavia without explanation; railway transportation was halted, and Yugoslav ships were hindered in their use of the Danube. All in all, from July 1948 through August 1950, over one thousand petty but irritating border incidents and violations of Yugoslav territory took place, resulting in the shooting of border guards and bloody skirmishes, each of which was made potentially more grave by the threat, always present, that Stalin might seize upon the incident to invade Yugoslavia. Why Stalin did not order an invasion of Yugoslavia is difficult to say. Perhaps he was overly confident that Tito would collapse, perhaps an invasion by Soviet troops would have too deeply disturbed the peoples of the other satellites, or perhaps he was afraid that invasion might provoke a general conflagration in the world.

Tito was being punished for the crimes of independence and nationalism, and, as always, Stalin could not be satisfied simply with issuing a reprimand; his instinct was to destroy completely the man who stood in his way. Patently, his domestic technique of rule was being extended to his international relations; this was, indeed, precisely the issue, for Stalin considered Yugoslavia's internal political arrangements to be his own domestic concern—the country was one of his satellites, almost a part of the Soviet Union. Tito, however, interpreted the matter quite differently: he was chief of a national state; his peoples' interest were his, and he would serve these interests even if to do so meant that he must forcefully oppose the man who ruled the Soviet Union.

Tito and his colleagues had not wanted the break with Stalin; the old man's willfulness had forced them to it. Loyal

[8] Ministry of Foreign Affairs of Yugoslavia, pp. 174–177.

communists, they had only tried to reason with him, but at least in this matter, he was past reason. He could not believe that any kind of communism other than his own could exist. Yet, unaccountably, after the break, Tito lived and prospered in defiance, and his ideologists even elaborated new arguments to prove that Yugoslav Marxism was far more orthodox, more faithful to Marx, than the Soviet brand.

Stalin's failure to bend Tito to his will was a defeat of immense significance, for it marked a major change in the power structure of the communist world and in the strength of Stalin's own authority. No longer was he the sole communist oracle, the "one true light" automatically commanding the allegiance of all communists. Now there were two independent, national centers of ideological truth, each drawing part of its strength from the fact that its leader ruled a nation. Never again would Stalin's words in the arena of world communism be quite as overpowering as they had been, for the contending voice of another successful prophet and ruler steadily challenged his authority. And for the evolution of the Cold War the Stalin-Tito conflict had a further impact. To Western observers of the struggle the evidence of Stalin's brutal treatment of a "friendly" power, presented when the Yugoslav government published its correspondence relating to the conflict with Stalin, reinforced their assessment of Stalin as an aggressive and unreasoning brute who could only be made to listen to reason by force.

Concurrently with the Yugoslav crisis the world witnessed a further demonstration of Stalin's intransigence—or so the events were interpreted by the statesmen of the West. In June 1948, Stalin blocked off the West's communications with Berlin. This city, situated deep in the Soviet Zone of Germany, remained divided into four occupation zones, and the Western powers regarded the parts they occupied as free and democratic. Blockade of Berlin's narrow access routes from the Western Zones of Germany appeared to signify Stalin's intention to take over all of Berlin and force the other occupying powers to withdraw.

Stalin's reasons for establishing the blockade were several. Control of all Germany was the prize being struggled over, and he undoubtedly wanted to prevent the Allies from consolidating their zones of Germany into a new pro-Western state, since this would have tipped the balance to their side. More immediately, a currency reform that the Western powers established in their zones in June 1948 promised to weaken further the Eastern Zone in its economic relations with the others. Success by the communists in their effort to drive the Western powers out of Berlin would have placed the entire city in their hands and would have seriously damaged both the prestige of the United States and its image as the "defender of democracy." The result might well have been an increase in the prestige and influence of the Soviet Union in all of Germany. In addition, success would have meant to the communists the end of a relationship that was damaging East Germany's economy and bleeding the East Zone of its best professional people, many of whom were slipping across to the West in Berlin.

The United States, France, and Great Britain, however, refused to be driven out; the blockade of railway and highway access to the city was overcome by the Berlin Air Lift, which operated until May 12, 1949, and provided the city with a precarious but adequate supply of food and fuel by air. Stalin's effort to win control in Germany failed. Moreover, any hope Stalin may have had of frightening the small powers away from the United States by this threat of war was dispelled by the failure of the blockade. In March 1949 the North Atlantic Treaty Organization (NATO) was established. Twelve nations of the West united in a mutual defense pact providing for combined action through a common military force, and General Dwight D. Eisenhower was named to command the new Supreme Headquarters of the Allied Powers in Europe.

The blockade also brought other consequences, for the confrontation over Berlin had confirmed previous indications that Stalin would never give up the Eastern Zone of Germany and would never permit a reunion of the German zones under the principles of Western democracy. Since the Western powers, for their part, could not accept reunion under communist sponsorship, they encouraged the German states in the Western zones to organize an independent government. On September 12, 1949, the Federal Republic of Germany came into being, although it did not gain full sovereignty until 1955. In October

1949, Stalin responded with the establishment of the German Democratic Republic, the new name given the Soviet Occupation Zone of Germany.

By late 1949, Stalin had reasons to reconsider his belligerent policies, and appeared to be doing so. We cannot, of course, know what he was thinking, but the context of his thought is clear enough, and some of his motives seem evident. Certainly, by September 1949, his empire in Eastern Europe was well under control. Stalin-like purges of overly independent national communist leaders were being brought to completion, and the Soviet system was being forcefully imposed upon each nation. In addition, the world situation was hardening; although Stalin's grasp of the satellites was firm, Greece and Turkey had been drawn securely into the Western sphere of influence. The governments and economies of France and Italy were gaining strength, so that the earlier hope of quick communist victories in those nations had now waned. And in Germany, the Western powers had given forceful evidence not only of their determination to stay in Berlin, but also of their intent to maintain military forces in Western Germany to protect the efforts of a democratic government in building a new Germany.

It must have been clear to Stalin that his aggressive thrusts westward had created more hostility than was good for Soviet interests. Winston Churchill epitomized the conclusions and the perplexities of many Western observers in his speech at the Massachusetts Institute of Technology, in March 1949, when he asked a question that Stalin himself might well have pondered: "Why have they deliberately acted for three long years so as to unite the free world against them?" Churchill did not answer the question, but he pointed out that "thanks to the harsh external pressure" of the Russians, "unities and associations are being established by many nations throughout the free world with a speed and a reality which would not [otherwise] have been achieved for generations."[9]

But if Stalin now undertook a more subtle policy—a policy of propaganda for world peace and a cautious search for détente

[9] Winston S. Churchill, *In the Balance: Speeches 1949 and 1950* (Houghton Mifflin Company, Boston, 1951), pp. 48, 50, 51.

—his change of direction was not immediately perceived by the rest of the world. The journalists and statesmen of noncommunist nations were so caught up in their oft-repeated theories of an aggressive world communist movement directed by Stalin with Machiavellian cunning and in accordance with a Marxist blueprint of conquest that the subtle signs of change he put forth were not taken seriously. Meanwhile, certain world events that *were* perceived did little to bring about calm and peaceful negotiations. In China, for example, after long years of struggle, the communist, Mao Tse-tung, came to power late in 1949. Communist leaders could now boast, and loudly did so, that one-third of the world was communist and that this augured well for the future in the conflict with Western imperialism. Mao's long visit (December 16, 1949–February 17, 1950) to Moscow in search of Soviet advice, technical assistance, and financial credits emphatically underlined the dominant role Stalin intended to play in this new communist nation and added to Western fears that they faced a world communist hegemony.

If Chinese developments did not sufficiently confuse the situation, what happened in Korea did. Here, by agreement with the United States, the Soviet Union at the end of the war had occupied northern Korea down to the 38th parallel. And here in 1948, a Soviet-like, satellite state was set up—the People's Republic of Korea. The new state was provided with a large army, trained and in some units commanded by Soviet officers. Across the 38th parallel American forces were still occupying Southern Korea; however, in January 1950, the United States secretary of defense, Louis Johnson, announced that the United States could not much longer continue to carry out this duty. Acting probably on this assurance of American disinterest and. enjoying strong Soviet military planning and logistical support as well as Stalin's blessing, if not his direct orders to move, the North Korean armies on June 25, 1950, crossed the 38th parallel to attack South Korea.

Mr. Johnson's statement had been in error; the United States decided that Korea must be held. The ensuing struggle, lasting into 1952, pitted the Americans, with allied troops drawn from several United Nations countries, against Chinese and North Korean troops armed with Stalin's help. Thus Stalin fought this war by proxy, yet the clear evidence of his guidance and belligerence in this arena did much to increase doubts among the Western powers regarding his change of policy in the West. Stalin once again had succeeded in embattling the world. It seemed he could be halted only by force.

The Overtaken Dictator

Within the Soviet Union after the war, while Stalin faced many difficulties, one, arising from circumstances as well as from his character, was fundamental. An evolving system had overtaken its dictator. In the 1930s, as has been argued in previous pages, some form of coercive totalitarianism was probably essential to accomplish the modernization of the Soviet Union with the excessive speed its leadership deemed imperative. But the very processes of modernization that Stalin instituted had, by the postwar period, made obsolete the regime of the 1930s.

In the earlier period, Stalin himself had initiated and then streamlined an educational system that proceeded to turn out millions of highly specialized and well-indoctrinated technicians, managers, scientists, and engineers. While these people were in the process of being trained and while hundreds of new industries and offices were only slowly getting underway, the dictator had been essential to exercise a kind of omnipotent and arbitrary direction, deciding himself or through his most trusted lieutenants what should be done in many fields. So, too, throughout the period of the first plans, the rude and fearful pressures of the autocrat were needed to drive the society forward, not only because it still lacked sufficient numbers of competent and trustworthy middle-level administrators, but also because of other inadequacies stemming from a history of underdevelopment. In an environment of ignorant workers and peasants and backward nationalist groups whose written tongue often did not yet exist and whose religion was akin to simple animism, the successful achievement of most reforms undoubtedly demanded a Great Tsar, a Lenin-inspired Ivan the Terrible, whose dread decisions had to be obeyed on penalty of death. Similarly for those who had been deprived of their

religion by the atheist communists, there was a need for a substitute symbol, a figure with godlike authority, whose commands would ring with omnipotence and awe-inspiring terror.
Thus it had been for the Soviet masses in the 1930s.

But as the system matured, producing its millions of experts trained in the rational disciplines of the sciences, experienced at administration and decision making and habituated
to responsiblility, the shape of the society and the character of
its needs changed in significant ways. The apparatus of party
and government, which Stalin had so frequently reorganized
in the fluid years before the war, was now staffed by competent
and decisive men and women who possessed technical knowledge far exceeding his. Even more significantly, the bureaucracies developed lives of their own—their own imperatives
and momentum—so that the omnipotent dictator increasingly
found himself fenced about by technically efficient bureaucracies
led by officials whose very skill and knowledge made it absolutely essential that they tell him what he could and could not do.
Economists and heads of industrial ministeries were professionally obliged to warn him that if he chose to make an arbitrary decision based primarily on his power to do so he might
very well ruin production prospects for many years. His generals were professionally obliged to warn him away from one
or another military adventure and to compel him to give
adequate support to the development of weapons systems their
studies recommended. Leading men in his party, no longer
heavy-fisted revolutionaries, but highly educated economists
and engineers, could write learned books, as did E. Varga and
N. Voznesensky, posing views that seriously challenged Stalin's
primitive Marxism and supporting their views with arguments
that were hard to answer. In sum, the newly educated society
—the millions of scientists and technicians, economists, managers, teachers, and workers who had matured under Stalin—
could no longer be treated in the same manner as the illiterate,
passive multitudes of the 1930s. Stalin had created his own trap,
a system of offices and officials, of informed and sophisticated
routines, without which the Soviet Union could not continue
to function and grow.

In this environment, Stalin, while perhaps comprehending

the significance of the changes he had wrought, was never able to accept the implied constraints of the changes upon his own power. Instead of welcoming the new era, listening to his advisers, and permitting bureaucracies and bureaucrats to function according to their own rational imperatives, he persisted in fighting to preserve his control. Desperately he struggled to retain his personal right to swing a heavy hand and to say the final word in all things. The incredible determination that had first driven him to try to create a system absolutely amenable to his bidding now kept him incessantly searching for new ways to make the system respond more efficiently. What he refused to admit was that his continued irrational and arbitrary intervention now rendered the machine less effective than it was capable of being.

Thus, after the war and until his death Stalin fought the very machine he had built, because it had grown beyond him. This was a desperate and dysfunctional effort to maintain his earlier authority intact. He was, in these last years, at war with the party, with the state apparatus, with the society he had helped to create, and with the skilled technicians he had helped to train. Unable to recognize any authority but his own, the embattled dictator thrashed about, enmeshed and crippled by the growing powers of his own bureaucracies. In the struggle to preserve his former freedom to act at will, he continued to employ the fiercest weapons of terror and violence, attempting to manipulate people and institutions exactly as he had in earlier years. He remained convinced that these methods alone could ensure the continued existence of the perfect social machine perfectly controlled, but in fact his techniques were outmoded, his ability to fathom new social conditions was limited, and his solutions no longer sufficed.

While he was probably quite sane through these years, his failure to comprehend the new realities of Soviet life and his insistence upon applying unrealistic antidotes to imagined social ills often made his influence seem virtually that of a madman. Frustrated, angry, obsessively concerned with spurious plots and conspiracies, trusting almost no one, and working with a vision of Soviet society that existed only in his own mind, the declining *Vozhd* obstructed further progress even while willing it.

After the war he continued to hold the highest positions both in the party, as General Secretary, and in the state apparatus, as Chairman of the Council of Ministers (the old Council of Commissars, renamed in 1946). In these positions he maintained his customary style of leadership, continuing to rule the party as an instrument of personal government and ignoring various agencies and rules at will. The Politburo did not meet regularly, if it met at all, and he capriciously ignored it, casually arranging substitute committees to perform its work. Khrushchev, in his "Secret Speech," spoke of various commissions and committees Stalin set up on his own, with Politburo members—"quintets, sextets, septets, and novenaries"—in order to evade open discussion of one or another issue in the Politburo.[10] In similar fashion, Stalin ignored the requirements of the party statutes to meet regularly with the Central Committee, delaying a meeting of the Party Congress for thirteen years, from 1939 until 1952. Meanwhile, at his bidding, his personal secretariat under the direction of Poskrebyshev, controlled and manipulated the secret police, the security forces, the state administrative apparatus, and, of course, the party itself, playing man against man and bureaucracy against bureaucracy to preserve the dictator's predominance.

While Stalin personally directed the party and all other agencies within the state apparatus, he naturally required many reliable, second-level lieutenants to head up republican party organizations, central government agencies, sections of the party secretariat, the police, the army, the industrial ministries, and so on. These men, while enjoying very great authority within their respective fields, were held on tight leashes by Stalin's habit of playing them off against one another. He constantly encouraged rivalries for favor and power, probably because the practice kept these men all the more pliant to his will. Through the postwar years, first one man, then another seemed to enjoy his special trust.

But his power to rule absolutely had diminshed. Because of age, ill-health, and the increasing complexity of governing a huge industrial state, Stalin was now vulnerable to the machi-

[10] Nikita Khrushchev, *The Crimes of the Stalin Era* (The New Leader, New York, 1962), p. S62.

nations of his own subordinates. Moreover, as time passed there was growing reason why each of Stalin's lieutenants should more frantically seek to increase his own power. While no one dared to discuss openly how much longer Stalin might rule, the problem of succession was potentially a matter of life-and-death for all his chief assistants as well as for the numerous cliques of officials and hangers-on who looked to one or another of them for patronage. Consequently, the fiercely ambitious men around Stalin pushed and jostled for position, schemed how to disgrace or destroy their opponents, whispered accusations against their rivals into the old man's ears, and offered him doctored documents to prove a rival's guilt or disloyalty.

In a sense Stalin's position began to resemble that of Lenin after the latter's early strokes, for Stalin now was carefully isolated from the outside; he could learn about what was going on in the world only from men like Zhdanov, Malenkov, Beria, Khrushchev, Molotov, and Kaganovich, or from men who were their employees. And at least some of these men were busy filling his mind with malicious lies about the others and puffing up their own accomplishments, while taking care to hide their vicious internecine intrigues. In this atmosphere of Byzantine duplicity and conspiracy, which he had himself created, Stalin well understood that he must fear such a man as Beria, for example, whose control of the secret police and security apparatus and its vast economic empire gave him immense opportunity to do evil. Thus Stalin incessantly, fervently, and with apparent desperation, studied the men around him, wondering whom to trust and whom to destroy.

"Stalin was a very distrustful man," Khrushchev told the delegates to the Twentieth Congress of the Party: "sickly suspicious; we know this from our work with him. He could look at a man and say: 'Why are your eyes so shifty today?' or 'Why are you turning so much today and avoiding to look me directly in the eyes?' The sickly suspicion created in him a general distrust even toward eminent party workers whom he had known for years. . . . A situation was created where one could not express one's own will."[11] And after the war: "Stalin became

[11] Khrushchev, p. S34.

more capricious, irritable and brutal; in particular his suspicion grew. His persecution mania reached unbelievable dimensions."[12] That he knew he had created a gang of willing and cunning "yes-men" who would do anything to gain his favor, and that he was contemptuous of them, his daughter Alliluyeva demonstrates in a description of his response to their efforts to render him obsequious honor, when he muttered with fine contempt, "They open their mouths and yell like fools." And on another occasion he referred to the "court circle" scornfully: "Ah, you damned caste."[13]

The party itself was a mass party of 5.7 million early in 1945; its numbers rose to 6.3 million in September 1947 and to 6.9 million in late 1952. In these years, it was no longer the mass of revolutionary but relatively untutored zealots it had been in the earlier years. Instead, it represented the elite of the population; its leaders had diligently recruited the educated people, the engineers and scientists; and in its lower ranks, even those who represented themselves as workers or peasants, were predominantly men and women who had found positions of some authority in the state hierarchies, in economic endeavor, and in cultural work. Free to work actively and intelligently, this party could undoubtedly have played a vigorous and useful role, but it was trammeled. Under the fiercely centralized and personal rule of Stalin, the full capacities of the new elite could not be exercised.

Beneath the Central Secretariat, a small group of *apparatchiki*—the party secretaries and paid officials at all levels—exercised the tight control over the party that kept it a compliant and virtually blind tool of the dictator. The precepts of Marxism-Leninism, while still dinned into all ears, had long since given way in practice to another principle, that of *partiinost,* absolute loyalty to the party and its current line. Only by practicing *partiinost*—comparable to accepting as absolute truth each day's *Pravda*—could the average party member perform in the required manner, without questioning twists

[12] Khrushchev, p. S45–S46.
[13] Svetlana Alliluyeva, *Twenty Letters to a Friend* (Harper & Row, New York, 1967), pp. 166, 201.

and turns of policy and theory that would have been deeply disturbing had he tried to rationalize them according to his understanding of Marxism-Leninism and of reality.

Although the party penetrated into all other branches of Soviet life, although most of its members played some role in the state or the economy and many helped to govern the nation, its influence actually declined during Stalin's last years. His position as Chairman of the Council of Ministers gave increased importance to the state apparatus, and his habit of manipulating one branch of the power structure against the others prevented the party from becoming the dominant element. In a very real sense, however, although he remained Russia's dictator, he was no longer in command of the nation's governing structure; rather, he nagged at it, attacking now one of its discrete parts, now another, setting man against man and group against group, recalling by his actions his days as an underground revolutionary and as a revolutionary reformer. But he was incapable of fathoming the workings of the gigantic machine he had created. Indeed, as the machine forged ahead, multiplying its offices and its officials, he came in his last years to suspect that some vast new conspiracy was wresting the power from his hands. Finally, becoming convinced of this, he was to turn in a frenzy to a new series of purges.

Economic Progress

Whatever the faults of Stalin's system of administration, the Soviet industrial drive forged ahead with impressive results. To a significant degree the ambitious reconstruction aims of the Fourth Five-Year Plan were achieved, as were, for the most part, overall targets for growth. Gross industrial production actually exceeded the plan figures, the production of coal, electricity, oil, steel, tractors, and other products overfulfilling their planned quotas. By contrast consumer goods production as usual fell somewhat below the plan, and in agriculture, grain production fell far short of expectations.

While industrial production leaped upwards, there were awkward shortcomings in the new growth. Overcentralization and the Stalinist emphasis upon greater production rather than upon the selective production of much-needed goods negatively influenced the development of new products and the innovation of new industries in such fields as plastics, fuels, and chemicals. Within existing industries the continued concentration upon volume of production tended to discourage the development of new styles and improved models. On the other hand, managers able to come up with spectacular new ideas frequently obtained funds that should have gone to less dramatic but more essential industries. With many industrial ministries competing for funds, the greater weight of investment consistently went to the favored heavy industries and to research and production of military goods; this meant that less popular but nonetheless important industries were bound to suffer. Finally, confusions arose over the Fifth Five-Year Plan, supposedly begun in 1951. Although no announcement of it was made in that year, and although there was no draft of it until the Nineteenth Party Congress in October 1952, the plan approved then was scheduled to operate in part retroactively, from 1951 through 1955.

The economic Achilles' heel after the war continued to be agriculture. Despite the enormous importance of the agricultural problem and the serious crises perennially affecting this area, Stalin actually paid very little attention to agricultural production or to conditions in the rural areas. According to Khrushchev he did not visit farms and had no detailed knowledge of peasant attitudes, and what ideas and information he received were fed to him by politically conditioned informants, whose exaggerated statistics led him to completely unrealistic conclusions.

After the war, still believing that the peasant must support industrialization, Stalin continued policies designed to squeeze out of peasant incomes capital for investment in industry. In consequence, during the fourth plan the collective farmers (*kolkhozniki*) continued to live at subsistence levels or worse, frequently compelled to sell their produce to the state at prices well below the costs of production. Without adequate draft animals, tractors, and capital, the work of reconstruction in agriculture inched forward slowly, under conditions of want reminiscent of the early days of collectivization. The combination of overcentralization, too much intervention from above, low prices, and incentive pay that in effect encouraged the peasant to avoid work on the collective farm if he could, spelled continuous, painful failure.

A severe drought, the worst in the twentieth century, hit the country in January 1947. The catastrophe moved Stalin in 1948 to announce the sort of grandiose solution to agricultural problems that he increasingly tended to favor in all matters during these years. The agricultural environment itself was to be transformed. He ordered the planting of a great shelter belt of trees in the southeast portion of the country in order to protect the southern lands from drying winds. Pretentious plans for irrigation and reclamation were added. Naturally the major expense of this new effort was to be born by the peasant. Although such plans were put into operation, they were pursued only while Stalin lived and were quickly discarded after his death.

Other efforts to cope with agricultural problems during Stalin's last years were made by Nikita Khrushchev, who became one of the party's principal experts in agricultural affairs in 1950. His first step that year was to begin the amalgamation of collective farms. A total of some 250,000 collective farms existing at the beginning of 1950 had been reduced by the end of 1952 to 94,000. One reason for pushing amalgamation was that many farms were too small to operate efficiently. More important, however, were the problems of management and control. Competent chairmen and agricultural specialists were at a premium, and party members interested or knowledgeable in agriculture were lacking in sufficient numbers to establish primary party organizations on all farms or to provide good leadership. With amalgamation better use could be made of administrators, all the larger farms could have primary party organizations, and Machine Tractor Stations could service fewer separate units.

Despite all the crash programs of this period, however, agricultural production remained poor. Grain production in 1950, as well as in 1952, was below the 1940 level. Similarly, the production of potatoes and the number of cows failed to regain their 1940 levels. Blame for these failures rested only partially with the system's inability to stimulate the peasants to increase production. Shortcomings of labor and machinery, the result of war casualties, and Stalin's continued determination to draw capital from agriculture, all combined to keep an already inefficient system from improving.

Assault on the Intellectuals

Given Stalin's compulsion to achieve total control, it was perhaps predictable that he would continue after the war to seek to preserve and strengthen his role as sole arbiter of all intellectual and cultural matters. Embedded deeply in his urge for the perfect-machine-functioning-perfectly lay his conviction that the human cogs should be guided in all things by the one truth he alone could dispense. There were many reasons at the end of the war why the restoration of ideological purity and reassertion of the party's control over all intellectual activities were thought to be particularly urgent. Some sixty-five million Soviet citizens had lived for a time under the rule of German occupation forces, exposed to the contaminating influence of Nazi propaganda; there was need to cleanse these citizens and revive their faith in the socialist system the Germans had vilified.

Additionally, some five or six million other Soviet citizens had been taken prisoner or had voluntarily defected to the Germans, subsequently working in labor gangs as far west as the coasts of Brittany and Normandy. They, along with the officers, soldiers, and even the journalists, who had marched to Berlin and Prague during the war and after, were thought to be infected by their experiences; indeed many had made friends in the West, developed an admiration for things Western, and compared the institutions of the West favorably with those of their homeland. In Stalin's view these people were diseased and had to be quarantined until they could be cured by indoctrination and rehabilitation; thus thousands were thrown into prisons and concentration camps as they crossed the border on their way home, guilty of having been too long abroad and suspected as carriers of pro-Western sympathies.

There were other reasons as well why Stalin believed a major campaign to recapture total intellectual-political leader-

ship was necessary. In the annexed territories—Estonia, Lithuania, Latvia, Eastern Poland, and the western portions of the
Ukraine—Soviet policy required the reshaping of noncommunist institutions, from religious organizations and private farms
to schools and government bodies. The aim was to bestow upon
the largely unwilling people of these regions the benefits of
socialism and to persuade them that they were happy to be a part
of the Soviet Union (even though thousands actively struggled
against the changes for many years).

Deeper within the Soviet Union itself, there were other
intellectual and cultural issues to be set straight. During the
war Stalin had heavily emphasized the Russian character of the
struggle, striving to take advantage of the fervent patriotism of
Soviet citizens who more enthusiastically defended the Russian
homeland than Soviet communism. He had also stimulated the
various ethnic minority groups to support the war by arguing
that Russian leadership from Alexander Nevsky forward had always been a liberating and enlightening influence and that by
supporting the Russian struggle the minorities were contribut-
ing to their own advancement. With the war over he sought to
continue his exploitation of the patriots' love for Mother Russia.
But everywhere in the Soviet Union, workers and peasants, who
had listened to promises of greater freedoms after the war, were
hostile and resistant to the effort to keep up the pressures as if
they were still fighting the Germans. Stalin also found the ethnic
minorities reluctant to accede to Russian leadership and superiority. Ukrainians and White Russians, some of whom had
joined pro-Nazi partisan groups during the war to fight Stalin's
armies and some of whom had organized partisan groups to defend their own independence, were slow to open their arms to
the party's Russian chauvinism. Similarly, in the southeastern
borderlands, Moslem and Turkic peoples staunchly defended
their own heroes and religious leaders, refusing to exchange
them for Russian heroes.

In the universities and academies of sciences, where the
party's controls had been relaxed during the fighting, there was
need now to reestablish discipline and control in order to curb
the limited autonomy and authority Soviet scientists and
scholars had developed. Steps were already being taken during

the last year of the war to reestablish the party's rights to decree the intellectual line for all Soviet citizens. Following this, Stalin's postwar campaign against the intellectuals began in early August 1946, when the Central Committee issued a decree demanding greater *partiinost* from party members working in the educational system. The decree specifically attacked two Leningrad literary reviews for publishing materials allegedly slandering the Russian people, which portrayed the latter as "primitive, uncultured, stupid, and vulgar." Following up this attack journals were closed, famous writers came under attack, and Zhdanov proceeded to set forth in precise detail the ideological position Soviet writers were henceforth to take:

> The imperialists, their ideological henchmen, their writers and journalists, their politicians and diplomats, are trying to slander our country in every way they can, to represent it in a wrong light, to slander socialism. Under these conditions the task of Soviet literature is not only to return blow for blow against all this vile slander and these attacks upon our Soviet culture, upon socialism, but also boldly to attack bourgeois culture which is in a state of degeneration and decay.[14]

The writers' tasks, Zhdanov further explained, were to oppose bourgeois culture, with its "rotten and decaying" foundation, to show the "great new qualities of the Soviet people," to "help light the road ahead," and to "help the party and the people to educate our youth in the spirit of supreme devotion to the Soviet order, in the spirit of supreme service of the interests of the people."[15]

Men and women who would not toe the party line saw their publications suppressed and were arrested or frightened into silence. The superiority of the Great Russian culture and the Soviet system to all others became predominant themes of the new propaganda campaign. With xenophobic intensity and scant regard for historical truth, the communist press claimed for Russian scientists and inventors important scientific discoveries and inventions previously credited to Westerners. Russian or

---

[14] A. Zhdanov, "On Cultural Policy," in U.S. Representatives' Committee on Foreign Affairs, *The Strategy and Tactics of World Communism,* Document No. 619 (U.S. Government Printing Office, Washington, D.C., 1948), p. 179.
[15] Zhdanov, pp. 179–180.

Soviet accomplishments of every sort were set against those of Western nations, with the intention always of persuading the Soviet citizen that his own culture was the only good culture and that what he had seen during his sojourn in Czechoslovakia, Poland, or Germany was decadent and despicable.

Such arguments were difficult to swallow for those who had been abroad. Moreover, as mentioned above, the Russian chauvinism of the party line offended many representatives of minorities groups who took pride in their own languages and literatures and who revered and emulated their own poets and heroes. In the postwar era legendary non-Russian priests, khans, and princes were denounced by Stalin's propagandists as remnants of the tsarist and capitalist past, and writers who eulogized such hero figures were told to rewrite their stories and histories with the correct emphasis.

In 1948 Stalin's extreme Russian chauvinism and his anti-Western position were heightened still further by the establishment of the state of Israel. Russia's Jews, always unpopular in the Soviet Union, now glimpsed the possibility of emigrating to their own national homeland. To Stalin their sentiments were an indication that the Jews were dividing their allegiance, and he moved to intensify the level of anti-Semitism in the country. With the beginning of the *Zhdanovshchina,* as the repression of the intellectuals during this period is called, Soviet writers who admired Western ideas and literature were branded "cosmopolitans." Subsequently, the term "rootless cosmopolitan" was applied to the Jews, and Jewish culture was systematically suppressed. In 1949 all Yiddish publications and the Yiddish theater were shut down and "in 1952 virtually all leaders of Jewish culture were shot. . . ."[16]

Artists, literary people, and Jews were not the only ones who suffered from Stalin's effort to reestablish his absolute control over intellectual matters. Academia came under similar attack. Mention has already been made of the relative independence that had developed in some university circles and academies of science. Not only were these centers dangerous in Stalin's eyes as possible areas of independent thought, but

[16] Leonard Schapiro, *The Communist Party of the Soviet Union* (Random House, New York, 1960), p. 538.

equally threatening was the fact that scientists and scholars now held influential positions in the organs of the party responsible for controlling thought. Assaulting the bastions of scholarly opinion, Stalin sought to reinstate the predominance of the party over the academy, to restore the right of the former to rule on matters of philosophy, linguistics, biology, and psychology.

In June 1947, Zhdanov condemned certain philosophers who held posts in the influential Directorate of Propaganda, a section of the party's Secretariat, for their admiration of Western philosophers, and successfully ousted them from this body. In July and August 1948, the party underwrote the theories of the pseudogeneticist, T. D. Lysenko, who fervently responded by acknowledging his gratitude to the party, the government, and "Comrade Stalin personally." Thereafter Lysenko's dominance in genetics was to pervert that science and, until the early 1960s, to hamper serious men working in the field. Stalin similarly intervened in the controversy over the theories of the linguist, N. Ya. Marr, again primarily to make the point that the party's line rather than the academicians' would be followed in this field. And in psychology, Stalin's desire to find ways to make the human machine respond to his bidding as he wished it to led him to support the revival of Pavlovian psychology.

Stalin also injected himself forcefully into still another area of scientific controversy when, in early 1952, he published his own book, *Economic Problems of Socialism in the USSR*. At issue was the interpretation by the Soviet economist, E. Varga, of the changes that had taken place in capitalist society as a result of World War II. Varga had concluded that there would be no serious capitalist economic crisis for a decade or more. In fact, the capitalist states, he thought, might very well achieve significant social reforms without destroying their governmental systems, and he saw the colonial nations as moving gradually toward independence. Most significant of all, because it profoundly challenged Stalin's orthodox position, Varga's study implied that neither intra-imperialist nor anti-Soviet wars were inevitable.

Stalin's book, coming after considerable discussion of Varga's theories by other men, laid down the official line on all these points. The crisis in world capitalism was declared to be

imminent; intra-imperialist wars were definitely to be anticipated; and the only sensible conclusion to reach was that imperialism had to be destroyed. The Institute of World Economy
and World Politics of the Academy of Sciences, Varga's base
of power, was reformed and the leadership handed to his opponents in early 1948. Varga himself was removed from public
life.

In every area of Soviet affairs, Stalin thus demonstrated
his fierce determination to lay down the law. But his objective,
which was nothing less than to legislate all thought, to shackle
and distort even the sciences if they could enhance his control
over Soviet society, lay beyond the realm of the possible. Stalin's
firm belief that it *was* possible indicates that in his own eyes he
stood apart from and above the system as a godlike arbiter of all
things, the ultimate and only source of law and truth in the
Soviet Union. He had come a long way since the early underground days in Baku.

Last Purges and Stalin's Death

There were deep overtones of irrationalism, perhaps even
madness, in Stalin's efforts to achieve greater control after 1945.
Compounding his frustrations in the last years was the very
impossibility of dictating a whole society's thought and behavior,
particularly when that society was well educated, volatile, and
progressing rapidly toward ever greater knowledge and complexity. Pressed by political, economic, and intellectual problems at home, by expanding difficulties in the satellites, by the
rise of Communist China and the war in Korea, and by his distrust of the men around him, Stalin sought a way out. It is not
surprising that under the weight of these pressures his mind
should have wandered back to the times when his authority to
command had been unquestioned, nor that he should have reverted to the most efficacious technique he knew for having
his own way—the purge. There were to be several purges in
the postwar era, each of them a frightening phenomenon, raising
tensions and fears to feverish heights.

Andrei Zhdanov, Stalin's principal agent in the Cominform and in directing the assault on the intellectuals, died in

late August 1948. He had, until his rise to national office, served as Secretary of the powerful Leningrad party organization, and even after he left Leningrad, his continued informal leadership of the Leningrad apparat appears to have greatly strengthened his national power position. Within a few months after his death, the Leningrad party organization suffered an extensive purge that destroyed the careers and lives of many who had been close to him. Among the victims were Nicholas Voznesensky, a member of the Politburo since 1947, Chairman of Gosplan (the National Planning Office) since 1938, and a Deputy Chairman of the Council of Ministers since 1939. Other victims were the former member of the Secretariat of the Central Committee, A. A. Kuznetsov (Zhdanov's successor as First Secretary at Leningrad), and Kuznetsov's successor, P. S. Popkov.

Georgi Malenkov, who had been Zhdanov's fiercest rival for Stalin's favor and who now became Stalin's chief lieutenant, has been credited with carrying out the purge of the Leningrad party organization according to later accounts of this purge by Nikita Khrushchev, A. N. Shelepin, head of the KGB (Committee of State Security) under Khrushchev, and P. N. Demichev, Chairman of the Moscow City party organization and a member of the Central Committee Secretariat. Presumably, Malenkov was cleaning out a nest of opponents in order to establish his own influence at Leningrad. It is hardly possible, however, that this sort of violence could have occurred without Stalin's authorization, and indeed, all three of the men mentioned above have publicly declared that Stalin was personally involved. Khrushchev said in his Secret Speech that the "Leningrad Affair" was "the result of the willfulness which Stalin exercised against party cadres." "As we have now proven," Khrushchev said, "this case was fabricated."[17]

In late 1951 and early 1952, Stalin charged that he had discovered a conspiracy in the so-called Mingrelian nationalist organization, in the Republic of Georgia (Mingrelia is a small area within that republic). There, he claimed, nationalists were conspiring for the overthrow of the Soviet power in Georgia "with the help of imperialist powers." The charge's grim over-

[17] Khrushchev, p. S45.

tones, reminiscent of Stalin's struggles with the Georgians in the early 1920s, make one wonder if he was indeed reliving the past. In the events that followed, several Mingrelians were removed from office and arrested. Because Beria (Chief of the Ministry of Internal Affairs [MVD], the successor to the NKVD), one of the most powerful of all Soviet leaders, was himself a Mingrelian and deeply involved in Georgian political affairs, it has been assumed by some scholars that Stalin may have been testing the ground for an attempt to purge Beria himself. The evidence, however, is too thin to permit more than speculation.

The meeting of the Nineteenth Party Congress in early October 1952 took place amid a rising tide of arrests, terror, and unexplained reshuffling of men at the higher levels of the party that looked to many as if Stalin were preparing for a general purge of the party's top levels. When this was followed, on January 13, by *Pravda*'s ominous announcement of the case of the "Saboteur-Doctors," fears mounted. Seven distinguished doctors, five of them Jewish, were charged with forming a "terrorist group who made it their aim to cut short the lives of active public figures of the Soviet Union through sabotage medical treatment." *Pravda* further stated that the doctors had confessed to having killed Andrei Zhdanov and A. S. Shcher-bakov, a Secretary of the Central Committee, and had worked to "undermine the health of leading personnel, to put them out of action." Among their other intended victims were named Marshals A. M. Vasilevsky, I. S. Konev, and S. M. Shtemenko. The formal report, as it appeared in *Pravda,* went on to say:

> It has been established that all the murderer-doctors, who had become monsters in human form, trampling the sacred banner of science and desecrating the honor of scientists, were enrolled by foreign intelligence services as hired agents.
>
> Most of the participants in the terrorist group . . . were connected with the international Jewish bourgeois nationalist organization, 'Joint,' established by American intelligence for the alleged purpose of providing material aid to Jews in other countries. In actual fact this organization, under direction of American intelligence, conducts extensive espionage, terrorist and other subversive work in many countries, including the Soviet Union.

In 1956, Khrushchev was to say, "We felt . . . that the case of the arrested doctors was questionable. We knew some of these people, because they had once treated us. When we examined this 'case' after Stalin's death, we found it to be fabricated from beginning to end." Insisting that Stalin had "set up" or rigged the "Doctors' Case," Khrushchev announced the rehabilitation of all of the doctors, including the two who apparently had died while in prison.[18]

As this case has since been interpreted, primarily by Khrushchev during his subsequent efforts to exonerate the party of all past misdeeds and to blame the dead dictator instead, the "Doctors' Plot" signaled Stalin's intention to widen the purge to attack the party leadership. Beria, Voroshilov, and Molotov, Khrushchev implied, were probably intended victims, along with Mikoyan, some remaining adherents of Varga and Voznesensky, and other Jews and Western sympathizers.

To what extent Khrushchev's charges may be accepted, it is impossible to tell. When he made them he was speaking to party members who knew as much about the recent past as he did and would have been quick to catch him out. At the same time, he was adroitly attempting to lay many crimes in Stalin's lap and thus clear the party of blame. In subsequent public statements at the Twenty-Second Party Congress, he and other speakers presented new evidence of the tormented, nightmarish atmosphere in which, early in 1953, the work of the party and government was carried on, an atmosphere in which eminent party members drifted silently, chilled by thoughts of what was to come. The evidence is convincing.

Whatever Stalin's plans, he was not to live long enough to implement them. In the first days of March 1953, he suffered what a team of doctors identified as a hemorrhage of the brain and lay paralyzed and unconscious for many hours. While he lay dying, his henchmen looked on and began plotting how to overcome one another. Beria and Malenkov prepared to seize the initiative, leaving Khrushchev, Bulganin, and Molotov to organize a defensive alliance. On March 5, death came. The machine man, the man of steel, had finally ended his dictator-

[18] Khrushchev, pp. S49–S50.

ship. As he quietly slipped from the center of power, he left a vacuum, like the eye of a storm, circled by viciously contending rivals who had been longing for his death but who now suddenly stood aghast before the fact.

It is one of the ironies of history that the passing of this man, who may have been hated during his lifetime by more of his contemporaries than any other man in history, was witnessed and sensitively recorded by his daughter, Alliluyeva, perhaps the one person who could most sympathetically see him as a suffering human being. She depicts him at that moment as a rude but lonely old man whose passing was, like any man's death, tragic. In her memoirs, *Twenty Letters to a Friend*, she wrote: "During those last days, when he found peace at last on his deathbed and his face became beautiful and serene, I felt my heart breaking from grief and love." She recalls seeing "Voroshilov, Kaganovich, Malenkov, Bulganin, and Khrushchev in tears," and she describes how the old servants at Stalin's country house sobbed tragically over his body. "All these men and women, who were servants of my father, loved him," she has written. "In little things he wasn't hard to please. On the contrary, he was courteous, unassuming and direct with those who waited on him. He never scolded anyone except the top men, the generals and the commandants of his bodyguard."[19]

Whatever his faults and his virtues, Stalin died like other men. His reign was ended, but the effects of his deeds would long continue to have immense influence both inside the Soviet Union and around the world.

[19] Alliluyeva, pp. 11–12.

CHAPTER SIX

Some Afterthoughts

To MAKE an exhaustive evaluation of the impact of Stalin's thirty years of rule upon the Soviet Union would entail the weighing and measuring of tangible and intangible factors too numerous to count. And to attempt to identify the historical consequences of Stalin and his era upon the Soviet Union and the rest of the world would be to explore far beyond the limits of this book. Nonetheless, we must try to sum up, if only in the briefest way, the major achievements of those thirty years and the state of Soviet society at Stalin's death.

The tremendous economic growth accomplished after 1928 is one of the most obvious and significant changes. Measures of gross national product, even when carefully adjusted to include all the qualifications that must be made for Soviet statistics, are at best rough and unsatisfactory estimates of economic progress; yet it must be acknowledged that the annual growth rate of Soviet GNP of 7 percent apparently achieved through the years 1950–1955 compared remarkably well with that of 4.3 percent for the United States during the same period. Absolute increases in certain key products provide concrete evidence of the progress achieved by Stalin's industrialization plans. The following figures are solid evidence of almost incredible advances.

	1928	1940	1950	1953
Pig iron (million tons)	3.3	14.9	19.2	27.4
Steel (million tons)	4.2	18.3	27.3	38.1
Electricity (million kilowatts)	5.0	48.2	91.2	134.4
Oil (million tons)	11.6	31.1	37.8	52.8
Coal (million tons)	35.5	166.0	261.1	320.4
Cement (million tons)	1.8	5.7	10.2	16.0
Tractors (thousands)	1.3	31.6	116.7	111.3
Cotton Cloth (million meters)	2.7	3.9	3.9	5.3
Leather footwear (million pairs)	58.0	211.0	203.4	238.1

Sources: *Narodnoe khozyaistvo SSSR v 1968,* pp. 190–198; *Strana sovietov za 50 let* (1967), pp. 53–54; for column 4, *Narodnoe khozyaistvo SSSR v 1958,* pp. 158–169.

Just as clearly demonstrated by statistics are the failures in agriculture through this period. In the following table the value of products is calculated in terms of 1965 prices, in millions of rubles.

	1913	1928*	1940	1950	1953
Grain	86.0	69.3	95.6	81.2	82.5
Potatoes	31.9	41.1	76.1	88.6	72.6
Meat (live)	5.0	4.2	4.7	4.9	5.8
Milk	29.4	29.3	33.6	35.3	36.5

*The column under 1928 actually presents the annual average production from 1924 through 1928.

Source: *Narodnoe khozyaistvo SSSR v 1968,* pp. 314–315.

Grain production in 1950 and 1953, it will be noted, was still below that of 1913, while meat and milk production showed only slight improvement. These failures, given the immense growth of population (from 159 million in 1913 to 188 million in 1953), signified a major economic disaster, which was worsened by the great increase of urban consumers during the period—from 28.5 million in 1913 to 80 million in January 1953. As late as 1950 agriculture had hardly regained pre-1928 levels, and between 1940 and 1953 the value of agricultural products rose only 4 percent. Thus although Stalin had created a whole new system of agricultural organization and political control, he had thoroughly botched the task of increasing production and productivity in agriculture.

Figures detailing the growth of the Soviet Union's economy only begin to suggest the advances that had been made in the overall modernization of the Soviet society. Another dramatically significant illustration was the military-scientific strength of the postwar USSR, demonstrated most convincingly by the announcement of the first Soviet atomic explosion in September 1949. This was followed, only a few months after Stalin's death, by the testing of the first Soviet thermonuclear device in August 1953. Added to these terrible weapons were newly built battleships, MIG planes that were highly effective in Korea, and a land army numbering in 1953 some 5.8 million men. The Soviet Union remained the second military power in the world.

Other fundamental consequences of Stalin's modernization are perhaps best presented in growth figures. For example, the number of wage and salary earners grew from 10.8 million in 1928 to 31.2 million in 1940, and to 43.7 million in 1953. The number of trained specialists (engineers, economists, doctors, managers, scientists, and the like) graduated each year from the middle schools (technicums) and the higher-level institutes and universities rose from 49,000 in the years 1918–1928 to 115,000 from 1929 to 1932. By 1951–1955, annual graduating classes in such specialists averaged 536,000 each year. Because of this educational expansion, the number of doctors and dentists in the Soviet Union rose from 70,000 in 1928 to 265,000 in 1950, and to 334,000 in 1955, and the number of scientific workers rose from 98,000 in 1940 to 192,000 in 1953.

Too often the education and training provided was poor, and certainly the numbers educated were never adequate to the need, so that the vast majority of semiprofessional and professional workers—at all levels—even in 1950 did not have sufficient formal training for the jobs they held. Most had gained their skills from practical experience. Nonetheless, although the accomplishment was spotty, such figures as those listed above, which are presented in every Soviet statistical handbook, tell the story of a society transformed, educated, and equipped to live and work within the framework of a rapidly changing and steadily more complex industrial environment. Nor were the specialists alone in feeling the educational impact, for the broad expansion of secondary and technical education also transformed the minds and interests of the millions. Some evidence of this change is provided by Soviet figures on the growth of libraries and books. The 29,000 libraries that existed in 1928 had increased to 145,000 by 1954, the year after Stalin's death; in the same period library holdings had grown from 72 million books and journals to 514 million. *Pravda* on May 4, 1952, announced that since the beginning of the Soviet era, one million books had been published "in a total of more than 14 billion copies." One implication of these staggering numbers is fairly obvious: by the early 1950s, many millions of Soviet citizens were poring over modernizing technical literature, as well as the works of Marx, Lenin, and Stalin, and as a result were thinking in ways unknown to them before Stalin.

In the complicated arena of politics, the single most important fact up to the moment of Stalin's death was his own preeminence in all things. While the system surged ahead, virtually without need of him, he continued frantically to tinker with the mechanism, freely drawing upon his absolute authority to do so. Even after reviewing Soviet history to this point, we find it difficult to grasp fully the immense, overpowering, and awesome weight of the dictator's technically absolute authority to change almost anything he wished; equally hard to grasp is the exaggerated submissiveness with which the society around him acceded to his every caprice.

Some sense of his exalted position is gained by examining the tribute in flattery that he levied upon all around him. Beginning in the early 1930s, the press, the schools, and his colleagues were required to speak—and presumably to think—of him almost as if he were superhuman, possessed of divine powers. By the early 1950s the eulogies and adulation had become habitual, both to Stalin and to those who endlessly repeated the gradiloquent praises of the god-man who led them. The state of this virtual worship of Stalin was well illustrated at the meeting of the Nineteenth Party Congress in October 1952. According to the format established by this time, Stalin himself first pontificated along with his erstwhile lieutenant, Georgi Malenkov. These main addresses were then followed by a long series of reports by party members of high rank, each report customarily sandwiching its information between lengthy, sonorous, and obsequious obeisances to Stalin.

At this Congress, although the high praise given the Chief Mechanic in no way exceeded what he had long received in the daily press, the swift succession of report after report provides a concentrated illustration of the incredible degree of public worship that Stalin by this time demanded and received.[1] The

[1] The following excerpts are from *The Current Digest of the Soviet Press,* edited by Leo Gruliow, Vol. IV: No. 48, p. 23; No. 49, pp. 22, 34, 35–36; No. 50, pp. 21, 28.

Ukrainian author, Alexander Korneichuk, promised in the name of his fellow Ukrainian writers to "gladden our motherland with new and talented works illumined by the brilliant ideas of the great friend of Soviet literature and arts, Comrade Stalin." Anastas Mikoyan (member of the Party Presidium and minister of foreign trade) spoke of the party's "praise to the genius Stalin, the great architect of communism," and went on to say: "Comrade Stalin illuminates our lives with the brilliant light of science." Mikhail Suslov, Presidium member and party theorist, emphasized his conviction that past victories had been won because "our country and the whole Soviet people are being led along Lenin's path with indestructible will and the greatest wisdom by the great genius of mankind, the beloved leader and teacher, Comrade Stalin." Carried away by his theme he supplemented this euphoric comment in a later paragraph: "It would be difficult to name a branch of science, culture or the arts, a sector of the ideological front, where the inspiring and guiding role of our great leader and teacher and the beneficent influence of his brilliant ideas are not felt." Ultimately, he called Stalin, "the coryphaeus [the leader of the chorus] of science. . . ."

Other high party officials termed Stalin "the inspired creator of all our victories," "our pride, our glory, our great leader and teacher," "our own beloved father and teacher of the people." As the Old Bolshevik and Presidium member, Lazar Kaganovich, expressed his admiration, "our party, our people, while building communism, are constantly enriched and armed by the brilliant theoretical work of the great Stalin." And the Old Bolshevik, Kliment Voroshilov, who had served with Stalin at Tsarytsin (later, Stalingrad) during the civil war, called for: "Glory to the great leader and teacher of the working people and of all progressive mankind, the brilliant architect of communism. . . ." Even then the ovations were not over. Stalin was proclaimed "the standard bearer of peace throughout the whole world," "the brilliant pilot of our party," "our brilliant commander," and so on, *ad nauseam*. His death left a great vacuum.

But while to some of the men who praised him Stalin may

indeed have seemed to merit their eulogies, his influence generally upon the moral quality of the party and its leadership, as well as upon the lower ranks of party and state, had been evil. The sycophantic chorus just described, which accompanied Stalin all through his last years, turned his underlings into yes-men, into fawning, terrified courtiers, who involved themselves in sordid Florentine intrigues for power and position behind his back. Stalin, of course, was fully aware of the fear he created and the moral depravity it produced among his aides; yet he persisted in manipulating with terror and demanding his tribute of adulation as if his only real pleasure lay in debasing the men in his entourage. Ultimately he appeared to enjoy a deep sadistic pleasure in his cruelty and to exercise a singular lack of restraint in his arrogance.

Two observers who have studied these characteristics of the *Vozhd* attribute them to a deep-seated lack of conscience. In the view of the American diplomat, George Kennan, a close and knowledgeable student of Stalin for many years, Stalin was "a man of incredible criminality, of a criminality effectively without limits; a man apparently foreign to the very experience of love, without pity or mercy. . . ."[2] The Yugoslav leader, Milovan Djilas, who had sat with Stalin at the table in the Kremlin where the midnight meetings were held, reached similar conclusions. Describing how, filled with admiration of the Soviet war effort, he literally worshiped Stalin, he once wrote: "Stalin was something more than a leader in battle. He was the incarnation of an idea, transfigured in Communist minds into pure idea, and thereby into something infallible and sinless. Stalin was the victorious battle today and the brotherhood of man tomorrow."[3] But after more extensive personal experience with the dictator, Djilas ultimately decided that to Stalin "will fall the glory of being the greatest Criminal in History." And Djilas summarized his conclusions by saying: "He knew that he was one of the cruelest, most des-

[2] George F. Kennan, *Russia and the West under Lenin and Stalin* (Little, Brown and Company, Boston, 1961), p. 254.
[3] Milovan Djilas, *Conversations with Stalin* (Harcourt Brace Jovanovich, New York, 1962), p. 57.

potic personalities in human history. But this did not worry him one bit, for he was convinced that he was executing the judgment of history. His conscience was troubled by nothing, despite the millions who had been destroyed in his name and by his order, despite the thousands of his closest collaborators whom he had murdered as traitors because they doubted that he was leading the country and people into happiness, equality and liberty."[4]

Regardless of how Stalin's character is defined, it fitted him for the unique position of power he had created. And obviously, after Stalin died, some great adjustment was necessary, for none of the second-level men could claim the role of the coryphaeus of science or the Great Criminal. Yet Stalin's political system, as has been argued in previous pages, was considerably more than personal authority and arbitrary power exercised at the caprice of a willful old man. Although he had been the *deux ex machina,* manipulating the discrete units of party and government more or less as he wished until the last years, the administrative machinery had become vast and its personnel had grown far more competent than at the beginning. This machine remained after the leader had left the scene, and it exercised far-reaching influence even without him. A party of 6.9 million members and candidates, under a strongly centralized hierarchy headed by the Presidium and Secretariat, interpenetrated government offices, universities and research academies, industrial plants, schools, military organizations, and youth and sports operations; and the leading officials of all these organizations were themselves communists. Thus the party's supervision and control were exercised directly everywhere.

Meanwhile the competence of party members had reached a high level. While 76 percent of those attending the Nineteenth Congress in October 1952 were over forty, the party as a whole was young, with 76 percent of its members having joined during World War II or after. Nearly 12 percent of the membership had complete or incomplete higher educations, and 22 percent

[4] Djilas, pp. 106, 187.

had completed their secondary education. An auxiliary corps of nearly 19 million Komsomols, members of the communist youth organization, formed a supplementary preparatory school for new party members and government officials and provided enthusiastic workers in areas where party members needed support.

Trusted officials of the party moved easily from one position to another, now holding an office in the Secretariat, now managing an industrial ministry or combine, now directing a republic or a city. And at the very top of the party-state hierarchies, tough and competent men of long experience—Molotov, Kaganovich, Suslov, Mikoyan, Khrushchev, Kosygin, and many others like them—were capable of effectively directing any of the major bureaucracies. In sum, while the machine Stalin had built had been, during his lifetime, dependent upon his personal will and driven by his brutalizing violence, it continued to function after his death perhaps because, after all, the men in charge did not need him quite as much as he had thought. One may recall that after announcing the "Doctors' Plot," he had scornfully told the members of the Politburo: "You are like blind kittens; what will happen without me? The country will perish because you do not know how to recognize enemies."[5] Perhaps he had built better than even he had realized, for he left men steeled by his schooling; these were Stalinists who would continue into the 1970s to do their utmost to preserve his system and much of the administrative machinery he had constructed, even while they blamed him for past mistakes.

The intellectual life and condition of Soviet people at different levels of Soviet society at Stalin's death present still other facets of the complex picture of Stalinist achievement. Stalin's efforts to control the intellectuals had created an artificial culture, a kind of dreamworld in which literature and art portrayed as real that which did not exist. Historians recorded events as they had never happened, fulfilling thus the tasks assigned by the party, and journalists faithfully reported that

[5] Nikita Khrushchev, *The Crimes of the Stalin Era* (The New Leader, New York, 1962), p. S49.

all the poor, the hungry, and the oppressed of Russia were "new men," enjoying happiness and plenty and eager to be led on to "radiant communism" by the great teacher.

Agitprop, the section of the Central Committee's Secretariat responsible for agitation and propaganda, set forth in explicit detail the missions of *partiinost* which the intellectuals were to serve. A parallel governmental "Committee on the Arts" extended control into government agencies, and a host of party-directed cultural organizations—such as the Union of Writers, the Union of Artists, and the Union of Soviet Composers—implemented the party's policies. Criticism from any of these units could ruin careers and destroy the lives of individual artists and writers, and frequently did. In the scholarly world, the academies of science received their budgets from the government and were thus influenced to perform as the party ideologues wished them do. Ministries of education, and industrial and other ministries that directed their own institutes, closely supervised the schools. Finally, all newspapers, journals, book publications, radio reporting—in sum, all formal means of communication—faithfully and endlessly presented the false pictures of Soviet reality and of the world that Stalin wished his people to believe.

Sensitive poets, composers, and painters, as well as the more sturdy adherents of original and creative thought, honest criticism, and objective scholarship, simply could not live in these conditions. Men paid lip service to the artificial culture and tried to live private lives based on some recognition of truth; but by 1953 they had been so long isolated, so long deliberately cut off from normal relations with artists and scholars in the outside world, that even the most sophisticated Soviet intellectual was shockingly ignorant and was far more influenced by Stalin's deliberate effort to carry out a national intellectual lobotomy than he could have realized.

A Soviet writer, Valentyn Moroz, has said that while Stalin was not instructed in cybernetics, he invented the "programmed man." Obviously, the success of the programming differed from person to person, and certain elements of the programs were assimilated more readily than others. But the messages of the programs were uniformly clear and unsubtle. A good Soviet citizen had to be anti-Western, anti-Semitic, chauvinistic, and driven by a passionate faith in the bright communist future. He had to accept whatever scientific principles the party found politically useful, even if this meant swallowing the absurdities of a Lysenko. He was required to esteem the socialist realism of Soviet hack writers as the greatest literature in the world, even while he read Pushkin and Tolstoy. Soviet poster art, stereotyped and lifeless but challenging the population to greater productivity, he was expected to judge as the only good art, in undisputed contrast to Western art, which he was to condemn as corrupt and decadent. Jazz, he had to pronounce evil, and a properly trained political ear would unerringly pick up the corrupt overtones of Western-influenced Soviet-composed sonatas. Above all, the good Soviet citizen had to acknowledge that the Stalinist social system was the one good system the world would ever know. Within such strictures, the "good man" was further conditioned by a communist-oriented "Protestant Ethic" to put forth hard and productive labor and to dedicate himself totally to the collective society.

Such emphasis upon at least overt acceptance of Stalin's dream façade of utopian theories, pseudoscience, socialist realism, and promises placed a great burden upon those whose business it was to communicate these images. For the artist—talented in poetry, prose, art, music, or the ballet—who could conform and who could be boastful about everything Russian, anti-Western, and parochial, almost no rewards were too great. Pampered intellectuals and artists enjoyed great prestige, dachas in the country, immensely high salaries, visits to the West, and acclaim by the party leadership. But those who could not easily conform, among them some of the greatest Soviet thinkers and scientists, could hope at best to concentrate upon scientific research, taking care to utter no unsolicited comments on political and social matters.

To a surprising degree the system worked, possibly because the central focus of most of the new intellectuals was technical and scientific and because they lived in a rapidly expanding economy, where all their best efforts were called forth and where the challenges were both exciting and exhausting. Working in the economy, the laboratories, schools, and other institutions of the society, these technical-professional intellectuals valued, above all else, efficiency. Their faith was in material progress, which in their minds included spiritual progress as well. They were loyal servants of the cause, for the long-run noble aims of that cause seemed more important to them than the ephemeral freedom of the poet or the artist, more important than objective scholarship, and more important than the untrammeled research of the pure scientist. They accepted intellectual bondage and moral servitude in the conviction that thus a humane and free society would be secured.

Of the social classes, the peasant remained the most generally dissatisfied and critical. Ruined by collectivization, he was still ruled and starved by a system he despised. Very few peasants received adequate pay, worked at jobs that interested them, or felt any hope in the future. Very few of their children could plan to go on to a higher education. Urban workers were better off and better satisfied, and as a consequence the younger generation of the cities went far beyond their elders in embracing the ideals and programs of the state. While responding sympathetically to the complaints of some intellectuals about terror and collectivization, urban youth accepted the right of the communists to govern and to set the goals for the nation. Stifling desires for greater personal freedom, they accepted the collectivist ideals of the leadership.

Meanwhile, beyond the pale of these free classes, the men and women behind the barbed wire of the labor camps carried on their dreary lives as best they could. They were a part of society and yet not a part of it; they had been shunted aside for alleged criminal thoughts and political crimes, although many of them were completely innocent. One cannot help but wonder what manner of critical discussions they pursued behind the walls of their confinement. The fine novels written in the 1960s by Alexander Solzhenitsyn, himself an inmate of a labor camp during the eight years before Stalin's death, have at least broken the ice by depicting the contempt and hatred of those inside for the man who had put them there.

Looking abroad at the international scene, Stalin appeared to have reason for personal satisfaction during his last years. With the Soviet expansion into the European satellites and the appearance of communist regimes in North Korea, North Vietnam, and China, one-third of the world's population had joined his camp, and he could claim credit for this. But the expansion created difficult problems as well, bringing international communism into a troublesome new phase and lifting to the surface embarrassing dissensions previously hidden. With the splitting off of Yugoslavia, Stalin, until then the infallible source of all communist truth, had found himself in a world where two infallible heads claimed the right to dispense revealed communist truth. Ordinarily in the past when Stalin had found himself thus threatened, logic was served by executing or banishing the upstart, but Tito carefully refrained from putting himself in the way of an assassin's axe. The leadership of the communist world became even more ambiguous in 1949, when Mao Tse-tung won all of mainland China for himself, and thus a third national communist leader, acting as the independent head of a sovereign nation, presented himself to the world as the only true and infallible successor of Lenin.

Further complicating Stalin's position were events in the Eastern European satellites, where bold and independent national communist leaders increasingly made evident their desire to decide for themselves, within the context of their own nations' interests, which aspects of the Soviet system they might adopt and which they would reject. These men, taking their cues in part from the examples of Tito and Mao, argued cautiously but stubbornly that the cultural and economic characteristics of their own nations must determine to a considerable degree the kind of communism that could be constructed.

With the appearance of other independent centers, a truth about Soviet communism that Stalin was never to admit became clear to the rest of the world. The great leader and teacher was *not* an international communist. The hodgepodge of theory, practice, institutional structures, and rules of thumb he insisted upon exporting to the new communist nations was, in fact, a *national* brew. He was blinded by his own parochialism, arrogance, and age, and what he believed to be an international panacea was actually a system created in a backward society by brutal methods. Exporting the Soviet system labeled as "international communism" and assuring his new converts and subjects that they could become good communists only by the most precise imitation of every facet of this system, Stalin ran head-on into something he had never suspected and was never fully to understand or accept.

The new communist states perceived Stalin as a nationalist; they resisted his organizational forms and techniques because these had been created for the Soviet Union and were in many cases less advanced than alternative institutions and methods already existing in the satellite states. Often the exported Soviet models would not work or were not needed in nations already culturally better developed than the Soviet Union or where conditions differed so greatly that Soviet forms could not be applied as one lays a template on a map. With megalomaniac forcefulness, however, Stalin attempted to foist his system upon other nations, behaving like any chauvinistic imperialist. Thus by expanding communism and helping to create other communist nations, Stalin had brought to the surface the profound contradiction of the Soviet claim that it was the model for all international socialism. He had served as the midwife to the birth of many national communist systems, but in doing so he had also destroyed his own right to dominate them, for the principle that still rules the national-state systems of this world is the national interest of each state rather than the national interest of the USSR. This was a complication Stalin died too soon to fathom or solve; his successors were to be endlessly plagued by it.

There was considerable confusion in his international policies at the end. By his aggressive Cold War policies, he had united the Western powers, and by his support of the communists of North Korea, he had kept them united. Simultaneously, he appeared to be attempting a measured withdrawal toward some kind of peaceful coexistence and a policy aimed at relaxing tensions that would allow him to chip away quietly at relations between Western states. Yet, while his emissaries at a wide variety of international meetings spoke loudly of peace, much of the world continued to doubt and fear him, unable to ignore his warlike postures and actions. The world itself had become too complicated for Stalin and the system he had created. Its diverse changing elements, represented by the many, new national communist states, the neutral Third World of developing nations, and the powerful network of capitalist states, posed problems that seemed to surround each step of the new giant power with uncertainty and danger.

The man of steel had done much good for Russia, and much harm to her people. He had magnified the power of the nation and greatly enhanced the influence of Marxist-Leninist-Stalinist doctrine around the world. But for the Soviet Union itself the usefulness of his techniques of society building was almost at an end. He died at an opportune moment, therefore, because the nation was moving beyond him, beyond Stalinism. The old rigid mold needed to be shattered and recast.

Yet despite the many changes made after Stalin's death, the imprint of his long reign remains deep and seemingly ineffaceable in Soviet society, and because its impact is daily renewed and perpetuated, its ultimate effect cannot be weighed. Nor can the legacy he left for the world soon be fully analyzed or comprehended, for this legacy continues to evolve and spread its influence into many minds and lands where men and women dream of utopia and where ambitious men lust for the power that can be won quickly by brave and ruthless leaders.

Bibliographical Note

Since books dealing with Soviet developments during Stalin's rule number in the thousands, this bibliography is necessarily limited to listing only *some* of the most useful works that have appeared in English. A more extensive bibliography is Walter Kolarz, *Books on Communism* (New York: Oxford University Press, 1964). In the area of international relations the best and most exhaustive bibliography is *Soviet Foreign Relations and World Communism,* compiled and edited by Thomas T. Hammond (Princeton, N.J.: Princeton University Press, 1965). More recent books are listed and analyzed in the *Slavic Review.*

Some of Stalin's most important writings in the 1920s are to be found in Joseph Stalin, *Problems of Leninism* (New York: International Publishers, 1928). A much more complete presentation is offered in the thirteen-volume translated *Works* (Moscow: Foreign Languages Publishing House, 1946–1955). Even this collection, however, does not include all of Stalin's writing, and the reader who wishes to acquaint himself with the fuller picture should turn to the valuable study by Robert H. McNeal, *Stalin's Works: An Annotated Bibliography* (Stanford, Calif.: Stanford University Press, 1967).

The best and most readable biography is still the work of Isaac Deutscher, *Stalin, A Political Biography* (New York and London: Oxford University Press, 1945), although it leaves much to be desired in objectivity and detail. Leon Trotsky's *Stalin: An Appraisal of the Man and His Influence,* edited and translated by Charles Malamuth (London: Hollis and Carter, Ltd., 1947), is invaluable. While it is a fierce and brilliant polemic by a man who hated and misunderstood Stalin, it contains much worthwhile information. The work of Boris

Souvarine, *Stalin* (New York: Longmans, Green, 1939), is an early, condemnatory effort; and the long essay by Robert H. McNeal in *The Bolshevik Tradition* (Englewood Cliffs, N.J.: Prentice-Hall, 1963) provides a bold and original interpretation based on very deep knowledge of Stalin. *Let History Judge* by the Soviet scholar Roy A. Medvedev (New York: Alfred A. Knopf, 1971) is a penetrating and enlightening study that provides much new information. Beyond this, little of great value has been published, although there are many illuminating insights in a number of memoirs. Especially worth noting are Milovan Djilas, *Conversations with Stalin* (New York: Harcourt Brace Jovanovich, 1962), Svetlana Alliluyeva, *Twenty Letters to a Friend* (New York: Harper & Row, 1967), and *Khrushchev Remembers* (Boston: Little, Brown and Company, 1970). The authorship of the latter work is attributed to Nikita Khrushchev, but while it seems plausible that he was the source of the information, much of the narrative appears to have been written, or perhaps transcribed from notes or tapes, by others.

The best study presently available of Lenin, his work, and his relations with Stalin is Adam Ulam's *The Bolsheviks: The Intellectual and Political History of the Triumph of Communism in Russia* (New York: Collier Books, 1968). The first two volumes of Isaac Deutscher's trilogy, *The Prophet Armed: Trotsky 1879–1921* and *The Prophet Unarmed: Trotsky 1921–1929* (New York: Vintage Books, 1965), provide excellent and extensive analyses of Trotsky-Stalin relations.

There are many general surveys of the Stalin era that offer the reader essential background material. The most exhaustive work—and a masterful one—is Edward Hallet Carr's *A History of Soviet Russia* (London and New York: Macmillan, 1950–1964), which has been published in six volumes covering the period from 1917 through 1926. A smaller but useful study by a distinguished student of government is *How Russia Is Ruled,* by Merle Fainsod (Cambridge, Mass.: Harvard University Press, 1965). John Maynard's book, *Russia in Flux* (New York: Macmillan, 1948), is especially noteworthy for its insights into the responses of workers and peasants to the changes Stalin introduced. Two Soviet works are both interesting and revealing because they present the communist viewpoint at two different times (under Stalin and several years after his death), and because they demonstrate what the Soviet student was required to read and believe through these years. The first, *The History of the Communist Party of the Soviet Union* (*Bolsheviks*), edited by a Commission of the Central Committee of the CPSU (New York: International Publishers, 1938), is a perfect illustration of Stalinist rewriting of history; the second, *History of the Communist Party of the Soviet Union,* prepared by B. N.

Ponomaryov et al. (Moscow: Foreign Languages Publishing House, 1960), presents the Khrushchevian version of Stalin's times. Still another contrasting survey of events from 1917 to 1939 is put forth by Raphael R. Abramovitch, a Menshevik, in *The Soviet Revolution, 1917–1939* (New York: International Universities Press, 1962).

Many excellent analyses of Marxist-Leninist ideology are available. Among the most useful are Alfred G. Meyer, *Marxism* (Cambridge, Mass.: Harvard University Press, 1954), Alfred G. Meyer, *Leninism* (Cambridge, Mass.: Harvard University Press, 1957), Herbert Marcuse, *Soviet Marxism: A Critical Analysis* (New York: Columbia University Press, 1958), George Lichtheim, *Marxism, A Historical and Critical Survey* (New York: Praeger, 1961), and the popularly written book by Robert V. Daniels, *The Nature of Communism* (New York: Vintage Books, 1962). Other important works dealing with various aspects of Soviet ideology are Milovan Djilas, *The New Class* (New York: Praeger, 1957), and Leon Trotsky, *The Permanent Revolution*, translated by Max Shachtman (New York: Pioneer, 1931).

Some of the finest scholarly efforts have been focused upon political analysis of the Communist party and its function. Especially outstanding are Leonard Schapiro's brilliant work, *The Communist Party of the Soviet Union* (New York: Random House, 1960), which traces the activities of the party from its formative years into the late 1950s, and the detailed study by John A. Armstrong, *The Politics of Totalitarianism* (New York: Random House, 1961). The most perceptive study of the opposition movements under Stalin is *The Conscience of the Revolution*, by Robert V. Daniels (Cambridge, Mass.: Harvard University Press, 1960). Somewhat dated but still useful attempts to analyze and explain Soviet political processes under Stalin are the following: W. W. Rostow, in collaboration with Alfred Levin and others, *The Dynamics of Soviet Society* (New York: Norton, 1953), Barrington Moore, Jr., *Soviet Politics: The Dilemma of Power* (Cambridge, Mass.: Harvard University Press, 1950), and the same author's *Terror and Progress, USSR* (Cambridge, Mass.: Harvard University Press, 1954). In the book *Power and Policy in the USSR* (New York: St. Martin's Press, 1961), Robert Conquest has carried out an exhaustive analysis of the dramatic events of Stalin's last years, such as the Doctors' Plot, the Leningrad Case, and the Mingrelian Affair.

An early effort to define the inner drives guiding the party under Lenin and Stalin was made by Nathan Leites, in his *The Operational Code of the Politburo* (New York: McGraw-Hill, 1951); and certainly one of the most important such analyses was presented to the world by Nikita S. Khrushchev in his Secret Speech to the Twentieth Congress of the Communist Party of the Soviet Union, which has been published under the title, *The Crimes of the Stalin Era* (New York: The New Leader, 1962). Robert C. Tucker, in *The Soviet Political Mind* (New York: Praeger, 1963), sets forth a number of original and provocative theories about Stalin's character, motivation, and impact upon Russia and the world.

On the thorny question of the nature and importance of totalitarianism, the works of the principal proponents are these: Carl J. Friedrich (ed.), *Totalitarianism* (Cambridge, Mass.: Harvard University Press, 1954), Carl J. Friedrich and Zbigniew K. Brzezinski, *Totalitarian Dictatorship and Autocracy* (Cambridge, Mass.: Harvard University Press, 1956), Hannah Arendt, *The Origins of Totalitarianism* (New York: Harcourt Brace Jovanovich, 1951), and Carl J. Friedrich, Michael Curtis, and Benjamin R. Barber, *Totalitarianism in Perspective* (New York: Praeger, 1969).

Still worth reading, although they have been superseded by many specialist studies in economics, are the surveys by Alexander Baykov, *The Development of the Soviet Economic System* (New York: Macmillan, 1948), and Maurice Dobb, *Soviet Economic Development Since 1917* (New York: International Publishers, 1948). Harry Schwartz, *Russia's Soviet Economy* (Englewood Cliffs, N.J.: Prentice-Hall, 1954), is a well-organized text by an American scholar. In *The Soviet Industrialization Debate (1924–1928)* (Cambridge, Mass.: Harvard University Press, 1960), Alexander Erlich carefully examines the complex debates that eventually led Stalin to the First Five-Year Plan. S. Swianiewicz, in *Forced Labor and Economic Development* (London: Oxford University Press, 1965), has attempted to relate the purges and their effects to Soviet efforts to industrialize.

Two excellent studies have examined the role of the Soviet industrial manager and the problems he faced under Stalin: David Granick, *Management of the Industrial Firm in the USSR* (New York: Columbia University Press, 1954), and Joseph Berliner, *Factory and Manager in the USSR* (Cambridge, Mass.: Harvard University Press, 1957). Scholarly research by Western students has corrected many Soviet boasts about their accomplishments. A useful example is the collection of essays dealing with many aspects of the economy and providing reliable new estimates—*The Development of the Soviet Economy: Plan and Performance,* edited by Vladimir G. Treml (New York: Praeger, 1968).

In the field of agriculture one of the most accurate and exhaustive early studies, still very important, is Naum Jasny's *The Socialist*

Agriculture of the Soviet Union (Stanford, Calif.: Stanford University Press, 1949). A set of excellent papers is to be found in *The Soviet Rural Community*, a work edited by James R. Millar (Urbana: University of Illinois Press, 1971). M. Lewin's *Russian Peasants and Soviet Power* (Evanston, Ill.: Northwestern University Press, 1968) is a recent and worthwhile study; and Fedor Belov, a former kolkhoz chairman, has described in grim detail the trials and tribulations of the collective farm where he worked immediately after the war in *The History of a Soviet Collective Farm* (New York: Praeger, 1955).

In the broad area of Soviet social conditions and processes under Stalin, where the topics of great interest are themselves almost too numerous to list, many fine studies have been written. Alex Inkeles' *Public Opinion in Soviet Russia* (Cambridge, Mass.: Harvard University Press, 1950) remains a fascinating account of how Stalin's regime used its communications network both for information and control. Harold J. Berman, *Justice in the USSR* (New York: Vintage Books, 1963), is a full and intelligent exposition of Soviet-Marxist theories of law and of the impact such law has on the citizen.

Shortly after World War II, several studies were made of the Soviet social system, based on exhaustive interviews of Soviet citizens who had left the country during the war, as military prisoners, slave laborers, or defectors. Two of the most engrossing are: Alex Inkeles and Raymond A. Bauer, *The Soviet Citizen: Daily Life in a Totalitarian Society* (Cambridge, Mass.: Harvard University Press, 1959), and the shorter study, published earlier by Inkeles, Bauer, and Clyde Kluckhohn, *How the Soviet System Works* (Cambridge, Mass.: Harvard University Press, 1956). Equally absorbing is Merle Fainsod, *Smolensk under Soviet Rule* (Cambridge, Mass.: Harvard University Press, 1958). This book, based on the party archives of Smolensk captured by the Germans and subsequently handed over to the Americans, presents a richly detailed picture of relationships within the party and between party and citizens. Soviet youth and the organizational means devised to control it are very well portrayed by Ralph R. Fisher, Jr., *Pattern for Soviet Youth* (New York: Columbia University Press, 1959). The evolution of the trade unions is examined by Isaac Deutscher, *Soviet Trade Unions* (London and New York: Royal Institute of International Affairs, 1950), and the same subject is searchingly explored in Solomon M. Schwarz, *Labor in the Soviet Union* (New York: Praeger, 1951).

The complex problems of Soviet nationalities policies in the pre-Stalinist years are capably discussed by Richard Pipes in *The Formation of the Soviet Union: Communism and Nationalism, 1917–*

1923 (Cambridge, Mass.: Harvard University Press, 1954). Walter Kolarz has produced a fine general study of nationality policies, *Russia and Her Colonies* (London: Phillip, 1952), and has examined more specifically the history and conditions of several minorities in a second book, *The Peoples of the Soviet Far East* (London: Phillip, 1954). Soviet treatment of Jews is carefully and reliably set forth in Solomon M. Schwarz, *The Jews in the Soviet Union* (Syracuse, N.Y.: Syracuse University Press, 1951), and in Salo Baron, *The Russian Jew under Tsar and Soviet* (New York: Macmillan, 1964). Robert S. Sullivant's book, *Soviet Politics and the Ukraine, 1917–1957* (New York: Columbia University Press, 1962), is an outstanding and objective scholarly study of the Soviet Union's second largest national group; and John A. Armstrong, *Ukrainian Nationalism, 1939–1945* (New York: Columbia University Press, 1955), is a well-documented account of Ukrainian nationalist activities before and during the war.

The purges of the 1930s deserve the attention of any careful student of Stalin's times, both as a political and as a social phenomenon, for the purges and the concentration camps directly impinged upon the lives of millions of Soviet citizens. The official transcripts of the court proceedings provide an authentic picture of the trials that is overwhelming. For these transcripts, see People's Commissariat of Justice of the USSR, *The Case of the Trotskyite-Zinovievite Centre, August 19–24, 1936* (Moscow: People's Commissariat of Justice, 1936); see also, People's Commissariat of Justice of the USSR, *Report of Court Proceedings in the Case of the Anti-Soviet Trotskyite Center, Moscow, January 23–30, 1937* (New York: Howard Fertig, 1967). For the court transcript and an important analysis of the Bukharin trial in March 1938, see Robert C. Tucker (ed.), *The Great Purge Trial* (New York: Grosset & Dunlap, 1965). Robert Conquest's book, *The Great Terror* (New York: Macmillan, 1969), is the best comprehensive study of the purges.

A useful scholarly effort to summarize and appraise the size and the consequences of forced labor is the work of David J. Dallin and B. N. Nikolaevsky, *Forced Labor in Soviet Russia* (New Haven, Conn.: Yale University Press, 1947). Much more interesting is the account by two scholars, a German scientist and a Russian historian, who served time in Soviet prisons and thus record observed facts. This is the book by F. Beck and W. Godin (pseudonyms), *Russian Purge and the Extraction of Confession* (New York: Viking Press, 1951). Many personal narratives have been written by men and women who lived through months or years of the labor camps. Among these, the following are outstanding: Alexander Weissberg, *Accused* (New York: Simon and

Schuster, 1951), Elinor Lipper, *Eleven Years in Soviet Prison Camps* (London: Hollis and Carter, 1951), Jerzy Gliksman, *Tell the West* (New York: Gresham Press, 1948), and Vladimir Petrov, *Empire of Fear* (London: Eyre and Spottiswoode, 1951).

In the area of literature and the arts, a number of excellent studies are available. Among the surveys of Soviet literature, a readable work that deserves mention is Marc Slonim, *Soviet Russian Literature: Writers and Problems, 1917–1967* (New York: Oxford University Press, 1967), and a discerning and sensitive treatment is Edward J. Brown, *Russian Literature Since the Revolution* (New York: Collier Books, 1963). Another survey of great insight is Gleb Struve's work, *Soviet Russian Literature, 1917–1950* (Norman: University of Oklahoma Press, 1951); and a fourth work, Vera Alexandrovna, *A History of Soviet Literature, 1917–1964* (New York: Doubleday, 1964), presents thoughtful analyses of the works and ideas of Soviet writers.

Somewhat more limited in nature, but useful because of their special focus upon the regime's control over literature, are the works of Edward J. Brown, *The Proletarian Episode in Russian Literature* (New York: Columbia University Press, 1953), and Harold Swayze, *Political Control of Literature in the USSR, 1946–1959* (Cambridge, Mass.: Harvard University Press, 1962). In this connection, a scholarly study, *The Positive Hero in Russian Literature,* by Rufus W. Mathewson (New York: Columbia University Press, 1958), effectively illustrates the influence of ideology and tradition upon Soviet literature. The best way to study Soviet writing is, of course, to read the authors themselves. Dramatic and vivid pieces may be found in the book edited by Patricia Blake and Max Hayward, *Dissonant Voices in Soviet Literature* (New York: Pantheon, 1962), in the collection published by Joshua Kunitz, *Russian Literature Since the Revolution* (London: Boni and Gaer, 1948), and in Bernard Guilbert Guerney's *An Anthology of Russian Literature in the Soviet Period from Gorki to Pasternak* (New York: Vintage Books, 1960).

With respect to the other arts, the book by Andrei Olkhovsky, *Music under the Soviets: The Agony of an Art* (New York: Praeger, 1955), is a grim and depressing picture of the sufferings of the musician under Stalin. Jay Leyda's *Kino: A History of the Russian and Soviet Film* (New York: Macmillan, 1960) is a careful survey in which the course of political history is given its due influence. Nikolai A. Gorchakov's study, *The Theatre in Soviet Russia* (New York: Columbia University Press, 1957), traces the evolution of the Soviet theater up to 1952.

Much first-rate work has been done in the field of education. James Bowen's *Soviet Education: Anton Makarenko and the Years of Experiment* (Madison: University of Wisconsin Press, 1962) is an excellent and full introduction to the ideas of the revolutionary and influential educational theories of Makarenko. Two studies by George S. Counts and Lucia P. Lodge, dealing with political control and the character of Soviet education, are well documented and useful. They are *The Country of the Blind: The Soviet System of Mind Control* (Boston: Houghton Mifflin, 1949) and *The Challenge of Soviet Education* (New York and London: McGraw-Hill, 1957). A demonstration of the thought of Soviet educators is jarringly presented in the translations from a Soviet textbook on pedagogy in Boris P. Esipov and N. K. Goncharov, *I Want To Be Like Stalin* (New York: John Day, 1947). Finally, Nicholas DeWitt's *Soviet Professional Manpower: Its Education, Training and Supply* (Washington, D.C.: National Science Foundation, 1955) is a careful judgment of the accomplishments of the previous twenty-five years. DeWitt's massive and exhaustive subsequent work, *Education and Professional Employment in the USSR* (Washington, D.C.: National Science Foundation, 1962), although concerned primarily with the reforms of 1958 and after, supplies substantial information on the earlier period.

The life of the Orthodox Church in "Godless Russia" has not been easy; yet for a variety of reasons the Church continued to exercise wide influence under Stalin. *The Russian Church and the Soviet State, 1917–1950,* by John S. Curtiss (Boston: Little, Brown and Company, 1953), is a sound inquiry into Church-State relations, while the less objective work by Matthew Spinka, *The Church in Soviet Russia* (London and New York: Oxford University Press, 1956), places emphasis upon the efforts of the Patriarch to maintain a certain degree of independence. *Religion in the Soviet Union,* by Walter Kolarz (London: Macmillan, 1961), examines the destinies of a number of religious groups.

The Red Army and its wars have produced many studies. For the civil war, the second volume of *The Russian Revolution,* by William H. Chamberlin (New York: Universal Library, 1965), is one of the most balanced treatments. Arthur E. Adams's *Bolsheviks in the Ukraine* (New Haven, Conn.: Yale University Press, 1962) is a careful account of Lenin's efforts to subdue the Ukraine, and Paul Avrich tells the story of the Kronstadt revolt in precise and well-documented detail in *Kronstadt 1921* (Princeton, N.J.: Princeton University Press, 1970). Useful broader surveys of the army's history have been written by

Dimitri Fedotoff White, *The Growth of the Red Army* (Princeton, N.J.: Princeton University Press, 1944), and by Basil H. Liddell Hart in *The Soviet Army* (London: Weidenfeld and Nicolson, 1956). The most exhaustive and informative political analysis is John Erickson's very excellent *The Soviet High Command, 1918–1941* (London: Macmillan, 1962).

There are many accounts of World War II and of separate battles between German and Soviet forces. One of the more popular books is by Paul Carell, *Hitler Moves East, 1941–1943* (Boston: Little, Brown and Company, 1965); a second, which deals much more fully with wartime conditions, is Alexander Werth's *Russia at War, 1941–1945* (New York: Dutton, 1964). Leon Gouré, *The Siege of Leningrad* (Stanford, Calif.: Stanford University Press, 1962), presents a meticulously documented and terrifying account of the Germans' efforts to bombard and starve that city out of existence. And Alexander Dallin, *German Rule in Russia, 1941–1945* (New York: St. Martin's Press, 1957), sets forth a long and solid analysis of German occupation policies. *Soviet Military Doctrine,* by Raymond L. Garthoff (New York: The Free Press, 1953), is an extensive exploration of Soviet political-military relationships, military principles, and the organization and operation of the various military services. Of the many memoirs written both by German and Soviet generals, *Marshal Zhukov's Greatest Battles,* by Georgi K. Zhukov (New York: Harper & Row, 1969), is particularly valuable for its detailed record of conversations about military matters and wartime decisions between Zhukov and Stalin.

In foreign relations, several collections of documents are fundamental to effective study. Among the most important are the works edited by Jane Degras, *Documents on Soviet Foreign Policy* (London: Oxford University Press, 1951, 1952, 1953), three volumes that cover the period from 1917 through 1941. *The Communist International,* also edited by Jane Degras (London and New York: Oxford University Press, 1956, 1960), is an essential, two-volume collection on Comintern affairs. A very well-edited work by Xenia Eudin and Robert C. North is *Soviet Russia and the East, 1920–1927: A Documentary Survey* (Stanford, Calif.: Stanford University Press, 1957). A two-volume collection of considerable significance is Xenia Eudin and Robert Slusser, *Soviet Foreign Policy, 1928–1934: Documents and Materials* (University Park: The Pennsylvania State University Press, 1966, 1967).

For the period of World War II, a number of documentary collections are indispensable. One of these is the work edited by R. J. Sontag and J. S. Beddie, *Nazi-Soviet Relations, 1939–1941* (Washington,

D.C.: U.S. Government Printing Office, 1948). The most valuable set of documents on Allied relations during the war published by the Soviets is: Ministry of Foreign Affairs of the USSR, *Correspondence between the Chairman of the Council of Ministers of the USSR and the Presidents of the USA and the Prime Ministers of Great Britain during the Great Patriotic War of 1941–1945* (2 vols., Moscow: Foreign Languages Publishing House, 1957). The U.S. State Department Series, *Foreign Relations of the United States: Diplomatic Papers,* includes several volumes useful for the study of Soviet foreign relations beginning in 1917. One of the most valuable of these, published by the U.S. Government Printing Office, Washington, D.C., in 1955, bears the subtitle: *The Conferences at Malta and Yalta 1945.* For a shocking but reliable insight into Soviet relations with the satellite states after the war, see Ministry of Foreign Affairs of the Federal People's Republic of Yugoslavia, *White Book on Aggressive Activities by the Governments of the USSR, Poland, Czechoslovakia, Hungary, Rumania, Bulgaria and Albania towards Yugoslavia* (Belgrade: Ministry of Foreign Affairs, 1951).

The difficulty of producing reliable surveys of Soviet foreign affairs has deterred the writing of volumes in this area. Several of those published, however, are of immense value. Among these is the two-volume work of Louis Fischer, *The Soviets in World Affairs* (London: Cape, 1930). Dealing with the first twelve years of Soviet policy, Fischer writes well about people and events he knew intimately. Max Beloff's two-volume study, *The Foreign Policy of Soviet Russia, 1929–1941* (London and New York: Oxford University Press, 1949), has long been the principal work in this period. The best single volume covering the whole period from 1917 to 1967 is Adam B. Ulam's *Expansion and Coexistence* (New York: Praeger, 1968); this is an erudite and sophisticated study by a leading American scholar.

A few of the most important studies devoted to special aspects of Soviet foreign relations should also be mentioned. Conrad Brandt's *Stalin's Failure in China, 1924–1927* (Cambridge, Mass.: Harvard University Press, 1958) is a careful and reliable study. Franz Borkenau's pioneer work, *The Communist International* (London: Faber & Faber, 1938), is still the principal book in its field. One of the finest studies of relations during World War II is William H. McNeill's *America, Britain and Russia: Their Cooperation and Conflict, 1941–1946* (London and New York: Oxford University Press, 1953). Vladimir Dedijer, *The Battle That Stalin Lost* (New York: Viking Press, 1970, 1971), offers some new ideas on the Tito-Stalin conflict by a man who was deeply involved in it. Martin F. Herz, *Beginnings of the Cold War* (Bloomington: The Indiana University Press, 1967), presents a compact and somewhat defensive American view, and Marshal D. Shulman, *Stalin's Foreign Policy Reappraised* (New York: Atheneum, 1965), is a provocatively "contrary" interpretation of Stalin's motives and behavior after the war, which has stimulated much salutary "reappraisal" of earlier Cold War interpretations.

While many memoirs contain vital information regarding Stalin's foreign relations, only a few of the most important titles can be noted here. Of these, first mention should be made of the several volumes of Winston Churchill's memoirs, which have been cited in the text. Alexander Barmine, a former Soviet diplomat, describes the problems of serving Stalin in *One Who Survived* (New York: Putnam, 1945); and Gustav Hilger and Alfred G. Meyer, in *The Incompatible Allies* (New York: Macmillan, 1953), present the views of a German diplomat in Moscow in the years before Hitler invaded the Soviet Union. American interpretations by men who participated in the events have been written by James F. Byrnes, *Speaking Frankly* (New York: Harper & Row, 1947), and Edward R. Stettinius, Jr., *Roosevelt and the Russians* (New York: Doubleday, 1949). And George F. Kennan, one of the finest of American students of Soviet foreign policy, has much of interest and significance to say in his *Memoirs, 1925–1950* (Boston: Little, Brown and Company, 1967).

Many other insights into Stalin's times are available in numerous other works. For their titles and for judgments of their value, the interested reader is referred again to the extensive bibliographies mentioned at the beginning of this brief list.

Index

233

Rhineland, 91
Ribbentrop, Joachim von, 125–128, 134
Rokossovsky, Konstantin, 153
Roosevelt, Franklin D., 139, 140, 144, 148–151, 153, 155, 156, 158, 160, 161, 163
Rostov, siege of, 143
Rumania, 125, 127, 131, 142, 153, 154, 161, 164, 166, 176
Rundstedt, Gerd von, 134, 142
Russia (*see* Soviet Union)
Russian chauvinism, 198, 200, 217, 220
Russian Orthodox Church, 167
Russian Social Democratic Labor party, 2
Rykov, Aleksei, 26–27, 29, 53, 76, 107

Sabotage, 73, 98, 100
Schulenburg, Friedrich, 124, 128, 131, 134
Secret police, Soviet, 54, 61, 70, 73, 79, 93, 97, 98, 100, 102, 175, 191
Serebryakov, Leonid, 105–106
Sevastopol, siege of, 143
Shcherbakov, A. S., 204
Shelepin, A. N., 203
Shock-brigades, Soviet, 65–66, 74, 120
Shtemenko, S. M., 204
Siberia, 57, 100, 109, 119
Sikorski, Wladyslaw, 147
Slavs, 142
Smolensk under Soviet Rule, 70
Social justice, 43
Socialism in one country, theory of, 30–33, 44, 122
Socialist accumulation, 35
Socialist emulation, 66, 82

Socialist realism, 115, 217
Socialist utopia, 121
Solzhenitsyn, Alexander, 218
Southern Sakhalin, 161
Soviet-Chinese Company, 161
Soviet Communist party, 1–2; Central Committee, 13, 16, 18, 21, 22, 25–27, 29, 36, 54, 76, 108, 112, 191, 199; civil war, impact on, 5; Control Commission, 18, 19, 25, 76, 98, 100; Directorate of Propaganda, 201; educational backgrounds of members, 39, 193, 214–215; Eighteenth Congress, 96; factionalism in, 18–19, 25, 28; Fifteenth Congress, 44–45; First Five-Year Plan and, 75–80; Fourteenth Congress, 27, 28, 31, 36; Left Opposition, 28, 29, 35, 45, 46, 52, 66, 74, 102–103, 107; Leningrad organization, 27, 28, 37, 52, 102, 104, 203; membership growth, 37, 193; militarization of, 4–5; nationality policy, 13–14; Nineteenth Congress, 195, 204, 211–212, 214; Orgburo, 16, 27, 36–37; Politburo, 10, 11, 16, 20, 22, 26–29, 36–37, 53, 76, 102, 103, 105, 112, 191; purges, 98–110, 112–114, 117, 118, 186, 202–205; Right, 46, 75, 76, 107; Secretariat, 16–18, 27, 36–37; Seventeenth Congress, 90, 103, 108; Sixteenth Conference, 76; Stalin as leader of, 36–41; Stalin's struggle for power in, 17–29; Tenth Congress, 18; Thirteenth Conference, 19; Thirteenth Congress, 24; Twelfth Congress, 18; Twentieth Congress, 103–104, 192; Twenty-Second Congress, 104, 205; Unit-

Soviet Union *(cont.)*
Machine Tractor Stations, 61–
62, 85, 196; and Manchuria, 93–
94, 165; mastering techniques,
81–82; Menshevik party, 109;
military-scientific strength, postwar, 209; New Economic Policy,
7, 29, 34–35, 42–43, 75, 107; new
power position, postwar, 165–
167; and Norway, 141; October
Revolution, 4, 97; oil production, 85–87, 169, 170; overcentralization, 194–196; peasants, 3,
35, 36, 43–45, 51–56, 60–62, 66,
73, 218; Poland and, 127–129,
149–155, 159–164, 175, 180; population (1917), 3; population
growth, 34, 209; population
shifts, 58–59; postwar, 165–210;
pre-1917 government, 3; public
organizations, control of, 119–
120; Rumania and, 125, 127, 131,
142, 153, 154, 161, 164; Second
Bolshevik Revolution, 47, 74–
75, 80, 97; Second Five-Year
Plan, 81–86, 101; secret police,
54, 61, 70, 73, 79, 93, 97, 98, 100,
102, 175, 191; shock-brigades,
65–66, 74, 120; Social Revolutionary party, 109; societal
change, 189; and Spain, 86, 93;
Stakhanovite movement, 82–83,
102; Stalin's impact on, 207–221;
state farms, 61, 85, 115; steel production, 66, 81, 85, 169; taxes, 35,
36, 61; technical and industrial
experts, importation of, 71–73;
technical schools, increase in,
72; Third Five-Year Plan, 86–
87; thought control, 115–121,
171, 216; trade unions, 70, 76,

Soviet Union *(cont.)*
120; transportation systems, 49;
United States and, 89, 139, 143–
144, 148–151, 153, 155, 156, 158,
160, 161, 163, 173, 179, 185; urban population, growth of, 52,
68; and Vietnam, 219; wages,
49, 64–65, 83; war casualties,
166; work incentives, 65–66, 83;
and World War II, 134–167;
youth organizations, 66, 119,
214, 215; and Yugoslavia, 132,
164, 166, 176, 180–184, 219. *See
also* Stalin, Joseph
Spain, civil war in, 86, 93; France
and, 93; Germany and, 86, 93;
Great Britain and, 93; Italy and,
86, 93; Popular Front policy, 92–
93; Soviet Union and, 86, 93
Stakhanov, A. G., 82–83
Stalin, Joseph, 5, 8, 10–16; administrative talent, 15, 16, 39; assault
on intellectuals, 197–202, 215–
218; birth of, 11; as Chairman of
the Commission of Commissars,
135; as Chairman of the Council
of Ministers, 191, 194; character
of, 13, 190, 206, 213–214; as
Chief of the State Defense Committee, 135–136; Churchill's
visits to, 144–145, 153–155; Cold
War policies, 172–188; as Commander-in-Chief, 135–136; as
Commissar of Nationalities, 15;
death of, 205–206; dualistic policy, 32–33; education, 11–12;
eulogies to, 116, 211–213; exile,
13, 14; foreign policy (1920s and
1930s), 87–97; as General Secretary of the Communist party, 16,
23, 191; ill-health, 191–192; as